SRI LANKAN ETHNIC CRISIS

TOWARDS A
RESOLUTION

To: Jodi Jensen
Executive Director
PRA

With the compliments of
the author.

R.B. Herath

info@rbherath.com
www.rbherath.com

R. B. HERATH

Sri Lankan Ethnic Crisis

Towards
A
Resolution

Trafford Publishing/Victoria, Canada

National Library of Canada Cataloguing in Publication

Herath, R. B.,
    Sri Lankan ethnic crisis : towards a resolution / R.B. Herath.

Includes bibliographical references and index.
ISBN 1-55369-793-6

    1. Sri Lanka—Ethnic relations. 2. Sri Lanka—Politics and government.
I. Title.

DS489.2.H47 2002   954.9303   C2002-903863-4

TRAFFORD

Trafford Publishing
Suite 6E, 2333 Government St., Victoria, B.C. V8T 4P4, CANADA
Phone   250-383-6864   Toll-free   1-888-232-4444 (Canada & US)
Fax   250-383-6804   E-mail   sales@trafford.com
Web site   www.trafford.com   TRAFFORD PUBLISHING IS A DIVISION OF TRAFFORD HOLDINGS LTD.
Trafford Catalogue #02-0606   www.trafford.com/robots/02-0606.html

10   9   8   7   6   5   4   3   2

Sri Lankan Ethnic Crisis: Towards a Resolution

R. B. Herath

This book is dedicated to the loving memory of my parents, grandparents and teachers.

Acknowledgements

I benefited from the discussions with many Sri Lankans and others with a diversity of views in the writing of this book. I express my sincere appreciation to all of them. They are too numerous to mention by name. I also wish to thank a friend, who wishes to be anonymous, whose critical and dissenting views were useful in the writing of this book.

After completing the manuscript, my friends, Henry and Seela Subasinghe, Chelliah T. Premarajah, Poppy Preena, and Neil and Arzeena Turner reviewed it from the reader's perspective. Their comments helped give a final touch to it. K. (Karu) and Padma Karunaratne converted the final version of the manuscript to a digital print-ready form.

Dr. Hari Sharma, Professor Emeritus of Sociology of the Simon Fraser University, British Columbia, Canada, and President of the South Asian Network for Secularism and Democracy and the International South Asian Forum in Canada kindly undertook to write a foreword for the book. Henry and Seela contributed to the back cover with an endorsement.

Swati Bhagat, a web designer, designed the front cover. It shows a traditional Sri Lankan oil lamp lit and placed inside a map of Sri Lanka, signifying an auspicious new beginning for the country.

Venerable Ajahn Sona, the Abbot of the Birken Forest Buddhist Monastery in Princeton, and Venerable Chitapunno, a resident monk of the Monastery, kindly answered from Buddhist perspectives some questions I had on the role of Buddhist monks in politics. They also helped me understand the principles of good governance and the qualities essential for a good leader as taught by the Buddha.

Last but not least, I wish to thank my family for giving the support I needed to write this book. My wife, Hemamala, gave her fullest cooperation and assistance in completing it. Her own knowledge and experience on Sri Lankan affairs became a great asset in writing the book. Our children helped in every possible manner. They were the first lines of help in grammar and computer difficulties.

Although many people have contributed to the book in numerous ways, I alone am solely responsible for the views expressed in it.

7359 – 128A Street   R. B. Herath
Surrey, British Columbia
Canada V3W 7G9
E-mail: heraths@familynet.bc.ca

June 2002

CONTENTS

List of Maps:

List of Tables

List of Charts

About the author

The author was born and raised in Sri Lanka. He was a toddler when the country gained independence in 1948. He grew up amidst the changes that shaped the country to what it is today. He was concerned about the future of the country, and contributed towards reducing ethnic divisiveness among its people. He did this first as a student leader in his high school and university days, and later as an active participant in national politics.

In October 1979, he co-founded and led a democratic political party in Sri Lanka by the name Podujana Party (meaning Peoples' party) with a vision of 'One Lanka – One Nation, One Nation – One Family.' This political party prepared for the general election scheduled for 1983. This election, however, did not take place; the incumbent government postponed the election to 1989. Meanwhile, the LTTE turned the ethnic crisis of the country into a separatist war in 1983, taking control of its democratic political process. In the aftermath of the commotion that followed, the author left the country in 1984. He now lives in Canada.

He has travelled to many countries in the world, and worked as an engineer, university teacher, development planner and a public service administrator in six of them: Sri Lanka, the United Kingdom, Tanzania, Kenya, Zambia, and Canada. In his teaching assignment at the University of Dar-es-Salaam, Tanzania, he was promoted from Lecturer to Senior Lecturer in 1975. In his work-assignment in Zambia as the national co-ordinator of a special rural development program (Intensive Development Zones), he represented that country in a number of bilateral and multilateral conferences sponsored by the United Nations. At these conferences he presented varied country review reports on agriculture and rural development. In 1984, he was registered with the United Nations Centre for Human Settlements as an expert in Rural Physical Planning and Water Supply- Infrastructure. Presently he is working with the government of British Columbia, Canada, and deals with, among other things, First Nations' issues in managing and allocating Crown land. Wherever he travelled or lived, he always took keen interest to study the ways of governance in plural societies. He has an excellent knowledge of the international scene. After settling in Canada, he conducted extensive research on the Sri Lankan ethnic crisis. He now has a special message of peace and reconciliation to those committed to bring a lasting solution to the ethnic crisis in Sri Lanka. This book is written to convey that message.

This is the first time a person outside social science academia and the journalistic world has written a book on the Sri Lankan ethnic crisis. This is also the first time that a book written on the subject suggests a co-ordinated resolution to the crisis with a comprehensive model of governance for Sri Lanka.

The author has written and published three books on Sri Lankan topics before, one in English and the other two in Sinhalese, a vernacular language of Sri Lanka. The author wrote these books after a constitutional change in the country, renaming it as The Democratic Socialist Republic of Sri Lanka. The book in English, Democratic Socialism, discusses the pre-requisites of democracy. One of the books in Sinhalese, Sri Lanka Desapalanaya, Ayanna, Aayanna, Eyanna, Eeyanna (translation reads as A, B, C, D of Sri Lankan Politics) analyses the contemporary political system of Sri Lanka. The other, Desappremayen Udavadiwa Darudariyanta Kavivalinma Liyu Lipiyak (translation reads as A Letter to Our Children in Poems Written through Patriotism) is a book of poems. It gives a message of mutual respect, love and unity to the children of Sri Lanka in a child's diction. The government of Sri Lanka purchased a number of copies of this book for distribution among its schools and municipal libraries.

In 1989, while he was in Zambia, he wrote and directed a stage drama, Angulimala, depicting a story from Buddhist literature. Later he wrote and directed two other stage dramas in Canada based on historical heroic events in Sri Lanka, Hoisting the British Flag and Keppetipola Heroism, for the 50th Sri Lankan Independence anniversary celebrations held at Michael J. Fox Theatre in Burnaby, British Columbia, Canada, on 7 March1998. The author was one of the two Overall Co-ordinators of this event.

Currently, he is a member of the Board of Directors of the South Asian Network for Secularism and Democracy (SANSAD) in Canada, and an active member of the International South Asian Forum (INSAF). He possesses a Bachelor's degree from the University of Ceylon and a post-graduate degree from the University of Birmingham in the United Kingdom. He is married and has three children.

Foreword

It has been a pleasure to have known R. B. Herath for the last several years - as a person, and as a co-worker on the Board of Directors of "South Asian Network for Secularism and Democracy" (SANSAD).

As an organisation, SANSAD strives to bring together the diverse segments of the South Asian Diaspora living in British Columbia, Canada: people who have brought with them the rich cultural heritage from the lands of Bangladesh, India, Nepal, Pakistan and Sri Lanka. Cutting across the barriers of language, religion, national identities and affinity to the countries of origin, SANSAD strives to promote mutual respect among the people, peaceful resolution of conflicts between the countries of the region, the values of social justice, secularism and democracy, and upholding the rights of all minorities within the framework of democratic polity in plural societies.

"RB," as he is fondly known among his friends, has been a valuable asset as a Director of SANSAD. He has brought long years of political experience, consummate love for his country of origin Sri Lanka, an internationalist perspective, and above all a firm commitment to the values of democracy, secularism, and social justice. His being a Sinhalese did not affect his ability to look at the totality of the Sri Lankan situation in a proper historical and objective way. The earlier background paper on the Sri Lankan ethnic crisis he (along with other Sri Lankan Directors of SANSAD) produced was a very useful tool for an educational program organised in the South Asian community. I am glad that RB has now completed a book length study of the ethnic crisis in Sri Lanka. I feel honoured to be asked by him to read the manuscript of this book and write a few words as a foreword.

Sri Lanka, as a nation-state, is not exceptional in having a great deal of diversity among its people: diversity based upon religions practised, languages spoken, tribal or clan-based affinities, or varying histories of ancestral settlements in the land. Such diversity is found in practically every country of the world. Even in Western Europe (where the modern Nation State emerged after centuries of long struggle against monarchy, landed aristocracy and feudal order, and where the State eventually became an expression of the "national" character) there are still differences among the people based upon identifiable primordial affinities. However, those differences - in most cases, at least - could be accommodated due to the long process of consolidation of democratic norms and institutions. The situation is vastly different in post-colonial societies. What we have as national boundaries are constructs and legacies of the colonial rule. Centuries of colonial domination deprived these societies of the natural, necessary and long process of nation building. Whatever social differentiation based upon new class formations and economic developments might have occurred was thwarted. On the contrary, old feudal and pre-capitalist relations of production were reinforced and nurtured; and traditional differences based upon primordial identities (religion, language, etc.) were deepened, accentuated and turned into cleavages. If a new class emerged, it was the class of political and bureaucratic compradors, who could be relied upon, and who eventually emerged as the privileged, and often dynastic, elite in the post-colonial situation. Such has been the scene in most of the ex-colonial world; definitely so in the South Asian region. Conflicts based upon ethnic, linguistic or religious factors have been rampant. And they have acquired ominous character if the legitimate economic, political and cultural aspirations of distinct identities remain denied or are suppressed - especially through majoritarian self-righteousness and arrogance.

The conflict between the Sinhalese majority and Tamil minority in Sri Lanka is somewhat of an exceptional case due to the prolonged civil war that has been raging there, and because of the internationalisation of the conflict. RB rightly labels it as an "ethnic crisis". His book is a thorough and dispassionate account of the Sri Lankan history through different stages. In a most ruthless manner he nails down the root causes of the civil war which is now almost twenty years old, and has taken a toll of tens of thousands of lives. It is also a systematic study of the political and constitutional shifts and alliances over the period of five decades, which have so far failed to find a proper solution to the Sinhalese – Tamil conflict.

The most important aspect of the book is the earnestness with which RB makes a case for an entirely a new political beginning: to devise a new constitutional and political framework that would aim to secure full democratic and participatory rights to the various segments of Sri Lankan people.

It is a book that should be read by everyone interested in the phenomenon of identity politics, and in matters of democratic processes to ensure the civil, human, and political rights of the entire citizenry. And most certainly it is a book that should be read by all Sri Lankans, living in Sri Lanka or abroad. Hopefully, the book will generate the necessary and much-needed dialogue among the people as RB so earnestly desires.

Hari P. Sharma, Ph.D.
Professor Emeritus of Sociology
Simon Fraser University, British Columbia, Canada
President, South Asian Network for Secularism and Democracy (SANSAD), and President, International South Asia Forum (INSAF)

15 June 2002

Acronyms

BLP	Bolshevik Party
CIC	Ceylon Indian Congress
CNC	Ceylon National Congress
CP	Communist Party
CWC	Ceylon Workers Congress
DDC	District Development Council
DIG	Deputy Inspector General of Police
DPLF	Democratic people's Liberation Front
DWC	Democratic Workers Congress
ENLF	Eelam National Liberation Front
EPDP	Eelam People's Democratic Party
EPRLF	Eelam People's Revolutionary Liberation Front
EROS	Eelam Revolutionary Organization of Students
FP	Federal Party
IPKF	Indian Peace Keeping Force
JVP	Janatha Vimukthi Peramuna
LP	Labour Party
LSSP	Lanka Sama Samaja Party
LTTE	Liberation Tigers of Tamil Eelam
MOU	Memorandum of Understanding
MP	Member of Parliament
NUA	National Unity Alliance
PA	People's Alliance
PLF	People's Liberation Front (JVP)
PLOTE	People's Liberation Organization of Tamil Eelam
PP	Podujana Party
SAARC	South Asian Area for Regional Cooperation
SLFP	Sri Lanka Freedom Party
SLMC	Sri Lanka Muslim Congress
SLMC	Sri Lankan Muslim Congress
SLMM	Sri Lankan Monitoring Mission
SMS	Sinhala Maha Sabha
TC	All Ceylon Tamil Congress
TELO	Tamil Eelam Liberation Organization
TUF	Tamil United Front
TULF	Tamil United Liberation Front
TULF	Tamil United Liberation Front
UCPF	Upcountry People's Front

UK	United Kingdom
UNF	United national front
UNP	United National Party
USA	United States of America

CHAPTER 1: INTRODUCTION

The purpose of this book is to examine the Sinhala -Tamil ethnic crisis in Sri Lanka and to contribute towards a democratic process to resolve it. The crisis climaxed in the early 1980s as a civil war. This civil war has already claimed more than 65,000 lives and displaced more than 670,000 people from their homes. The civilians living on both sides of the warfront have suffered from the cessation of civil society, indiscriminate killings of innocent people, extortion, kidnappings, rape, and other war crimes. Those who have become victims of suicide bombers were a President, three cabinet ministers, and many other prominent political leaders.

The Liberation Tigers of Tamil Eelam (LTTE), a militant group within the largest ethnic minority in the country, the Tamils, started the civil war to establish a separate state for Tamils in the northern and eastern provinces of Sri Lanka. There are about 3.5 million Tamils altogether in the country out of the total population of 19.5 million (18%). The rest of the population consists of about 14.4 million Sinhalese (74%), 1.4 million Muslims (7%), 60,000 Malays (0.3%), 60,000 Burghers (0.3%), and 40,000 others of different ethnic identities (0.2%). The Sinhalese are predominantly Buddhists, while the Tamils are predominantly Hindus. According to 1981 census, 55.16% of the Tamils live in the Northern and Eastern Provinces, and the rest are concentrated in the central highlands and the urban areas outside the Northern and Eastern Provinces. Those settled in the central highlands, about a million, have a separate identity as Indian Tamils. They are descendants from the indentured Indians brought to the country during British colonialism in the nineteenth century for work in the colonial plantations. The Tamils who had domiciled in the country before that are generally referred to as Sri Lankan Tamils. Almost 74% of the Sri Lankan Tamils and 10% of the Indian Tamils live in the Northern and eastern Provinces.

The ethnic crisis and war in Sri Lanka has had implications beyond its borders. India had initially assisted in the training of the military cadres of the LTTE. In 1987, India sent thousands of its troops to Sri Lanka for peacekeeping purposes. The LTTE waged war against the members of the Indian peace keeping force and eventually together with the Sri Lankan government made India withdraw its forces in 1990. By this time the Indian army had already lost 1,150 troops to LTTE guns. Later, Indian Prime

1

Minister Rajiv Gandhi was assassinated by a LTTE female suicide bomber. Subsequently in 1992 the Indian government has proscribed the LTTE as a terrorist organization. Ever since, neither the central government of India nor any of its State governments has shown interest in playing a direct role in resolving the Sri Lankan ethnic crisis.

Since the early 1980s when the Sri Lankan ethnic crisis took on its violent war phase the international community had shown concern. Thousands of Sri Lankans who took refuge in India and many western countries had further influenced the separatist war. There had been a growing concern and pressure from the international community on the Sri Lankan government and the LTTE to resolve the crisis in a peaceful manner. In this context the activities of some members of the Sri Lankan Tamil diaspora to financially and otherwise support the LTTE have become a contentious issue in many countries in the world. The United States of America (USA), Canada, the United Kingdom (UK), and Australia, where the Sri Lankan Tamil Diaspora is concentrated, have followed the Indian example and proscribed the LTTE as a terrorist organization.

Some of the factors that may have contributed to the ethnic crisis in Sri Lanka may have a long history. However the escalation of the crisis to a separatist war is largely due to three recent, post-independence factors. Firstly, the country's constitution at its independence in 1948 had many shortcomings. It ignored the basic issues of equality, fundamental human rights and even citizenship. As a result, it left the doors open for inequality, discrimination, disenfranchisement, and the eventual conflicts in the country over ethnicity and religion. Post-independent governments have revised the constitution on two separate occasions, in 1972 and 1978. The revisions, however, failed to address the shortcomings of the country's constitution, and, instead, further aggravated issues of fundamental rights and discrimination.

Secondly, some post-independent politicians of the country have pursued shortcuts to power by resorting to divisive, chauvinist policies, taking undue advantage of the shortcomings of the country's constitution. After coming to power, these leaders have passed laws and regulations that discriminated against the minorities in the country. This has generated chauvinism among the majority Sinhalese and the largest minority, Tamils. Before the European colonization of the country, the Sinhalese and Tamils of Sri Lanka had lived separately for more than two centuries in three kingdoms, two Sinhalese (Kotte and Kandyan kingdoms) and one Tamil (Jaffna kingdom). Sinhalese kingdoms in the country date back to more than 2500 years. South Indian invasions and conquests had led to the rule of some of the Sinhalese kingdoms in the northern plain by foreigners from time to time. The leaders of post independent governments and the LTTE often represent and interpret this history in ways to legitimize their respective positions on the present ethnic divide.

Thirdly, the post-independent economy of the country has failed to create sufficient employment opportunities to its growing numbers of educated youth. Sri Lanka has been internationally noted for its very successful social development, particularly in education and health. But the slow economy failed to create adequate employment opportunities for the educated youth. This has made the limited opportunities in employment highly competitive. As a result, there was an increase in the need and competition for post-secondary education as well. In time, these matters became political issues among the different ethnic groups. Every group wanted a fair share of the limited opportunities. The leaders of the different ethnic groups, however, did not see eye to eye as to how to achieve that objective. The government dominated by Sinhalese leaders, advocated that the new opportunities in the public sector employment and higher education should be on a quota basis on the strength of the population of each group. The government argued that such a system was fair, as it could eventually correct the existing over-representation of Tamils in the public service and higher learning institutions. The leaders of the Tamil community, however, argued that it would be very unfair to follow such a policy. They insisted on selection to the public service and higher education institutions purely on the basis of merit. At one point, the government set two separate standards for the university entrance requirements, one for Sinhalese and the other for Tamils. These separate standards were applicable even when a Sinhalese student and a Tamil student sat for the same subjects in one language, say English.

Thus, the factors that contributed to the escalation of the Sinhala -Tamil ethnic crisis in Sri Lanka are both political and economic in nature. Many critics have commented on both these aspects. While the author recognizes the significance and importance of both, this book is confined to the political aspect of the crisis.

The post-independence governments of Sri Lanka attempted to bring about a solution to the ethnic crisis through a political settlement. However, they have so far failed to untangle the crisis and to bring lasting peace. In their attempts to solve the ethnic crisis, leaders of some post-independence governments had shown a willingness to correct the wrongs they had done to the Tamil community. For example, the government led by Prime Minister S. W. R. D. Bandaranaike had passed a bill in parliament making Sinhala the only official language of the country in June 1956. A year later, however, he entered into a special agreement with S. J. V. Chelvanayagam, the leader of the Federal Party representing the Tamil community. This agreement accepted Tamil too as an official language in the north and east and the need to allow a "reasonable use of the Tamil language" in the other provinces. This agreement known as the Bandaranaike-Chelvanayagam Pact had provisions for the setting up of Regional Councils with adequate decentralized powers in the provinces. It also had a commitment not to change the majority status of Tamil population in the north and east with the settlement of Sinhalese colonists. In addition, there were to be negotiations with the representatives of the Indian Tamils in the central highlands, who had been defranchised in 1949, on the question of their citizenship. Bandaranaike, however, could fulfil only one of these promises; he enacted the Tamil language (Special Provisions) Act of 1958 allowing reasonable use of Tamil in administration. He failed to implement the rest of the promises due to strong protests by his own supporters. The assassination of Prime Minster Bandaranaike by a Sinhalese Buddhist monk is in some ways linked to these protests.

A subsequent government led by Prime Minister Dudley Senanayake entered into a similar agreement with Chelvanayagam in 1965. Senanayake created regulations making Tamil the language of administration and law in the north and east and assured relief to Tamil public servants victimized by the Sinhala Only Act of 1956. He too, however, failed to implement the agreement in full due to strong protests by the extremist elements within the Sinhalese majority.

After the commencement of the separatist war there have been peace talks between the warring parties in 1985/6, 1990, and 1994/5, with and without cease-fires. These peace talks continued for months and ended without reaching a mutually acceptable solution to end the ethnic crisis. According to critics, every time peace talks broke down, the LTTE had returned to the warfront with more military strength than ever before. As a result, they say, the peace talks have only resulted in further deepening the crisis. Later in 2000, the government tabled in the country's legislature a devolution package modeled on the Indian federal system for a vote. The government, however, had to withdraw it from the parliamentary agenda after a few days due to strong protests from the same extremist elements within the Sinhalese majority.

The government of Sri Lanka and the LTTE have once again initiated a peace process in 2002. As the first step of this new peace initiative, the two warring parties have signed a Memorandum of Understanding (MOU) with a cease-fire arrangement on 22 February 2002. According to the LTTE, it has not yet decided to drop its call for a separate state. It treats this as an issue to be discussed at the peace talks now expected to follow. According to critics, the global war on terrorism launched by the United States of America and allied forces will significantly influence the LTTE to accept a political solution to the ethnic crisis in Sri Lanka within the context of one country. The global war on terrorism is, however, not a solution in itself to eradicate the root cause of the ethnic crisis in Sri Lanka.

There are numerous reasons for the failure of the efforts so far made by the post-independence governments to find a lasting solution to the ethnic crisis. In the first place, post-independent leaders never had a cohesive program in the country for the national consolidation and integration of all its peoples as one nation. If there was such a program, the government should have been able to identify and correct the shortcomings of the constitution at the earliest opportunity, closing the doors for inequality and discrimination. In the absence of such a program, the political opportunists in the country became successful in their attempts to gain power by resorting to divisive, ethnic and chauvinist politics. In turn, this led to more inequalities and discrimination, even with constitutional amendments. Thus, since independence Sri Lanka was preparing itself not to bridge the differences that existed among the different ethnic groups in the country, but to aggravate them.

In the process, some of these post-independent politicians turned many innocent peace-loving people in the country into political activists in support of their divisive, chauvinist policies. These leaders had succeeded in doing this by propagating their divisive, chauvinist policies in a disguised form of Sri Lankan nationalism. These leaders have interpreted Sinhalese-Buddhist nationalism as Sri Lankan nationalism, ignoring the ethnic and religious diversity of the country. They also advocated that only a unitary system of government could deliver the benefits of such a brand of nationalism. In pursuit of their course, these post-independent leaders have made federalism an anathema in the minds of the majority Sinhalese-Buddhists. In the process, their political activists, including some Buddhist monks, have become the most formidable opponents to any form of reconciliatory action, including federalism, as a solution to the ethnic crisis.

The dynamics of the power struggle within the two-party system that evolved after independence is another critical factor contributing to the escalation of the ethnic crisis. Whenever either of the two main parties took a step towards minority rights, the other had postured as the crusader of the interests of the majority. These two political parties have continued to rule the country since independence on their own or in coalition with minor parties, changing office back and forth.

The manner in which the post-independent governments attempted to address minority issues is also questionable. Their corrective efforts were secretive in nature. The discussions on possible corrections were strictly limited to the leaders of the government and the concerned minority groups. After striking a deal in those secret talks, they expected the whole country to accept it. Every time this happened, however, the government leaders had to face strong objections and protests from the Sinhalese, especially the extremist elements among them, some from among the government's own supporters. This clearly demonstrates the lack of a proper democratic process in the country for resolving its ethnic crisis. The leaders of the two main political parties have built an elite and dynastic-type rule in the country. For them, critics say, democracy ends at the ballot box. They fight elections on specific platforms. Once voted to power, however, they appear to disregard the promises they have made to the people.

The constitutional requirement for a two-thirds majority support in the legislature to establish a new form of government has become another problem in resolving the ethnic crisis. The constitution requires such a majority to change any of its provisions. Since the introduction of the proportionate representative electoral system in 1978, however, it has become difficult for any one political party or group to win enough seats in the legislature to have two-third majority on any issue. This is one reason why the devolution package tabled in the legislature in the year 2000 was not passed.

It also appears that the efforts of the government at the peace talks held so far have revolved around the need to address minority issues due to discriminative laws and regulations. The need to formulate a new system of governance for the country, with an altogether new constitution acceptable to all the ethnic groups, was not in focus. Before independence there was a definite proposal for such an altogether new system of government. It was a proposal to have a federal system of government giving the different ethnic groups in the country the power to rule themselves within the context of one, Sri Lankan nation. The representatives of the former Kandyan kingdom tabled the proposal at the sittings of two constitutional commissions appointed by the British government, in 1927 and 1946. Neither the departing colonialists nor the non-Kandyan Sinhalese or Tamil leaders supported the proposal at the commission sittings. There were, however, no protests or objections to the proposal from the Sinhalese or Buddhists as such. This proposal will be referred to later in the book in the context of its relevance to the present ethnic crisis.

The above is a brief outline of the ethnic crisis and civil war in Sri Lanka. The body of this book, after this introductory chapter, analyses the crisis in Sri Lanka in more detail and suggests a possible solution that may benefit all its peoples. The second chapter gives a historic background to the crisis. It takes the reader through three phases of Sri Lankan history: pre-colonial, colonial and post-colonial. It is useful for the reader to know the historic background of the crisis to fully understand its present complexities. The third chapter identifies the root cause of the crisis and explains 10 factors that have contributed to its escalation into a separatist war since independence in 1948. The fourth chapter stresses the importance of having an altogether new political beginning for Sri Lanka as a multi-ethnic, independent nation. It perhaps encapsulates the purpose of this book to suggest a way out of the crisis and work towards a solution. This chapter also discusses the varied governing systems developed in other democracies in the world, and proposes a new democratic governing model for Sri Lanka. The model addresses the ethnic issues in Sri Lanka and formulates a way to establish genuine democracy in the country, giving the power of self-determination to all its peoples. This chapter also explains how the country may be able to implement such a new model of democratic governance within the present political climate. The fifth and final chapter calls upon all Sri Lankans to take up the challenge of being part of the central decision making process in making their country a place fit to live in for all. The model of governance described in the book is, however, not a hard and fast blue print for immediate implementation. It is a basis for a dialogue among all concerned Sri Lankans living in Sri Lanka and abroad. Hopefully, it may provide a pathway for a peaceful and viable solution to the ethnic crisis in Sri Lanka on a permanent basis.

CHAPTER 2: HISTORIC BACKGROUND

Pre-Colonial Era

No one knows for sure the actual beginning of the human occupation of Sri Lanka. Historians only make good guesses based on whatever information available to them. K. M. de Silva, one time Chair of History at the University of Peradeniya, Sri Lanka, suggests that "judging from existing information about pre-historic times on the Indian subcontinent, homo sapiens probably first appeared in Sri Lanka about 500,000 B.C."[1] There is no evidence to prove this suggestion. According to him and other historians the earliest archaeological objects, such as implements made of stone and skeletal remains found on the island, date back to the subsequent Paleolithic culture of the second Stone Age period. C. R. de Silva, who was also a Chair of History at the University of Peradeniya, Sri Lanka, explains that such archaeological evidence has "enabled archaeologists to build up a picture of what is generally known as the 'Balangoda cultures.' This culture prevailed over most of the island from perhaps 10,000 BC to the sixth century BC and indeed survived in the remoter forested regions of the island up to the Christian era."[2]

Historians agree that the Balangoda man had Australoid characteristics and lived in caves. Originally, he fed only on meat, which he ate without cooking. Later, some time in the first millennium, he gained the ability to make fire, shape stone tools and had some knowledge of agriculture and drilling techniques. By this time, the Balangoda culture had resembled that of neighbouring south India. This shows the probability that at this time the people who lived in the region too may have been in some form of interaction across the Palk Strait.[3] A number of experts have expressed their opinions about the nature and extent of this interaction. A. J. Wilson sums up these opinions, "Historians such as A. L. Basham have expressed the view that Dravidian (South Indian) infiltration into Ceylon must have been going on from the earliest historical times and before. G. C. Mendis holds that the Veddhas, the pre-Aryan aboriginal tribe of hunters who lived till recent times (still living) in certain parts of the island, were probably from (Dravidian) South India and crossed to the island on foot before it became separated from the mainland by the ocean (at its narrowest point the Strait is about 20 miles wide). C. R. de Silva

SRI LANKAN HISTORY
Pre-Colonial Era

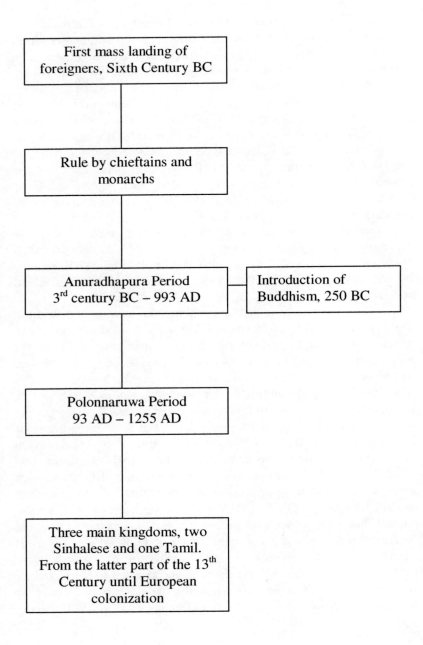

in 1994 confirmed this thesis on the basis of S. U. Deraniyagala's work: 'People who lived in the early Iron Age in Sri Lanka were diverse in their origin.... from north and south India as well as the Australoid peoples of the island.' The jurist H. W. Tambiah expressed the opinion in 1968 that recent archaeological finds in Ceylon showed the pre-Vijayan civilization to have been Dravidian."[4]

It is also possible that the Balangoda man was influenced by the Hoabinhian culture of Southeast Asia now believed to be the cradle of human civilization. According to historians, the Hoabinhians used stone tools and pottery and practiced agriculture thousands of years earlier than in India, China, or West Asia. There is evidence to show Hoabinhians' influence on the neighbouring countries, including the Philippines, Indonesia, Burma, Thailand, Malaysia, and even Madagascar. There is, however, no evidence to show any link between the Hoabinhians and the Balangoda people. Nevertheless, it is probable that the Hoabinhians used the sea routes through Sri Lanka, and settled on the island in significant numbers.[5] C. R. de Silva says, "However, no definite trace of such settlement has yet been found."[6]

The geographical location of Sri Lanka in the Indian Ocean has been a major cause of foreign influence. The Straits of Malacca and the Sunda Strait, the gateways from the East and South East Asia to the Indian Ocean, and the Straits of Hormuz and Bab-el-Mandeb where the sailors from Europe and West Asia entered the Indian Ocean were all within two thousand miles from the island. In early times, it was the winds and ocean currents that determined the maritime routes in the Indian Ocean for the sailors who arrived there from these two directions. As a result, Sri Lanka became a centre of naval and commercial interaction. The sailors who landed on the island at this time may have come from many parts of the world, the majority from neighbouring countries.

With its breath-taking scenary and rare natural resources : gems, emery, pearls, spices, and ivory, Sri Lanka was a haven of opportunities for sailors in the Indian Ocean. Some of the sailors, however, had only tourist interests in the island. They enjoyed the beauty, serenity and the wildlife of the island and then left for their intended destinations. Others settled in the island, making it their permanent home. Some of those who settled engaged in foreign trade, exporting mainly Sri Lankan spices to the rest of the world. The settlers who did not engage in foreign trade resorted to agriculture and other means of living, using new technologies and skills that they had brought to the island from wherever they had come. In time the indiginous community freely assimilated some of these foreign visitors.

Early Settlers

The sailors that were brought to the island's shoreline by the winds and ocean currents generally came in small groups. Any exception to this might have been easily noticed and remembered by the islanders. According to Mahavamsa,[7] the most important of the earliest chronicles of the island, the first mass landing of foreigners on Sri Lankan soil occurred in 483 B.C. It was a group of sailors from North India, led by a North Indian prince called Vijaya. According to Mahavamsa, Vijaya was a son of Sinhabahu, the ruler of Sinhapura in Latadesa in Northern India. Sinhabahu appeared to have exiled his son and 700 of his closest companions by ship, as their conduct had infuriated him and his subjects. Vijaya and his companions are said to have first landed at a port on the West Coast of India north of Bombay to a hostile reception, before eventually landing on the northwest coast of Sri Lanka near Mannar. According to the chronicle, Vijaya's arrival on the island coincided with the passing away of the Buddha in North India.

There is some doubt among historians about the place of origin of Vijaya in Northern India. There is also doubt as to whether Vijaya was a historic figure or a mere name (meaning victory) symbolizing the successful migration or invasion of the island by North Indians. Some evidence in Mahavamsa suggests that there were mass migrations from both the eastern and western coasts of Northern India. According to the legendary story of Vijaya, after arriving in the island, he accepted Kuveni, a daughter of a local chief, as his first consort, and became a ruler in the island. This is said to be the beginning of the Sinhala or Sinhalese identity and dynastic rule of Sri Lanka.

The mass migration of North Indians to the island had a big impact on its aboriginal culture. The North Indian newcomers were relatively more sophisticated people, with iron tools, advanced agricultural, trading, and communication techniques. They started to use iron ploughs in preparing the land for paddy cultivation. The indigenous community of the Balangoda culture had to adopt to the new ways or relocate inland to the forests. The migrants did, however, integrate with some of the indigenous people of the island. The indigenous people who refused to assimilate the new comers retreated to forests and continued to live as before. The dependents of the indigenous people who withdrew were referred to as Veddhas. They are the adivasis or aboriginals of the island.

The Mahavamsa also records that after living with Kuveni for some time, Vijaya rejected and exiled her, and brought a princess from South India, a daughter of a Pandyan ruler of Madura, as his queen. This South Indian princess is said to have brought a number of maidens who later became the wives of Vijaya's followers. This shows that their descendents, the Sinhalese, are not direct descendents of North Indians. C. R. de Silva explains, "These stories seem to indicate that whatever was the origin of the Sinhala identity the people whom it eventually encompassed were not just settlers from North India alone but also the product of some intermarriage with the earlier inhabitants of Sri Lanka and with migrants from South India."[8]

The Mahavamsa and other early chronicles depict Vijaya and his line of successors as kings of the whole island. According to inscriptional evidence, this is, however, not correct. The inscriptions clearly indicate that there were a number of independent power bases ruled by chieftains in various parts of the island. The Mahavamsa itself provides clear evidence for this. According to Mahavamsa, Vijaya and his early successors had established their power in the Malvatu Oya region of the country and ruled from Upatissagama. Then, there was a ruler, Pandukhabhaya, who reigned the lower reaches of Mahaveli Ganga. Pandukhabaya had eventually triumphed over the Uptissagama regime, and moved the capital to Anuradhapura on the northern plain of the island. Anuradhapura remained as an important power centre of the island for more than one thousand years.

Inscriptional evidence also shows that Anuradhapura rulers or chieftains did not have continuous and undisputed control over the whole country or even over the whole of the northern plain. A number of independent power bases seemed to have existed at various times of this period, to the east, northwest and north of Anuradhapura on the northern plain and outside the plain. Such independent power bases outside the northern plain included the mountainous centre of the island and Kataragama in the south.

Sinhalese-Buddhist Identity

Despite such territorial divisions among early chieftains, the different groups of migrants and aboriginal inhabitants who assimilated them began to develop a common and distinctive culture, characterized by an agricultural economy based on advanced techniques of irrigation and farming. The introduction of Buddhism to the island in the third century BC and its subsequent spread within the country became a force of crystallization and consolidation of this common culture. In time, the different languages of the migrants, including those who originally arrived on the island from South India and the aboriginals of the island spoke, evolved into one language-identity, Sinhala or Sinhalese. According to experts, inscriptions that followed show little variation in language and script throughout the island. This was how a Sinhalese identity, with a common language, religion and culture, began on the island. Sinhalese is considered as an Indo-European language. This supports the history of migrants coming from North India.

One of the unique distinctions of the Sinhalese culture that evolved was the central role Buddhism played in it. Buddhism was a driving force that united people in their communities. The rulers of the day, like their subjects, held Buddhist monks in reverence, and were fully committed to safeguard and protect their interests. Throughout the country the rulers, monks and the laity, worked together for the advancement of their common language and religion, Sinhalese and Buddhism respectively, and for their unique way of life.

Advanced Hydraulic Civilisation

The advanced irrigation system Sinhalese Buddhists developed on the northern plain was unique in many ways. Ravindralal Anthonis says, "... no contemporary civilization in any part of the then-known world had a superior (irrigation) system."[9] It consisted of thousands of man-made reservoirs called 'wewas' and an extensive network of water conveyance and distribution canals crisscrossing the northern plain. Anthonis reports that according to Surveyor General R. L. Brohier, a 1904 count had disclosed 11,200 wewas in the Anuradhapura and Northern provinces alone.[10] Sri Lankan engineers at the time appear to have had an amazing knowledge of trigonometry and structural engineering and hydraulic principles. They built reservoir dams with properly designed structural foundations and a high level of soil compaction to withstand heavy pressure and last thousands of years. They had designed special hydraulic structures to regulate the flow of water from these dams during times of irrigation and flood. By the third century BC, they invented a valve pit called bisokotuwa,[11] the prototype of sluices which regulate the outflow from contemporary reservoirs. The principle of 'hydraulic jump,' which is comparatively new in the rest of the world, had been effectively used in their designs. The irrigation canals they built had this and other amazing hydraulic features. K. M. de Silva gives some specific details of few irrigation structures that testify to the highly advanced engineering technology at the time, "Engineering milestones included the Kantalai tank built by King Mahasena (274 – 302 AD). It covered 4, 560 acres, was fed by a canal 25 miles long, and was contained by a dam 50 feet high. Even more superior in technology was the Kalawewa constructed by King Dhatusena (460 – 478 AD). It encompassed seven square miles and had a dam 3 ½ miles long and 36 to 58 feet high with a spill of hammered granite. A canal 54 miles long and 40 feet wide linked it to the city of Anuradhapura and played an integral role in the development of that ancient capital. The first 17 miles of this canal, known as the Yoda Ela or Giants' Canal, had a gradient of only six inches' slope per mile. Subsequent centuries saw even more remarkable developments in the irrigation of Sri Lanka."[12]

The Buddhist stupas or dagobas and sculptural works that sprang up in the country at the same time blended well with the irrigation works. The stupas were and are still objects of veneration, as they usually enshrined relics of the Buddha and his well known early disciples. The stupas are solid hemispherical bodies of varying sizes. Two of them, Abhayagiri and Jetavanarama are taller than Egypt's third pyramid at Gaza. According to K. M. de Silva, the tallest, Jetavanarama, which is more than 400 feet high, may be the largest monument in the Buddhist world.[13] He further explains, "It towers above St. Paul's Cathedral in London and nearly matches the height of St. Peter's in the Vatican."[14] The engineering, architectural and sculpturing expertise of the early Sri Lankans, evident from the ruins of these religious works and the sophisticated irrigation system explained earlier, remains monumental and amazes the modern experts and tourists alike.

The politics of the Sinhalese dynasties were often in the hands of the chieftains, the local rulers. In time the stronger chieftains appeared to have gradually extended their territory and power, resulting in the fall of some independent power centers and the rise of new and expanded territories from time to time. Having conquered a significant portion of the island, some of the chieftains ascended to royal status as Kings and Queens. In addition to inter-chieftaincy conflicts, the dynastic rule at the time was characterized by family feuds, succession-wars, and internal rebellions. Despite this, the Anuradhapura rule had remained as the major Sinhalese rule in the island.

South Indian Invasions

By the second century BC, however, the Anuradhapura rule of the northern plain became a target for South Indian invasions. After their first successful invasion, two South Indian Tamil warriors, Sena and Guttika, ruled the Anuradhapura regime for twenty years, from 177 to 157 BC. Thereafter the Anuradhapura regime was ruled by South Indian warriors from 145 to 101 BC, 103 to 89 BC, 231 to 240 AD, and from 429 to 455 AD. Then came the 993 AD South Indian Chola invasion. This time, after capturing Anuradhapura, the invaders moved the capital to Polonnaruwa. There were two periods of South Indian rule in Polonnaruwa, first from 993 to 1070 AD and later from 1212 to 1255 AD For five years, from 1056 to 1061 AD the south and southwest of the country also came under the South Indian rulers of Polonnaruwa.

Mahavamsa depicts the reigns of these South Indian rulers as particularly opprobrious, dismal periods of Sri Lankan history, characterized by torture, extortion, plunder, and destruction of Buddhism. Modern historians cast doubt upon such interpretation of what may have actually happened during these periods. Modern historians generally believe that some of these South Indian rulers, especially those who came before the fourth or fifth century A.D, were themselves Buddhists or had been supportive of their Buddhist subjects' way of life. For example, the South Indian ruler Elara (145 to 101 BC) had enjoyed considerable support from Sinhalese Buddhists, and there is no evidence at all that Buddhism suffered in the area during his period. However, Mahavamsa records that the whole purpose of the campaign of the Sinhalese Buddhist prince Dutthugamani, who later triumphed over Elara, was to restore Buddhism. C. R. de Silva says, "it is likely that the authors of Mahavamsa, living and writing at a time when Sinhala-Tamil tensions were high, had re-interpreted the story of Dutthugamani in the light of contemporary events."[15]

Mahavamsa also records that at the time of his passing, the Buddha had spoken to Sakka, the Lord of gods, about Vijaya's arrival in Sri Lanka, which is believed to have happened at the very same time. According to the chronicle, the Buddha told Sakka[16] that with the arrival of Vijaya and his 700 followers, Buddhism would flourish in the island, and had asked him to carefully protect Vijaya and his followers and Lanka (Wilhelm Geiger (Trans.), The Mahavamsa, p.55.). This story in the Mahavamsa no doubt had given the Sinhalese a special identity in Buddhist history. In time, the safeguarding and fostering of Buddhism became a strong force of unification and a powerful and popular political platform among the Sinhalese people.

Modern historians and academics, however, are not sure whether this story is true or just a legendary creation of the Buddhist monks who wrote Mahavamsa, as in the case of Dutthugamani. It may be possible that the authors of the Mahavamsa created a legend to energize Sinhalese people against contemporary threats of invasion from the non-Buddhist warriors of South India. A. J. Wilson explains, "the legend of the Buddha handing over the entire island to the safe possession of the Sinhalese people was a historical myth designed to refute the Ceylon Tamil 'presumption' that the status of a 'founding race' could be shared between them."[17]

Whatever the facts of the case might be, the rise of three powerful Hindu militant dynasties, Pandya, Pallawa, and Chola, in South India after the seventh century brought a new dimension to the politics of the region. First the Pandyans who rose to power in the eighth century conquered the Anuradhapura regime during the rein of Sena 1 (833 – 853 AD). They ransacked Anuradhapura City and defeated its Sinhalese army at Mahatalithagama. Sena 1, however, later managed to persuade them to return to India by offering a large indemnity. According to historians, Tamil residents in the north of the country supported the Pandyans in this invasion. C. R. de Silva explains, "The Pandyan invading forces apparently found some support among the Tamils resident in the northern coastal area and the Sri Lankan forces were completely defeated at Mahatalithagama."[18]

From this time onwards, the Anuradhapura rulers concentrated their efforts in curbing the power of potential South Indian invaders. This drew the Anuradhapura rulers into South Indian dynastic wars among the Pandyans, Pallawas and Cholas. In 862 AD, during the rein of Sena 11 (853 – 887 AD) the Sinhalese army crossed the sea and seized Madura, the capital of the Pandyans, in support of a rebel son, Varaguna, of the Pandyan King, Srimara Srivallagha - at a time of a Pandyan-Pallawa war. This whole saga ended with Varaguna becoming the next king of the Pandyan kingdom.[19]

This type of military involvement of the Sinhalese army in South Indian dynastic struggles didn't always have a happy ending for Anuradhapura rulers. For example, the involvement of the Sri Lankan force in the Chola-Pandyan war in 915 AD turned suicidal for them. By this time Cholas had become the most powerful dynastic force in South India. When they went to war with the Pandyans, the Sri Lankan force took their side. Cholas finally won the war decisively defeating the Sri Lankan and Pandyan armies. After the war, the Pandyan king arrived in Sri Lanka and left the Pandyan royal jewels and insignia with Anuradhapura rulers. This type of Sri Lankan-Pandyan alliance brought the wrath of the mighty Cholas against Anuradhapura rulers. Ever since, Sri Lanka continued to remain a target for the Cholas, who later consolidated their power in the region. There were a number of Chola attacks after the 915 AD war; the strongest of all was the one that occurred in 993 AD. This time, the army that was sent to Sri Lanka by the Chola king, Rajaraja 1, captured and ransacked Anuradhapura, established its power over the northern plain, and started to rule the plain from Polonnaruwa. Polonnaruwa remained a seat of government in the island until 1255 AD, first in the hands of Cholas for 77 years till 1070 AD, then in the hands of Sinhalese rulers who regained power over the northern plain from 1070 to 1212 AD and finally in the hands of two South Indian warriors from 1212 to 1255 AD The South Indian warrior who defeated the last Sinhalese ruler in Polonnaruwa, Lilavati, the queen of Parakramabahu 1, in 1212 AD was a Pandyan Prince by the name of Parakramapandu. The last South Indian warrior who ruled from Polonnaruwa (1215 to 1255 AD) was a prince from Kalinga, Kalinga Magha.

Demise of Hydraulic Civilisation

The Sinhalese chronicles that appeared after Mahavamsa, including Chulavamsa, Nikaya Sangrahaya and Saddharmaratnakara, show that the periods of South Indian rule after 883 AD had been particularly disturbing, with chaos, looting and pillage on the northern plain. During these periods, the irrigation system that had been neglected or destroyed as a result of invasions and other reasons, if any, remained unattended. According to the chronicles, this situation, especially during the rein of Kalinga Magha, eventually led to the end of the hydraulic civilization on the northern plain.

It is possible that during such periods of chaos many Sinhalese people who lived on the northern plain may have migrated to the south. Such migration may have been at its peak in the thirteenth century when lawlessness and violence remained longer and more widespread on the northern plain, especially during the period of Kalinga Magha, as explained in Chulavamsa. If those with technical expertise and experience in operating and maintaining the sophisticated irrigation system of the time also left the area, restoration works would have become difficult or impossible. Under any event, South Indians that came and occupied the northern plain at that time may not have had the expertise and experience necessary to effectively manage such a sophisticated irrigation system.

As explained in the above mentioned chronicles and, indeed, in the writings of modern historians, some Sinhalese rulers who took control over the northern plain in between the periods of South Indian rulers spent much of their time in restoring its irrigation system. The contributions in this regard made by Vijayabahu 1 (1070 to 1110 AD) and Parakramabahu 1 (1153 to 1186 AD) in particular were extremely significant. Vijayabahu 1, who ruled in Polonnaruwa immediately after Cholas, did a great deal to restore the irrigation system, and Parakramabahu 1 further extended the system to the highest resplendent era of hydraulic civilization of the country's history. C. R. de Silva refers to early writings about Parakramabahu's contributions in his Sri Lanka: A History, "The Chulavamsa records that he (Prakramabahu) restored or built 165 dams, 3910 canals, 163 major tanks and 2376 minor tanks. Much of this must certainly represent restoration of the irrigation network of the Anuradhapura era, but Parakramabahu's reign certainly saw the extension of the network. The pride of place among new works went to the gigantic Parakrama Samudra near Polonnaruwa which was fed both by the old network via the Giritale tank and a new canal bringing water from a dam at Angamadilla on the Amban Ganga."[20]

Going by the above, it may be reasonable to assume that the beginning of the real end of the hydraulic civilization on the northern plain occurred only after Parakramabahu's reign. After Parakramabahu, Polonnaruwa remained in the hands of Sinhalese rulers for only 26 years, from 1186 to 1212 AD This was a period of instability, especially after the reign of Nissankamalla (1187 – 1196 AD), due to many dynastic conflicts among the Sinhalese and repeated Chola invasions from South India. There is, however, no evidence to suggest that there was significant neglect or disruption of the irrigation network during this period. This boils down to the belief expressed by Chulavamsa that the demise of the hydraulic civilization on the northern plain was primarily caused by South Indian invasions and the reportedly hideous rule that followed by the invaders in the early thirteenth century.

Some modern historians have different views as to what may have led to the demise of the hydraulic civilization on the northern plain. One such view is that the centralization of administration during the reign of Sinhalese kings, including Vijayabahu 1 and Parakramabahu 1, might have weakened the local initiative of people to maintain the irrigation network. Initially, the maintenance and repair of the network had been the responsibility of locally organized groups of people at the village level who directly benefited from it in terms of revenue, water or both. With a centralized system of administration, these local groups may have lost some of those benefits, thus frustrating them in their efforts in maintenance and repair of the irrigation network.

Another view expressed by some modern historians is that under any event there was a significant movement of people from the northern plain to the south and southwest, the wet zone, in search of more attractive land for settlement. The south and the southwest were much more attractive to settle because of better climatic conditions, fertile soil to grow a vast variety of food items, and adequate rainfall for cultivation with less reliance on irrigation. Initial settlers in the island may have avoided the wet zone as it was thickly forested. However, those who dared to go there may have proved the benefits of settling there. In time this may have led to mass movements of people to the wet zone. According to C. R. de Silva, such mass movements of people to the south may have begun "in the heyday of Polonnaruwa as a response to the increasingly high dues demanded of the peasant in Rajarata,"[21] meaning the northern plain. Even in this situation, it may be reasonable to think that the subsequent South Indian invasions by Cholas, Pandyans and Kalinga Magha and the tyrannical rule perpetrated by Parakramapandu and Magha in Polonnaruwa did intensify the movement of the people to the south.

Three Kingdoms, Two Sinhalese and One Tamil

The end of Magha's rule was also the end of Polonnaruwa era. Thereafter the old heartland of hydraulic civilization became an area

of dissension between Magha's forces and the Sinhalese army that
ousted Magha. During this period, Tamils on the northern plain
withdrew to the extreme north and created a new Tamil power base
in the Jaffna peninsula, which later emerged as a separate kingdom
toward the end of the thirteenth century. This also triggered an
influx of more Tamils from South India to the north. As the Tamils
moved to the extreme north, the Sinhalese people who lived on the
northern plain moved southward to the southwest and central
regions of the country.

These migrations of the Sinhalese people finally led to the
emergence of two powerful, separate Sinhalese kingdoms, one
based in the central hills, the Kandyan kingdom, and the other in the
southwest. The descendents of the Sinhalese of the Kandyan
kingdom are generally referred to as Kandyans, and the descendents
of the Sinhalese of the kingdom in the southwest as Low Country
Sinhalese.

The Kandyan kingdom had grown in strength and size ever
since its formation, and in time became the last of the Sinhalese
kingdoms of the island - until 1815 AD The Sinhalese power base in
the southwest and the Tamil kingdom in the north lasted until they
came under Portuguese rule in the sixteenth century. According to
historians, the Tamil kingdom in the north was also under Sinhalese
rule for a period of few decades during the time of Parakramabahu
VI (1412 – 1467 AD), who ruled from Kotte.

These three kingdoms developed well-defined separate
administrations. According to C. R. de Silva, the Sinhalese kings
ruled their kingdoms with the help of a number of ministers. In the
Kotte kingdom, the chief minister had the title of 'ekanayake.' The
central administration had a number of key positions:
'bhandaranayaka' in charge of the warehouses; 'adikarana
nayaka' in charge of justice, 'aramudalnayaka' in charge of
economic affairs; 'badunayaka' responsible for collecting taxes;
and so on (C. R. de Silva, Sri Lanka: A History, p.99).

The emergence of the three different kingdoms, centred
around the southwest, the centre and the extreme north, occurred
after Magha abandoned the historic agricultural base on the northern
plain and its irrigation system. This resulted in a gradual decline in
agricultural production and the revenues collected by governments.
At the same time there was a growing external demand for spices
due to increased trade in the Indian Ocean. In this situation, the
governments started on a new economic venture, the export of
spices, mainly cinnamon and pepper, with royal monopolies.

Colonial Era

European Colonisation

Vasco da Gama, a Portuguese national, discovered the oceanic route from Europe to India around the Cape of Good Hope in 1498 A. D. This discovery was one of the most important events in maritime history. Its consequences also had profound impact on countries in the Indian Ocean, politically, economically and culturally. Sri Lanka had its own share of this impact. Its first Portuguese contact was Lourenco de Almeida's fleet in 1505 AD. Sri Lanka was not an intended destination for the fleet; the adverse winds drove the fleet to the Sri Lankan coast. S. Arasaratnam explains, "Don Lourenco, son of the Portuguese viceroy of India, was cruising in the Indian Ocean from the new Portuguese fort at Cochin when he was blown to Colombo."[22]   These first European visitors to the island had a friendly audience with the Sinhalese king in Kotte, and left with "some cinnamon and two elephants, together with an impression of the commercial possibilities of the island."[23]

Among the international traders in the region at the time, Arabs played a significant role. They controlled an extensive shipping network in the area to supply spices and gems to European and Middle Eastern countries. In addition to spices and gems, these traders exported pearls, emery, incense, ivory and timber. Some of the Arabs who came for trading eventually settled in the island, especially on its western coast at points suitable for the berthing of ships - including Galle. At times they got involved in disputes among the Tamil kingdom in the north and the Sinhalese kingdom in the southwest. S. Arasaratnam explains. "In the fourteenth century, when the Sinhalese kings were being pressed by the expanding Tamil kingdom and its maritime influence, they came to rely more heavily on the southern Muslim community. When the Tamils attacked Colombo and Negombo, the Arabs organized the defense. The Tamils of the north and the Arabs were competitors, for the Tamil traders of the northern kingdom did considerable sailing of their own to the Indian coast and as far as Yemen. The decline of the Tamil power in the fifteenth century left the trade of the south completely in Muslim hands."[24] Despite their richness and navigable power and occasional involvement in the disputes between the Sinhalese and Tamil kingdoms, the Arabs never attempted to control the political affairs of the country.

In a subsequent visit to the island, the Portuguese entered into a commercial agreement with the Kotte king. By this agreement, the Kotte king promised the Portuguese a regular supply of cinnamon and permitted them to establish a residence in Colombo for the purpose of international trade (Arasaratnam, 125). In 1518 AD they built a fort in Colombo to protect their trade interests. They also asked the king to expel all Muslim traders (Arabs) from his ports, hoping to take over the entire foreign trade of the country. The king, however, refused to do so. Then they got involved in dynastic disputes in the native kingdoms based in Kotte and Jaffna, helping some rulers defeat their rivals. In time the Portuguese themselves gained control over parts of the coastal region of the island that came under the two native kingdoms. The Kotte kingdom came under their rule by 1521 AD and the Jaffna kingdom by 1591 AD. The Portuguese repeatedly attempted to conquer the kingdom in the central part of the country, the Kandyan Kingdom, but were never successful.

During their period of rule, the Portuguese introduced Christianity in the form of Catholicism to the island. In addition, they brought in Western styles of education and culture. According to historians, they destroyed Buddhist and Hindu temples and showed their intolerance to other religions. Further, they persecuted Muslim traders who lived along the coast and took full control of the Indian Ocean spice trade from the Arabs. Resistance to the Portuguese rule was centred on and was led by the Sinhalese kingdom in the central highlands.

In the early seventeenth century another European power, the Dutch, came to the region, trying to expand its trading empire in Asia. This resulted in a power struggle between the Portuguese and the Dutch. To take advantage of this situation, the Sinhalese king in the central highlands asked for support from the Dutch to oust the Portuguese from the island. To achieve this, the king made an alliance with the Dutch by agreeing to give them a share of the cinnamon lands in the highlands in exchange for subduing the Portuguese and returning the captured lands in the coastal areas to the Sinhalese kingdom. With the help of the Sinhalese people, the Dutch managed to defeat the Portuguese in the wars that followed,

SRI LANKAN HISTORY
Colonial Era

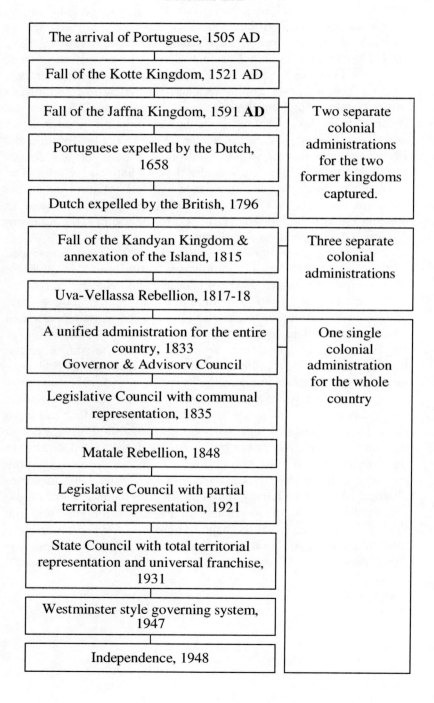

The arrival of Portuguese, 1505 AD

Fall of the Kotte Kingdom, 1521 AD

Fall of the Jaffna Kingdom, 1591 **AD**

Portuguese expelled by the Dutch, 1658

Dutch expelled by the British, 1796

Two separate colonial administrations for the two former kingdoms captured.

Fall of the Kandyan Kingdom & annexation of the Island, 1815

Uva-Vellassa Rebellion, 1817-18

Three separate colonial administrations

A unified administration for the entire country, 1833
Governor & Advisory Council

Legislative Council with communal representation, 1835

Matale Rebellion, 1848

Legislative Council with partial territorial representation, 1921

State Council with total territorial representation and universal franchise, 1931

Westminster style governing system, 1947

Independence, 1948

One single colonial administration for the whole country

but retained two of the major ports they captured, Galle and Negombo. Later, between 1638 AD and 1658 AD, the Dutch brought the entire area that was ruled by the Portuguese under their control. In time the Dutch too tried to subjugate the Sinhalese kingdom in the central highlands, but with no success.

The most significant change that took place in the island during the time of the Dutch rule was the introduction of the Roman-Dutch laws, that covered property and inheritance rights. Ever since, this law remained an important part of the legal system of the maritime regions of Sri Lanka. The other major developments that occurred during their period include the cultivation of spices in the lowlands and the establishment of cash-crop plantations of coffee, coconuts, sugarcane, cotton, and tobacco. According to historians, the Dutch were also intolerant of religions and cultures of the local people, but not to the extent of the Portuguese.

Despite their intolerance of the local way of life, both the Portuguese and the Dutch were more interested in export trading and making money than in ruling the local people. They left the administration of the coastal regions in the hands of the local people. With this arrangement, the administrative systems that existed before continued under these European rulers.

In the seventeenth and eighteenth centuries, a new group of Europeans – the British - became active in the Indian Ocean. They defeated the Dutch rulers in Sri Lanka and took over the lowlands of the island ruled by them in 1796 AD. After taking over, the British started to rule the lowlands the same way as the Portuguese and the Dutch did, without significantly changing the administrative systems in the area. In 1802 AD, Sri Lanka became a British Crown Colony under the official name of Ceylon. Ceylon is a derivative form of the word Ceilao, the name given to the island by the Portuguese. The British were also anxious to conquer the whole island, and sent a number of expeditions against the Sinhalese kingdom in the central highlands, the Kandyan kingdom. The Kandyan kingdom, however, managed to repel the expeditions militarily and remained intact until 1815 AD

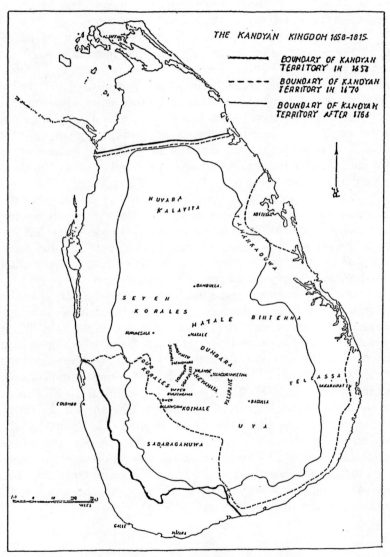

Source: C. R. de Silva, *Sri Lanka: A History*, np. (Reduced copy)

The fall of the Kandyan kingdom to the British in 1815 AD was primarily due to the unpopularity of its king among the local Chiefs. By this time the Chiefs were attempting to get rid of the king, and to crown one among themselves as the next Sinhalese king. In this attempt, they sought help from the British rulers of the maritime regions. The British rulers gladly agreed to come to their aid, and played an active role in ousting the king. But once the king was ousted, the British asked the Kandyan Chiefs to accept the British king as their king, instead of crowning one of the Chiefs as the next Sinhalese king. Having come this far, the Kandyan Chiefs were left with only two options, either to accept the British king as their king or to challenge the British army they themselves had invited into their territory. On the one hand they were not prepared to surrender the sovereignty of their independent nation to the British. On the other hand they were also not ready to wage war against the British army that had already entered their territory. Finally, the Chiefs agreed to accept the British king, if only the British were willing to give an irrevocable undertaking to a number of conditions, guaranteeing the preservation of Buddhism and Buddhist monks, the powers enjoyed by the Chiefs, and the customs, traditions and institutions of the Kandyan people. The British agreed to this proposition and entered into a written agreement with the Kandyan Chiefs, which was later ratified at a joint convention held on March 2, 1815 at the Palace in Kandy. This special agreement between the British and the Kandyan Chiefs later became known as "The 1815 Convention" or simply "the Kandyan Convention."

The Kandyan Convention

This historic agreement was between "His Excellency Lieutenant – General Robert Brownrigg, Governor and Commander-in-Chief in and over the British Settlements and Territories in the Island of Ceylon, acting in the name and on behalf of His Majesty George the Third, King, and His Royal Highness George Prince of Wales, Regent of the United Kingdom of Great Britain and Ireland, on the one part, and the Adikars, Dissaves, and other principle Chiefs of the Kandyan provinces, on behalf of the inhabitants, and in presence of the Mohottales, Coraals, Vidaans, and other subordinate head men from the several provinces, and of the people then and there assembled, on the other part."[25]   What was "agreed and established"[26] between these parties included the cruelties and oppressions of the deposed Kandyan king, his forfeiture of all claims to the throne, banishment of his relatives from the Kandyan provinces, vesting of the Kandyan provinces in the sovereign of the British empire, declaring Buddhism as inviolable and protection of Buddhist practices, monks, and places of worship, prohibition of bodily torture and limb or organ mutilation, the need for written warrant of the British Governor or Lieutenant-Governor for death sentence executions, the administration of civil and criminal justice and police over the Kandyan inhabitants of the Kandyan provinces, the administration of civil and criminal justice and police over non-Kandyans, civil or military, residing in or resorting to Kandyan provinces, priority of these agreements over temporary or partial proclamations, the management and collection of royal dues and revenues of the Kandyan provinces, and export–import trade dispositions. Basically, the Convention preserved intact the Buddhist religion, the powers of the Chiefs, and the customs and institutions of the natives. Appendix 1 gives the contents of this historic document in full.[27]

Three Separate Administrations

With this special agreement between the British and the Kandyan Chiefs, the entire island came under British rule. The British began to rule the Kandyan provinces, using their own administrative system. The administrative systems the British used to rule the maritime areas had also developed from those of the former kingdoms of the north and southwest, which had survived through the periods of previous European rulers, the Portuguese and the Dutch. The British had thus left the administration of the entire country in the hands of local people and their past systems.

Despite the Kandyan Convention and the continuance of the administration of the Kandyan provinces in the hands of local people, the events that followed in the country after 1815 had most devastating effects on Kandyans. The loss of their traditional land to colonial plantation projects, the spread of Christian missionary movement from the maritime provinces to the Kandyan areas, and the introduction of insurmountable new, colonial taxes were particularly devastating.

With the fall in the price of cinnamon and coffee taking its place in the world market, the Kandyan areas, which were best suited for coffee, became the hub of the colonial economy in the island. Another significant economic activity that contributed to the colonial economy at the time was graphite mining. These economic activities opened the floodgates for new opportunities for natives, especially in the Kandyan areas. The beneficiaries of these opportunities were, however, not Kandyans, but the traders, transporters, and the like from the maritime provinces, who had already acquired for several generations the skills and abilities, needed to prosper in a colonial economy. Under any event, the Kandyans as a whole were still not prepared to settle for foreign rule. They attempted to free their nation from British rule. This situation, in time, led to the decline of the relevance of the Kandyans in their own provinces and, indeed, in the rest of the country, and the emergence of a new brand of rich and powerful, non-Kandyan natives of national stature.

Uva-Vellassa Rebellion

At the same time, the influx of people from other parts of the country to the Kandyan provinces in search of the new opportunities further aggravated the land shortage in the Kandyan areas. Thus the Kandyan areas became a land of opportunities for Sri Lankan non-Kandyans and foreigners, at the expense of the Kandyans. The Kandyans' growing opposition to British rule within their territory first erupted in the form of a mass rebellion against the government in 1817-18.[28] It was first organized and led by ordinary people in Uva-Vellassa, and was later joined by many from other Kandyan areas. According to K. M. de Silva, "The rebellion of 1817-18 had its roots in the fact that the Kandyans had called in British help in 1815 for the sole purpose of eliminating an unpopular ruler. They had not contemplated the prospects of the establishment and continuation of British rule."[29] As the rebellion gained momentum, a few Kandyan traditional Chiefs, including Kappetipola and Madugalla, broke ranks with the British and joined the rebels. According to historians this rebellion was the most formidable insurrection the British ever faced in the island. It was of such gigantic proportion; the British had to get down extra cadres from neighbouring India to suppress it. Ever since the British had been extremely suspicious of the Kandyan people and seemed to have kept them at bay in the handling of the country's affairs. Immediately after crushing the rebellion, the British took a number of administrative and other initiatives to systematically obliterate the capability of Kandyans to stage similar rebellions in the future. For achieving this goal, the British wanted to reduce the powers of the Kandyan Chiefs and to stop using the Kandyan, local administration to govern the Kandyan provinces. In implementing the initiatives, the British put Kandyans under a new type of administration manned and managed by British personnel and their recruits selected on a nation-wide basis, in place of traditional Kandyan players. Then in 1831 the British government formally established an "Advisory Council" to assist the governor, and extended its powers to the Kandyan provinces.[30]

A Unified Administrative System

Two years later the British brought the entire country, including the Kotte and Jaffna regions, under a centralized system of administration in 1833, with its power base in Colombo. Ever since Colombo remained the capital of the unified island country. This was the fist time the whole country came under one single administration; even the native monarchs who had claimed all island control from time to time always depended on local administrative systems. It was a unification of three different administrative systems, which evolved and developed for centuries under the three former kingdoms. This unification of the colonial administration in 1833 led to the concentration of authority in the hands of the British Governor. It came about as a result of specific recommendations by the Colebrooke – Cameron Commission of 1832. As part of the administrative unification process, the British redefined the boundaries of the Kandyan provinces. The new provincial boundaries cut across the traditional divisions, and placed many Kandyan regions under maritime provinces. By this, the British wanted to obliterate the sense of identity among the Kandyans and reduce the risk of mass mobilizations against the British like the one in 1817 – 18.

With the new initiatives so taken by the British rulers after the 1817-18 rebellion, the Kandyans were heading for the worst times in the country's history. The occupation of their land for colonial plantation purposes continued with increasing vigour. The British rulers refused to recognize the native claims to land and came up with their own rules and regulations to decide on land ownership. For this they enacted a special land ordinance, the Crown Lands Encroachment Ordinance, in 1840. Michael Roberts and L. A. Wickramaratne explain, "The fundamental and inter-related objectives of this piece of legislation were to provide security of tenure and protect Crown forests from encroachment and claims, and by these means to establish a suitable foundation for agricultural improvement, so as to attract foreign capital and to permit the Crown to sell forest land to prospective planters." [31] By 1843, the number of major coffee plantations in the Kandyan areas shot up to 133 and by 1846 this number further increased to 600. With the loss of their land to plantation projects, the Kandyans also lost their homes, villages and their ways and means of living. As the plantations grew in number and size, the Kandyans became a forlorn flock in their own land. Meanwhile, more people who came from the maritime areas to work in the plantation sector settled in the Kandyan areas – exacerbating the already worsened land shortage. There were no signs this trend of events would slow down or reverse in a foreseeable future, as plantation agriculture for export had become the primary goal of the colonial government. The government had no regrets whatsoever for unscrupulously exploiting the Kandyan provinces for achieving its colonial goals at the expense of their natural owners.

In addition, the Kandyans' culture and religion were also under siege. The Christian missionaries became more active all over the island than ever before, now with state support. The government severed the state's connection with Buddhism, completely ignoring the Kandyan Convention. It had also enacted an excise policy encouraging the opening of taverns in the Kandyan areas in the 1830s, and introduced a series of new taxes, which the peasants found very difficult to pay. The Road Ordinance tax introduced in 1847 in particular was viewed as a strategy to force the peasants to contribute to improve plantation roads. All this contributed to the further strengthening of the Kandyan resolve to end the foreign rule by the British. The Kandyans were particularly concerned about the reluctance of the British to keep to their undertaking to Buddhism through the Kandyan Convention. On their part, the British may have encouraged this desperate situation of the Kandyans, thinking it would help prevent future potential Kandyan rebellions. However, this thinking was short-lived.

Matale Rebellion

By 1848, especially after the introduction of the Road Ordinance tax, the Kandyans' anger with the government culminated in the form of another bloody rebellion in the highlands, this time centred around Matale. At the peak of this rebellion, its leader, Gongalegoda Banda, was crowned at the historic Dambulla Buddhist temple as the next Sinhalese king of Sri Lanka. The British, however, later captured and publicly beheaded him in Matale town along with his accomplices. One of the accomplices beheaded was a Low Country Sinhalese, Puranappu, who had by then settled in the hill country. He also had played a leading role in the rebellion.

According to historians, this rebellion didn't grow to the same size and strength as that of Uva-Vellassa in 1817-18. It is not difficult to understand this, as the Matale rebellion broke out at a time when the British were fully prepared for such an eventuality. In fact they had taken all possible strategic measures to prevent such an event, ever since the Uva-Vellassa rebellion. By staging the 1848 Matale rebellion, disregarding such strategic measures and the systematic weakening of their economic base, Kandyans, together with non-Kandyans now living in Kandyan provinces, had shown in no uncertain terms their irrevocable commitment to safeguard Buddhism and to free themselves from foreign rule. It was left to the government to take note of their aspirations, in its future handling of the Kandyan areas, and, indeed, of the whole country. A close examination of what the British did, over the years that followed, shows that the 1848 Matale rebellion, although it failed in its objective had in fact tremendous effects on the lives of the native people.

Almost immediately after the rebellion the government changed its policy on Buddhism to be less rigid. K. M. de Silva explains, that at this stage the colonial government "conceded that there was an obligation to initiate and supervise the performance of specified legal functions, especially with regard to the Buddhist temporalities." [32] The other significant changes that followed include the following:

1852:   An Ordinance that "sought to assimilate the laws of the Kandyan provinces 'so far as regards the persons and properties of all persons other than Kandyans,' to that of the maritime regions." (De Silva, K.M., History of Sri Lanka, P. 315)

1856:   Irrigation Ordinance of 1856 – the revival of old Gamsabhas giving people the power to operate and maintain their irrigation schemes;

1859:   Ordinance 13 of 1859 – an amendment to the laws of marriage in the Kandyan Provinces, as requested by a group of Kandyan Chiefs;

1871:   Extension of the powers of Gamsabhas to cover other aspects of village life;

1877:   The refusal of Governor Gregory to a proposed
          introduction of a land tax;
1886:   Creation of one more Kandyan province, Uva;
1889:   Creation of still one more Kandyan province,
          Sabaragamuwa;
1889:   Nomi The nomination of a Kandyan to the Legislative
          Council for the very first time after 56 years of its
          existence, and the government's expectation that
          the Kandyan so nominated would also be a spokesperson
          for Buddhism.

Communal Representation

The constitutional structure of the country with a Governor and an Advisory Council remained intact until 1835. During this period, the country's sole authority was concentrated in the hands of the Governor. The Governor represented the British Crown on the island, and was also its sole ruler. This constitutional structure was changed in 1835 with the incorporation of both an Executive and Legislative Council. Initially, the Legislative Council consisted of 16 members: 10 colonial officials and six nominated unofficial members. The six unofficial members were nominated to represent the local people in the legislature, on a communal basis. The ratio kept by the government in nominating the six members was three Europeans and one each from among the Sinhalese, Tamils and Burghers. Burghers are a minority community of Eurasians, mainly of mixed Dutch - Sri Lankan or Portuguese - Sri Lankan descent.

The British didn't consider this Legislative Council as a representative assembly. Instead it served as an independent and reliable source of information for the Colonial Office in London, which would otherwise have to depend on the Governor alone. From the time of the Colebrooke–Cameron Commission that recommended the Executive and Legislative Council model in 1832, there was agitation for having elected representatives in the legislature. This, however, didn't come about till the beginning of the twentieth century. There was also sporadic agitation for a more representative institution in the country.

Incumbent Governors had the responsibility to nominate the six unofficial members of the Legislative Council to represent local people. Those nominated for the three European seats, the Burgher seat and the Tamil seat may have effectively represented their respective communities. But this cannot be said about the nominations made to represent the Sinhalese. For the first fifty-six years, all those nominated to represent the Sinhalese were Protestant Christians (who were converted to Christianity during Dutch and British rule), when a vast majority of the Sinhalese were Buddhist. Those who were nominated to represent the Sinhalese, in fact, had much more in common with the British rulers than with local people, whom they were supposed to represent. Incumbent Governors picked their nominees from those who had a track record of loyalty to the British. For example, the first Tamil member of the Council, Arumuganathapillai Coomaraswamy Mudaliyar (1783-1836) was known to have rendered service to the British in their attempt to gain control of the Kandyan kingdom in the early nineteenth century. The first Sinhalese appointed to the Council was J. G. Philipsz Panditharatne. [33]

In 1889, the British rulers created two additional unofficial seats in the Legislative Council, one for the Kandyans and the other for Muslims. The first Kandyan nominated for the Council, T. B. Panabokka, was also the first Buddhist ever nominated. The Governor at the time, Sir Arthur Gorden, expressed the hope that the Kandyan member should represent the Buddhist interests on the island. Historians see the nomination of a Kandyan to the Legislative Council in this manner as a concession to the widespread Buddhist revival movement.[34]

Buddhist Revival and Transformation

The Buddhist revival movement at the time was primarily designed to counteract the Christian missionary threat to Buddhism, especially in the areas where the Christian missionaries were most active. The most prominent activists in the Buddhist revival movement of the time were Mohottivatte Gunananda (1823 – 90), Colonel Olcott and Anagarika Dharmapala (1864-1933). Mohottivate Gunananda, a Buddhist monk and scholar, founded a Buddhist Society by the name "The Society for the Propagation of Buddhism" in 1862, in imitation of the Society for the Propagation of the Gospel. As part of his Buddhist revival work, he engaged in a series of public Buddhist-Christian debates, drawing nation-wide attention. These debates were held in five different places: Baddegama (1865), Varagoda (1865), Udanvita (1866), Gampola (1871), and Panadura (1873). The last debate held in Panadura continued for two days and became the most significant of all. The English-language press of Sri Lanka published this debate, which was a triumph for Gunananda, and as a result it became a subject of discussion among those interested in Buddhism, both within and outside the country. During the time of these debates there had also been some significant changes in the Sangha, the Buddhist clergy. Many had challenged some aspects of the Order, especially of the dominant Siyam Nikaya. As a result, a new Nikaya, Ramanna Nikaya, was established in 1864. These debates and the changes in the Order brought about new momentum to the Buddhist revival movement.

Colonel H. S. Olcott, a retired Colonel of the American Army, arrived in the island later in 1880. Madam Elena Oetrova Blavatsky accompanied him. By then, they had founded the Theosophical Society of New York, in 1875, and moved its headquarters to Adyar, Madras, in South India in 1879. After coming to Sri Lanka, they embraced Buddhism and founded the Buddhist Theosophical Society of Sri Lanka. Since then Colonel Olcott spent more of his time in Sri Lanka and became a major participant of its Buddhist revival movement. He created a Buddhist flag, which later became the emblem of the international Buddhist movement. He persuaded the colonial government to declare Vesak-day a public holiday, and introduced new ways of celebrating Vesak with Vesak-carols and Vesak-cards, modeled on Christian carols and cards. He also encouraged the formation of Young men's and Young Women's Buddhist Associations, and the establishment of Sunday schools in the villages. The Buddhist Theosophical Society that Colonel Olcott and Madam Blavatsky founded opened more than 200 new Buddhist schools in the country, including Ananda College in Colombo, Mahinda College in Galle, and Dharmaraja College in Kandy. Meanwhile, the Young Men's Buddhist Association supplied text books and other necessities to the Sunday schools in the villages and had conducted their formal examinations until a post-independent government took over the schools in 1961. All these Buddhist revival activities helped lay a strong foundation for further advancement of Buddhism in the country in an unprecedented manner.

Anagarika Dharmapala was born in 1864 and died in 1933. He was educated in Christian missionary schools in Colombo. Despite his Christian educational background, he showed interest in the Buddhist revival activities spearheaded by Colonel Olcott. In 1884, he was initiated into the Buddhist Theosophical Society, and spent some months with Colonel Olcott and Madam Blavatsky in Adyar studying Buddhism and Pali. Later the same year he returned to Sri Lanka and started to work as the manager of the Buddhist

Theosophical Society. He continued to play this role till 1890, with some minor interruptions. In this particular role, he edited and produced the Society's newspaper, Sandarasa. From about 1890 to 1906 he traveled widely outside Sri Lanka as a Buddhist missionary, first with Colonel Olcott and later on his own. In 1893, he represented Buddhism at the World Parliament of Religions in Chicago. In 1891, he founded the Maha Bodhi Society in India. Later, he shifted its headquarters to Sri Lanka, which later became the main centre for the spread of Buddhism outside the country, especially in the West. Even today it sponsors Sri Lankan Buddhist monasteries outside the country. Until about 1900, these activities of Dharmapala and the institutions he built both within and outside Sri Lanka were congenial to those of the Buddhist Theosophical Society and its founder, Colonel Olcott.

In the early 1900s, however, Dharmapala drifted away from the Buddhist Theosophical Society and its contemporary leaders, both physically and philosophically. The Theosophical Society, however, continued its mission, seeking universal brotherhood. According to the Society's beliefs, theosophy has no direct contradiction with any established religion in the world. Instead, it is believed to subsume all religions. In its mission for universal brotherhood, the Society had opened its doors for all the peoples of Sri Lanka, irrespective of religion, language or social or ethnic background. From the early 1900s Dharmapala did not have such a universal approach in whatever he did toward the Buddhist or nationalist movement in the country. On the Buddhist revival front, he narrowed down his interest group to Sinhalese-Buddhists. This changed the nature of the Buddhist revival movement in the country, from being universal to one with a racial and linguistic identity. On the nationalist front, he focused on the concept of Sinhalese-Buddhist nationalism in place of Sri Lankan nationalism. In 1906, he started his own newspaper called "Sinhala Bauddhaya," meaning the Sinhalese-Buddhist, and intensified his work on both Buddhist and nationalist fronts among the Sinhalese-Buddhists. He depended on Buddhist monks, who had always enjoyed respect and reverence from the public, to propagate his mission among the people. For this he redefined the role of the Buddhist monk, making social activism central to their day to day life. He openly called upon the monks to take the lead in reviving the people of the country, rescuing them from the Western influences on their religion, culture, and sovereignty. This call was well received by many Buddhist monks, especially due to the contemporary, ever increasing threat to Buddhism from Christian missionaries that had enjoyed government patronage. This, in turn, led to a period of rapid change in the role of the Buddhist monks, involving them more and more in social activism.

Throughout this period of change, some monks and a vast majority of the Sinhalese Buddhists of Sri Lanka believed that the change was a process of re-establishing the historic role of the monks in its early Buddhist era. It is important to note here that there is no specific, general injunction on the part of the founder of Buddhism, the Buddha, prohibiting monks from taking part in "social activism' or "political activities" as such. The main objective of the monks, however, has always remained as the attainment of nibbana, and as secondary objectives monks have always engaged themselves in preserving, teaching and spreading the teachings of the Buddha, the Dhamma. There is no doubt that in their role with these primary and secondary objectives in mind, Buddhist monks had always given mundane assistance to the laity in many ways. They had always performed Buddhist practices giving laypersons the moral boost they needed. Further, they had given moral advice on day to day mundane problems, and taken leadership in matters of social welfare and development work, especially in the village settings where they lived. By all these, the Buddhist monks, no doubt, held a central societal place in ancient Sri Lanka during the time of Sinhalese monarchial rule. The social and cultural changes that took place during centuries of colonialism had surely affected this societal central place the monks had once enjoyed. Thus, there was a genuine need for a change in the role of the Buddhist monks by the time of Anagarika Dharmapala. Perhaps, no one challenges that view. But whether or not the change in the role of Buddhist monks that took place during and after Dharmapala, incorporating social activism to its core, was a matter of going back to historical times, has become a moot point. For example, H. L. Seneviratne writes, "the conception of the role of the monks as social activism, widely believed by contemporary elite monks and the Sinhala Buddhist middle class to go back to two millennia, is in fact more convincingly traceable to the written and spoken words of Anagarika Dharmapala in the early decades of the twentieth century. Dharmapala's definition of the monastic role as dedication for national and moral renewal during the dark era of imperial domination went through rapid goal displacement within a short period of about three decades, giving birth to a worldly individualism in the monastery unprecedented in the history of South and Southeast Asian Buddhism."[35]

Going by the early monastic chronicles, however, the change articulated by Dharmapala for Buddhist monks was not inconsistent with the monastic life in the country's early history. According to the chronicles, the Sangha had profound influence on the people's life, not only morally, but also culturally and politically. The chronicles say the monks had been instrumental in making and unmaking the monarchial rulers of the time. Modern writers, on the other hand, do not share this view. H. L. Seneviratne writes in this regard, "We have no independent collaboration of this unrealistic and hyperbolic sounding claim, and we must be aware that this is a claim not of the Sangha as a whole but rather of a particular faction that managed to prevail over all others. This faction had a monopoly over writing propagandist books and could prevent them from being consigned to flames by hostile factions, thus controlling the sole 'mass medium' of the time."[36] According to modern historians and critics, during Dharmapala's time Buddhism in the country has evolved into a new form of Buddhism altogether. It is this new form of Buddhism, which some historians like to call "modernized Buddhism," that has prevailed in the country ever since.

Whether or not the change in the role of the Buddhist monks in the late nineteenth and early twentieth centuries is a revival of the past, it has become a dominant factor in the political struggles that followed both before and after independence in 1948. Before independence, the change in the role of the Buddhist monks became a catalyst in aggravating the pressure to end colonial rule. After independence, it forged Sinhalese-Buddhist nationalism to the front and centre of post-independent politics.

Talks on Constitutional Reforms

In the early nineteenth century, the British may have carefully designed the structure of the country's Legislative Council, with communal representation, as a means of governance of all the peoples of the island, who belonged to three distinct kingdoms in the past. Although the Low-country Sinhalese and the Tamils had already lived under a common foreign ruler (first the Portuguese and then the Dutch) for two centuries or more, they were still not ready to think in terms of one nation. In the case of Kandyans, their identity as a separate nation, the Kandyan Nation, was fresh in their minds. In a time like that, a Legislative Council with local representatives nominated on communal basis was not a recipe for effective unification and assimilation of the diverse communities to a single national identity. It is important to note, however, that all contributions made by nominated unofficial members in the Legislative Council had not been always partisan. They had shown their unity on many important matters of national interest.

The British argued, however, the Council as it was helped maintain a balance of power among the unofficial members, preventing any one community having sweeping powers over the others in the legislature. While, this argument had its own merit, critics argue that the Council with nominated members was a carefully crafted colonial system to divide-and-rule. Under any event, it had served the British well in ruling the country at the time, although it hadn't helped bring about a single national identity across the borders of the different communities.

Proposals for Federalism

By not having one of their representatives in the Council for the first 56 years or more of its existence, Kandyans had developed a sense of alienation from the process of governance of the unified Sri Lanka. In addition, the lack of a Buddhist representative in the Council during this period had particularly annoyed them. All this may have further strengthened their sense of a separate national identity as Kandyans. They also may have viewed the other communities and their leaders as collaborators and perpetrators of foreign rule. Kandyans had consistently shown their opposition to the British rule under one administration for the entire country, with or without a Legislative Council. They did not deviate from this position even after the nomination of a Kandyan to the Legislative Council. This was well demonstrated in their submissions to Royal Commissions subsequently appointed by the British government to study constitutional changes. Kandyans' submissions to these commissions, Donoughmore Commission of 1927 and Soulbury Commission of 1944 were not only consistent, but also precise and unambiguous. At the Donoughmore Commission, the Kandyan National Association representing the Kandyan view kept its distance from the Ceylon National Congress dominated by the elite of the Low-country Sinhalese and Tamils, and asked for a federal political structure for Sri Lanka. It explained to the Commission that in its view the majority of the grievances, which Kandyans had, were directly due to the centralization of the administration of the country in 1833. It argued that "the fundamental error of British statesmanship has been to treat the subject of political advancement of the peoples of Ceylon as one of the homogenous Ceylonese race." [37] Its specific proposal for a federal system of governance for the country was to have three autonomous units: one for the Kandyan provinces; one for the Northern and Eastern provinces, where Tamils were in a majority; and the other for the two low country provinces, Western and Southern. Later, Kandyans re-emphasized the same proposal at the Soulbury Commission in 1944. The British were, however, never agreeable to any form of federal system for the country.

It is extremely important to note here that at neither of these Royal Commissions, did the leaders of the other communities, the Low-country Sinhalese and Tamils, support the Kandyans' proposal of a federal system of government. Their actions during this period suggest that they were not ready for such a fundamental change to the existing unitary system of government, and all what they wanted was a constitutional process that would eventually lead to some form of transfer of power from the British to the native elite. At the Donoughmore Commission, the Ceylon National Congress on behalf of these non-Kandyan leaders had submitted, "we advisedly refrain from making any suggestion on the question of franchise or on the mode of allocating or distributing seats in the Legislative Council." [38] They further submitted that franchise should be restricted to those earning at least Rs.50.00 or more a month. Their reference to franchise came about as a response to a specific proposal of universal franchise brought forward to the Commission by the Young Lanka League, a breakaway group from the Ceylon National Congress led by A. E. Goonasinghe.

Ironically, S. W. R. D. Bandaranaike, who later became the idol of chauvinist politics in the country by advocating Sinhalese-Buddhist nationalism, was the only low country Sinhalese Congressman who had openly supported the idea of federalism advocated by Kandyans. This support was, however, not given at the constitutional deliberations in 1927 or 1944. In his statements on federalism outside these constitutional forums, Bandaranaike had referred to other countries, including the United States, Canada, Australia, and Switzerland, which had successfully established federal systems of government. According to him, Switzerland afforded a better example with three races, the French, Germans and Italians, united as one single, proud nation under a federal system of government.

One may wonder why Tamil leaders did not support the proposal for federalism at the time of the two Royal Commissions. One view was that Tamil leaders at the time did not want to promote federalism as Tamils were in the centre stage of the colonial government, with a disproportionate share of the public service. Obviously this had resulted from disproportionate opportunities Tamils enjoyed in western education under colonial powers, not only under the British, but also under the Dutch and the Portuguese. On a proportionate basis, Tamils had much more Missionary and other western education oriented schools than Sinhalese. Kandyan Sinhalese in particular had been exposed to western education only after 1815, two centuries behind Tamils and low country Sinhalese. Even then, the opportunities Kandyans received for western education were meager. With disproportionate opportunities in western education in their favour, Tamils may have secured a disproportionate amount of places in the colonial administration and professions. K. N. O. Dharmadasa explains, "In 1921, while the Sinhalese comprising 76 per cent of the total population (Europeans excluded) held only 46 per cent of the 'select professions' the Ceylon Tamils making up only 13 per cent of the population, held 31.9 per cent of them." [39] This situation itself, however, should not have stopped Tamil leaders at the time from looking towards the future in the context of the changing dynamics in the country's political system. It wouldn't have been difficult for them to think that the country would eventually free itself from colonial masters and establish a system where people would fight for equal opportunities, not only in education, but in other aspects as well. It may be possible that the Tamil leaders either did not have the political wisdom or maturity to look to the future or they simply depended on the colonial masters to secure the status quo.

Constitutional Changes Implemented

The British never agreed to establish a federal system of government as proposed by Kandyans. Instead, the British simply continued to rule the island with a centralized or unitary system of governance with the help of the Legislative Council, which was first established in 1833 and later evolved to a State Council with wider powers in 1931. All the constitutional changes brought about by the British rulers had been on the basis of a single colony with a unitary system of governance. The leaders of all communities nominated by the Governor to the Legislative Council had in general supported these changes, and had appeared to be making efforts to build bridges across their communities. From about 1890, there had been harmony among these leaders. Their words and actions had shown a sense of common commitment to bring all the peoples of the country under one banner within the context of one nation, a Ceylonese (Sri Lankan) Nation. They evolved a concept that Sinhalese (Kandyans and Low-country Sinhalese together) and Tamils were the "two majority communities" in the country, and appeared to have looked forward to a future where both Sinhalese and Tamils would embrace and cherish one single national identity. But events that occurred and constitutional changes that were implemented in and after 1918 only raised questions rather than provide answers as to how such aspirations of these leaders could have been met. The British never had the answers to the questions so raised even when they finally granted independence to the island in 1948.

In 1918, territorial representation was adopted in place of communal representation for the legislature. Although such a change would eventually affect the dynamics of power in the legislature against Tamils, their legislators supported the change. There is no question that the Tamil leaders in the legislature knew what would happen once such a change was implemented. Despite this they supported the change accepting it as inevitable, perhaps, going by the trend of politics in other countries in similar situations. Another reasoning for their support for territorial representation in the legislature is that they did not expect the Tamils to Sinhalese ratio in the legislature to change significantly, if the franchise were to extend only to the English educated. A.J.Wilson has expressed the latter view in his Sri Lankan Tamil Nationalism, (Vancouver, 2000).

In 1919 the Ceylon National Congress (CNC), comprised of leaders from all ethnic groups, was formed on a common platform for all the ethnic groups to work together to negotiate greater self-governance for Sri Lanka. Sir Ponnambalam Arunachalam, a Tamil, was the founding President of the CNC. Sinhalese leaders gladly accepted Sir Arunachalam's leadership in the CNC. The Tamil leaders' support for territorial representation in the legislature and the Sinhalese leaders' acceptance of a Tamil as the leader of the CNC demonstrate a clear commitment and willingness on both sides to continue to work together for the common good of all the peoples of the island.

The 1921 election was a partial transition to territorial electorates. It returned 13 Sinhalese against 3 Tamils. This changed the dynamics of the balance of power in the legislature against Tamils, even though Tamil legislators had supported territorial representation in the Legislative Council. At the time of communal representation, there was near equality in representation between the Sinhalese and Tamils in the legislature. Now after the 1921 election, Tamils had been reduced to a weakened minority in the legislature. Sections of Tamil politicians started to campaign for the restoration of the ratio of Tamils to Sinhalese in the legislature that existed before 1920. This perhaps was the beginning of minority-rights issues of Tamils in Sri Lanka.

The next major constitutional reform came about in 1931. It introduced universal franchise, a complete territorial system of electorates, and a "semi-responsible" self-government in domestic affairs, with a cabinet like council of ministers. CNC leaders, not only Tamils, but also Sinhalese, were totally against the introduction of universal franchise. With the introduction of universal franchise, Tamil leaders lost their hope of maintaining a more favourable ratio of Tamils to Sinhalese in the legislature.

The 1931 Council of ministers did not include Tamils and was characterized or perceived as pan-Sinhalese. This situation further reduced the Tamils' share of power in the affairs of the country. Tamil frustration and opposition to this worsening situation led to a demand for "fifty-fifty" representation, meaning that the minorities (Tamils, Muslims, Burghers, and others) though only 26 % of the population should have 50 % representation in the legislature. Tamil Leaders who advocated fifty-fifty representation broke away from the CNC and formed the Tamil Congress in October 1944, to prepare for their arguments for the next round of constitutional discussions.

Meanwhile, the Ceylon National Congress along with some other political organizations in the country formed the United National Party (UNP) in September 1946. Leaders of Muslims, whose mother tongue was also Tamil, broke ranks with Tamils and joined the UNP – as these leaders by then had realized that asking for a balanced representation was a lost cause.

The next round of constitutional changes came in 1947, with a Westminster style of governance and the granting of independence to Sri Lanka. A clause in the new Constitution for minority protection/rights was that no act of parliament should discriminate against any person or persons on the basis of religion, race or language, unless passed by a two-thirds majority. Additionally, a second chamber (the Senate) of 30 members, 15 elected by the house and the other 15 nominated by the Governor General on the advice of the Prime Minister, was introduced into the parliamentary system. It was envisaged that this might restrain any hasty legislation disadvantageous to minorities. More than 90 percent of the members in the house supported these constitutional changes, before they were finally enacted. The only dissenters were W. Dahanayake and I. X. Pereira, an appointed member.[40] The British government officially announced 'fully responsible status within the British Commonwealth of Nations' for the island on June 18, 1947.[41]

The August/September 1947 election was fought primarily on the basis of party politics. The political parties that ran for the election and won one or more seats included the United National Party (UNP – 1946), Lanka Sama Samaja Party (LSSP - 1935), Bolshevik Leninist Party (BLP – 1947), Communist Party (CP – 1943), Labour Party (LP – 1928), Ceylon Indian Congress (CIC – 1939), and the All Ceylon Tamil Congress (TC – 1944). In addition, there was a significant number of Independent members who took part in the election. Ninety-five members of Parliament (MPs) were to be elected for the 89 electoral districts in effect at the time, of which five were multi-member districts. Four of these five districts were two-member seats and the other a three-member seat. With the final counting of the ballots, the new legislature had the following party strengths: UNP - 42, LSSP - 10, TC - 6, CIC - 6, BLP - 5, CP - 3, LP - 1, and Independent – 22. Six more members were finally added to the list as appointed members to represent the underrepresented: Europeans, Burghers, and the like.

At this election, 61 of the 95 elected members had been voted in on the basis of their political ideologies, conservatism (UNP), liberalism (LP), and socialism or communism (LSSP, BLP, & CP), 22 as independents, and the remaining 12 members (TC & CIC) on policies that were ethnic based. The main platform of the TC at the election was to further stress on the demand for the fifty-fifty representation in the house. The electoral districts of the six TC members were from the north and the east, where a significant majority were Tamils, the descendents of early settlers from South India. The six CIC members had been voted to represent the interests of the Tamil population in the plantation sector, concentrated in the central hilly areas of the island. These Tamils were descendents of those who had been brought in from South

India by the British rulers in the nineteenth century as labour for the colonial plantations in the Kandyan areas. They were named Indian Tamils to distinguish them from Tamils domiciled in the country, mainly in the north and east, from pre-colonial times.

Post-Colonial Era

The government formed after the 1947 election had declared February 4, 1948 as the official Independence Day of the newly formed independent Sri Lanka (Ceylon), and celebrated it with all the fanfare and pomp customary for such celebrations. With the dawn of independence to the country, its entire people raised their expectations for a better future, socially, culturally, economically, and politically. They took inspiration from their past, before colonization. All the communities in the country were impatiently waiting to free themselves from the remnants of colonial bonds and to revive their language, religion, and culture. The nature and extent of such expectations and hope for the future was shared among all the communities. Language was one of the important issues in focus in all the communities, as both Sinhalese and Tamil speaking people had suffered under the English language during the time of the British. Even at the time of independence, only about one percent of the population could speak and write in English. Yet no one could send a telegram in Sinhalese or Tamil, even at a time of an emergency. In the case of Indian Tamils, the issue of impending defranchisement had not been settled. Unlike in some other colonies, the British did not accept them as their own citizens at the time of granting independence. Instead, the British washed their hands of the problem and asked the independent Sri Lankan government to find a solution. Thus the challenges that lay ahead at the time of independence were diverse and complex in nature.

The working arrangement of the new parliament was similar to that of the British parliament in Westminster, London. The floor was divided on a party basis and decisions were taken by majority vote. Elected representatives, Members of Parliament or MPs, generally voted on party lines. With all the MPs elected on the basis of territorial representation, it was clear that the fifty-fifty representation proposal of the TC was not an acceptable proposal. In this situation, the TC switched to a policy of "responsive cooperation," and its leader, G. G. Ponnambalam, joined the UNP government as a cabinet minister in early 1948. By this act the TC leader had sought to work with the "progressive minded Sinhalese" in looking after the interests of Tamils and other minorities in the country.

This change of TC policy was not acceptable to all the members of that party. It led to the break up of the Tamil Congress into two factions, one opting to go into coalition with the majority party forming government (UNP), and the other forming the Federal Party (FP) in 1949, demanding a federal system of government. A change to a federal system of government was a proposal the leaders of the Tamil community had previously not supported. The federal system sought by the Kandyans in 1927 and 1946 or by the FP at this time was not for the creation of separate states, but for autonomous governance in regions under a single Sri Lankan State or nation similar to what was being established in neighbouring India.

In the 1947 parliament the different political parties and their leaders, including the TC and its leader G. G. Ponnambalam, looked at the country as one state and one nation, the Sri Lankan (Ceylonese) Nation. D. S. Senanayake, the Prime Minister and the leader of the UNP, had shown strong commitment to a secular, unitary state as a means to unite the Sinhalese and Tamils, who were once divided among three kingdoms. Thus, there appeared to have been an open acceptance of the reality of a plural society and the need to work towards the legitimate interests of all the peoples (Sinhalese, Tamils, Muslims, Malays, Burghers, and others) within the context of an all island polity and Sri Lankan (Ceylonese) nationalism. Within a year or two, however, the differences between the Prime Minister and one of his own cabinet ministers, S. W. R. D. Bandaranaike, on the concept of Sri Lankan (Ceylonese) nationalism in the given multi-ethnic and religious environment developed into a major crisis. S. W. R. D. Bandaranike's version of Sri Lankan (Ceylonese) nationalism was a product of a mixture of his liberal political beliefs and inseparable link to the Sinhalese Buddhist revival movement in the country. He had gained a name in the country primarily through the activities of Sinhala Maha Sabha (SMS), a restructured political body of Sinhala Mahajana Sabha that was first started under the patronage of the Ceylon National Congress for the purpose of propagating its independence course in the rural districts. A vast majority of the people in these rural districts were Sinhalese Buddhists. As a responsible leader, he had the opportunity to educate the masses on the complexities of the contemporary multi-ethnic society vis-à-vis the dynastic times in the past and prepare them for a post-independent Sri Lanka with a secular government. But this did not happen. Instead, he emerged as a leader with a non-secular platform of Sinhalese-Buddhist nationalism. Meanwhile, no political party in the 1947 parliament, other than the CIC, was prepared to accept Indian Tamils as an integral element of Sri Lanka.

A Two-Party System

As the disputes between the Prime Minister and S. W. R. D. Bandaranaike grew, he finally resigned from the cabinet and the UNP and formed his own political party, the Sri Lanka Freedom Party (SLFP) in 1951. The UNP retained power in 1952. But in 1956 the SLFP with an electoral alliance with two Marxist Parties (LSSP and CP) won the election and formed the next government. This was the beginning of the development of a two-party system in the country, dominated by the UNP and SLFP. The governing power has since changed between these two major parties in the subsequent elections held in March 1960, July 1960, 1965, 1970, 1977, 1994 and 2001.

Parliamentary Acts passed by the house during the period of the UNP rule from 1947 to 1956 include the Public Security Act of 1947, The Trade Union (Amendment) Act of 1948, The Citizenship Act of 1948, The Indian and Pakistani Residents (Citizenship) Act of 1949, and The Parliamentary Election (Amendment) Act of 1949. The groups that were worst affected by the changes that followed were the Marxists and their trade union partners and the Tamil plantation workers (Indian Tamils). The Trade Union (Amendment) Act of 1948 laid down new restrictions for trade union movements, and the Citizenship Act of 1948 took away the citizenship and voting rights of Indian Tamils. The seven MPs representing the Indian Tamils in the parliament lost the ability to win or even contest parliament seats at the next election held in 1952. Taking away of the citizenship and voting rights of Indian Tamils was not perceived at that time as an act motivated because of their language, Tamil. As already mentioned, right from the very beginning no political party (other than CIC) was willing to accept Indian Tamils as an integral element and citizens of Sri Lanka.

The 1947-52 UNP government also started a new colonization program to relocate the landless in places where suitable vacant land was available. The northern and eastern provinces, which were predominantly occupied by Ceylon Tamils, came under this program. This led to changes in demographics in these provinces as a result of the Sinhalese families that were settled there. The taking away of the citizenship and voting rights of the Indian Tamils and this colonization program were later interpreted by Tamil leaders as "concealed agendas" of D. S. Senanayake and his UNP government against their communities. Until his untimely death in 1952, Prime Minister D. S. Senanayake managed to defend secularism and his government's actions in these matters as necessary and in the best interest of the country. His successor and son, Dudly Senanayake, however, was not so effective in defending this position.

In 1953 Dudley Senanayake resigned from the premier's position, and handed over the reign to Sir John Kottelawale, who opted to drop G. G. Ponnambalam, the leader of the TC, from his cabinet. The removal of G. G. Ponnambalam from the cabinet gave a disturbing signal to Tamils that "responsive cooperation" with Sinhalese leaders by Tamils as advocated by G. G. Ponnambalam was not going to work for them. This led to the immediate downfall of the TC and impulsive acceptance of the FP and its policies in Tamil speaking areas in the north and the east. Ever since the FP monopolized Tamil politics until it finally coalesced with other Tamil political groupings in the country under the name of Tamil United Front (TUF) in May 1972. This was later renamed Tamil United Liberation Front (TULF) in March 1975.

A Language Fiasco

After its defeat at the 1952 election, the SLFP brought the issue of language to the centre stage of the country's politics as a means to gather more support from the majority Sinhalese and win the next election. It did this by changing its language policy from 'Sinhala and Tamil as state languages' to "Sinhala Only.' This change resulted in a Sinhala Only movement in the country in support of the SLFP. The governing party, UNP, reacted to this new situation by changing its language policy too to Sinhala Only. As the next election drew nearer, both parties tried to defeat one another by a show of how much it supported this change. Then, on the eve of the election, the SLFP made an assertion that it would make Sinhala the only state language in the country within 24 hours of coming to power. This was the language policy of the SLFP when it finally formed the next government in 1956. The LSSP and CP had a no-contest pact with the SLFP at the 1956 election, but did not join in to form a coalition government.

The new government led by the SLFP with its leader, S. W. R. D. Bandaranaike, as Prime Minister had a mixed bag of policies, some Sinhalese nationalist and others socialist. Within two months, in June 1956, the new government legislated Sinhala as the country's only state language. This started a series of protest campaigns both inside and outside the legislature led by the leaders of the Federal party, which had now become the main political party representing Tamils. Through these protests the FP gained grounds on its four major demands and objectives: 1. Sinhala and Tamil to be recognized on an equal footing as state languages; 2. a federal system of government where the Northern and Eastern Provinces could share a union configuration with the other seven provinces in the country; 3. state aided colonization of the Northern and Eastern Provinces by Sinhalese to be ended; and 4. unity of all Tamil speaking people in the country, in particular the Ceylon Tamils, Tamil speaking Muslims in the Northern and Eastern Provinces, and the Indian Tamils, and a solution to the citizenship and voting rights issue of the Indian Tamils. Civil disobedience was one form of protest that had seriously affected the running of government in the northern and eastern provinces. At its national convention held in Trincomalee on August 19, 1956, the FP reiterated its four demands and gave an ultimatum to the government to form a federal system by August 20, 1957, threatening widespread non-violent protests in the event of the failure of the government to do so. This had brought Tamil speaking people all over the country to a formidable common front against the government.

After a year of FP protests and dissension, the government finally agreed to several concessions. The specific agreement reached between the government and the Federal Party that resulted in the concessions was signed by Prime Minister Bandaranaike and S. J. V. Chelvanayagam, the leader of the Federal Party, on July 26, 1957. This agreement later became more popularly known as the Bandaranaike-Chelvanayagam Pact or simply BC Pact (see Appendix 2). The concessions given by this agreement were primarily three-fold: 1. Tamil language was to be an official language, along with Sinhala, in the Northern and Eastern provinces for administrative purpose, and provisions for "reasonable use of the Tamil language" in the other seven provinces; 2. Regional Councils to be set up with adequate decentralized powers in the northern and eastern provinces; and 3. the settlement of Sinhalese colonists in the irrigation projects of the northern and eastern provinces to be restricted to maintain the existing majority status of the indigenous Tamil people in those provinces. On the question of citizenship and voting rights of Indian Tamils, the government agreed with the FP that it would separately negotiate with the leaders of the Indian Tamils, who had by then grouped under two camps, the Ceylon Workers' Congress (CWC) and the Democratic Workers' Congress (DWC).

The BC Pact was far from a final solution to the issues that had been raised by the FP. Despite this it was never implemented due to the events that followed. The moment the details of the Pact were made public, there was a storm of protests from many Sinhalese. Those who opposed it alleged that the Pact was a sell-out to Tamils and by signing it the Prime Minister had become an instrument to divide the country. The strongest opposition to the Pact came from the extremist elements of the Prime Minister's own party, the SLFP, orchestrated by some Buddhist monks, led by Baddegama Vimalavamsa,[42] who had actively supported the SLFP at the 1956 election. These monks performed satyagraha on the lawn of the Prime Minister's residence, and demanded abrogation of the Pact. The main opposition party in the parliament, the UNP, also showed its opposition to the Pact. Its protests against the Pact culminated in a 72-mile public march from Colombo to Kandy, which prematurely ended, as a result of a surprise human barricade organized by the SLFP at a strategic point on the road to Kandy. These protests by the main opposition party and the Prime Minister's own camp only exacerbated the already existing prejudices and animosity between Sinhalese and Tamils. In the heat of all this, the officials of the Ministry of Transport sent new buses in March/April 1958 from its newly nationalized public transport system with Sinhalese 'SRI' lettering on the number plates to Tamil speaking areas. This only added fuel to the growing fire. Tamils in the Northern and Eastern provinces protested the Sinhalese 'SRI' lettering on the number plates of the buses by replacing it with the same letter in Tamil script. In response to this act, Sinhalese extremists went on painting Sinhalese "SRI' on the perimeter walls of the houses occupied by Tamils in Colombo. While this was still going on an event that took place in the east triggered a nation-wide communal riot of unprecedented human disaster in May 1958. The government failed to give protection to Tamil people in this riot.

In August 1958, the government enacted the Tamil Language (Special Provisions) Act to allow reasonable use of Tamil in administration. This alone did not calm the FP or the people it represented. They wanted the government to honour the BC Pact in full. Meanwhile, Sinhalese extremist forces, both within and outside the SLFP, took the position that the Prime Minister had gone too far in appeasing the Tamil community, and thought of strategies to prevent him from implementing the remaining changes he had agreed to in the BC Pact. The Prime Minister was, thus, inescapably caught between these two opposing forces, with no apparent solution on his horizon. Then on September 26, 1959, a little more than a year after the enactment of the Tamil Language (Special Provisions) Act, an assassin - who was later proved to be a Buddhist monk in the Prime Minister's own political camp - gunned him down at short range at his residence, leaving behind a language-embroilment legacy.

At the next general election held in March 1960, the UNP returned to power with a slim majority. It ruled for four months and went to the polls again in July the same year, hoping to form a more stable government with a larger majority in the legislature. At the July election, however, the SLFP, now led by Sirimavo Bandaranaike, the widow of S. W. R. D. Bandaranaike, emerged victorious and formed the next government. She became the Prime Minister of this new government, creating history as the first woman Prime Minister in the world. At the election, she promised to continue with the policies of her late husband. But this did not happen. Her new government completely ignored the BC Pact, and, instead, implemented the 1956 Sinhala Only Act in its original form and rigour. In addition, it passed a new language bill that also directly affected the Tamil community, especially in the north and the east. This bill made Sinhala the only language of the courts in the country, including those in the northern and eastern provinces - where a vast majority was Tamil speaking.

When the UNP won the next election held in 1965, it formed a 'national government' with the support of the FP, under the leadership of Dudley Senanayake. The special agreement that brought the two parties together to form the government was popularly known as Dudley Senanayake – Chelvanayagam Pact or simply DC Pact of 1965 (see Appendix 3). In this Pact, Dudley Senanayake, the new Prime Minister, had agreed on five main issues:

1. Establishment of District Development Councils (DDCs) under the central government supervision;

2. An assurance not to disturb the existing demographic composition of the Northern and Eastern provinces (not to reduce Tamils to minority status in their own homeland), and to allocate the land available for colonization projects in the area on an agreed order of preference: first to Tamils living in the immediate vicinity; then to Tamils living in the same District; then to Tamils living in the two Provinces; then to Tamils in the rest of the country; and after all that to the overflow of Indian Tamils in the plantation areas;

3. Amendment of the Language Act making Tamil a parallel official language and the language of judicial administration in the Tamil provinces;

4. Safeguarding the rights of Tamil public servants who had not gained proficiency in the official language; and

5. Resolution of the citizenship and voting rights issue of the Indian Tamils in separate agreements with the two Indian Tamil organizations, CWC and DWC. (Sirima – Shastri Pact signed in early 60s had already made considerable progress in resolving this issue)

This agreement was consistent with the BC Pact the FP entered into with the SLFP in 1957, and included DDCs (with appointed members) instead of Regional Councils (with elected members) proposed by S. W. R. D. Bandaranaike with a specific order of preference in selecting colonists to be settled in the Tamil areas. In addition this new agreement had a commitment to safeguard the Tamil public servants that had not gained proficiency in Sinhalese. By 1968 there was some progress in some areas of the agreement. By Tamil Regulations of 1966, Tamil was made the language of administration and of the courts in the Northern and Eastern Provinces. The Prime Minister also had later assured some relief to Tamil public servants that had become victims of the Language Act of 1956. The Prime Minister, however, failed to implement DDC legislation due to increasing opposition from the Sinhalese, led by a Buddhist monk, Madihe Pannasiha.[43]

Thus the leaders of both major parties in the country, the SLFP and the UNP, had entered into special agreements or pacts with the FP to resolve the growing language crisis. But the extremist elements of the two major parties had consistently prevented them carrying out their agreements. At the same time, whenever any one major party tried to carry out its agreement with the FP, the other was there to discredit it for so doing.

The SLFP and its Marxist allies formed the next government in May 1970, with more than a two-thirds majority in the parliament. It changed the country's constitution in 1972 and extended its five-year term by two more years. While it was still preparing itself to deliver on its election platform, the new government was faced with a surprise-armed-uprising. It was staged not by any section of Tamils, but by a group of Sinhalese youth belonging to an underground Marxist movement called the Janatha Vimukthi Peramuna (JVP), in translation reading as People's Liberation Front. After a period of violence and armed confrontations, the government finally managed to bring the combatants under control. Despite its failure, the armed rebellion had tremendous effects in focusing the government's attention to the youth unrest particularly regarding education and unemployment. Being Marxist, the JVP was not believed to have any racial connotation, although its leaders at the time were all Sinhalese. It, however, had warned that there was a real threat of Indian expansionism and hegemonism in the region, and used that as one of its rallying points. The growth of the JVP, to the extent of being able to stage a bloody rebellion of such magnitude, clearly demonstrated the disenchantment of the Sinhalese youth with the other Marxist parties, mainly the LSSP and CP, which were now part of the government. More importantly, it showed the disenchantment of the youth with the entire parliamentary political system in the country for failing to solve the growing problems of poverty and unemployment, especially among the educated rural youth.

On the issue of Tamil language, the 1970 government didn't have anything new to offer to Tamils. Instead of finding solutions for reconciliation between Tamils and Sinhalese, the government introduced two major regulations for university entrance in 1971 and 1972 that particularly irked Tamil youth. The first of these two regulations established two different systems of standardization of marks for admission to universities, directed specifically in favour of Sinhalese students. The second established a district quota system in university admission, giving preference to rural areas, seriously affecting, among others, the Ceylon Tamil students in the North. K. M. de Silva explains the consequences of the first regulation, "The qualifying mark for admission to the medical faculties was 250 out of 400 for Tamil students, whereas it was only 229 for the Sinhalese. Worse still, this same pattern of a lower qualifying mark applied even when Sinhalese and Tamil students sat for the examination in English. In short, students sitting for the examinations in the same language, but belonging to two ethnic groups, had different qualifying marks."[44]

Tamil youth could not and did not accept the reasoning behind these regulations. For Tamil youth particularly in the Jaffna peninsula where land was scarce, these restrictions in educational opportunities became highly disadvantageous. This brought about a new dimension to language politics, with Tamil youth taking the lead in the affairs of Tamil political parties. Leaders of the Tamil political parties still wanted to continue with their usual way of non-violent protests against the regulations. The youth, however, did not see the usefulness in continuing with the same political tactics as before. Instead, they seemed ready to take a militant path in solving the language problem and pressurizing their party leaders to take such a course of action.

With its two-third majority in the house, the 1970 government also adopted a new constitution in 1972. This too was a blow to Tamil speaking people. The two main points at issue were language and religion. The new constitution had enshrined Sinhalese language and Buddhism with special provisions. It had given the Sinhalese language the status of the official language of the country, and Buddhism "the foremost place" with state protection, while "assuring to all other religions the rights secured by Section 18(I)d." By these special references to Sinhalese language and Buddhism, Tamils thought, the new constitution had discriminated against their language, Tamil, and their religion, Hinduism, and pushed them to a distinctly inferior position in the country. The UNP, which was now the main opposition party, had supported the new constitution in the Constituent Assembly.

In response to all this, leaders of all Tamil groupings and political parties, including the TC and FP, got together and set up a joint organization called the Tamil United Front (TUF) in May 1972, with a strong backing from Tamil youth. The main grouping of Indian Tamils in the hill country under Ceylon Workers Congress (CWC) also became an integral part of this joint organization. Tamil leaders and their parties still believed in a federal system of government with decentralized administration as a resolution to the growing ethnic problem in the country, but Tamil youth had now wanted nothing short of a separate state. Eventually, the official position of the FP, the main political grouping of Tamils in the North and the East, changed from unity in diversity with a federal system of government to self determination for Tamils with a separate nation. On 9th September 1973 the 12th National Convention of the Federal Party resolved, "... the Tamil-speaking people in Ceylon are in every way fully qualified to be regarded as a separate Nation by virtue of their language, culture, history, territory and the innate and intense desire to live as a separate nation, and that the only path for them .... is the establishment of the right to self-rule in their legitimate homeland based on the internationally recognized principle of the right to self-determination of every nation.."[45]

The leaders of the Federal Party then tried to bring together all the Tamil politicians in the country on this new resolve for a separate nation. By and large this was not a difficult task. Some Tamil leaders, however, disregarded this call for a separate nation and continued to work with the two major political parties in the country for a solution to the growing ethnic crisis within a unitary system of government. The tension that developed between these Tamil leaders and those who stood for separatism finally ended up in violence and assassinations committed by the separatist youth. The first Tamil leader who died in the hands of the separatist youth was Alfred Durayappah. A. J. Wilson explains, "In 1973 a group of Tamil youth led by the future military leader, Velupillai Prabhakaran, assassinated Alfred Durayappah, the SLFP organizer in Jaffna, a one-time MP (Member of Parliament) for Jaffna as well as a former Mayor. This, as later events showed, marked the beginning of a series of political murders." [46]

In their efforts to combat this situation and to maintain peace and order in the country, the Sri Lankan police came in direct confrontation with the separatist youth. In some of the events that followed the separatists blamed the police for using excessive force in dealing with them. The separatists also blamed the Sri Lankan government for not taking action against the police in those situations. Some critics say that the government's indifference and inaction in such situations moved the separatist youth to prepare for an armed struggle. One event that occurred in January 1974 became most significant in this regard. As A. Jeyaratnam Wilson explains, "An International Tamil Conference (the fourth in a series) was held on 3-10 January 1974. On its last day the police attacked a celebrating crowd with gas, bombs, police batons, rifle buts and other weapons. An independent commission comprising O. L. de Krester (chairman – a retired judge of the supreme court), V. Manicavasagar (also a retired supreme court judge) and Bishop Sabapathy Kulendran of the Church of South India in Jaffna condemned the action. It further reported that a policeman had fired at an electric cable, resulting in nine deaths. The government, as was only to be expected, took no action, and their indifference moved the Tamil youth to prepare for their armed struggle."[47]

The Emergence of the LTTE

A year later, in 1975 the TUF changed its name to Tamil United Liberation Front (TULF), emphasizing further radicalization of its policies. By this time, Tamil youth who were not satisfied with their leaders' non-militant approach to win their course had formed a militant wing. This militant wing later splintered into a number of groups, out of which the Liberation Tigers for Tamil Eelam (LTTE) emerged as the most dominant group by 1976.

Meanwhile, the 1973 to 76 period was also marred by anti – Muslim sentiments among Sinhalese as a result of some educational policies giving favoured treatment to Muslims. On a number of occasions in 1975 and 1976 these sentiments translated into communal riots. Riots in Gampola (1975) and Puttalam (1976) were the worst in this series. As the opposition to the new constitution and the educational changes was still heating up on a number of fronts within different ethnic groups, the Marxist allies of the government decided to leave the government and go on their own; LSSP left the government in 1975, and CP a year after that.

A Separatist War & Peace Talks

On the Tamil front, by 1976 Tamil people now mostly united nationwide under the banner of TULF had given up hope of ever having their problems solved under a framework of a unitary system of government or a federal system achieved by peaceful and/or non-violent constitutional process. Instead, they chose to fight the government for a separate nation. In the first National Convention of the TULF held on May 14, 1976, it adopted a resolution calling for all Tamil youth to "throw themselves fully in the sacred fight for liberation and to flinch not till the goal of the sovereign socialist state of Tamil Eelam is reached."[48] Thus, the language politics of Tamils that first started with equal representation in the Legislative Council in 1833, through a long period of struggles for fifty-fifty representation, responsive cooperation, and federalism, had finally ended up with a call for a civil war to establish a separate nation.

At the 1977 general election, the UNP came to power with more than two-thirds majority in the parliament. The SLFP that ruled the country from 1970 to 1977, first with the help of its Marxist allies and later on its own, was reduced from 91 seats to eight, and both its former Marxist allies lost all the seats they had in parliament. The FP that fought the election on the language issue gained the largest number of seats in the opposition, allowing its leader, Appapillai Amirthalingam, to become the Leader of Opposition in the legislature. The first major issue the new government had to deal with was a widespread Sinhalese – Tamil riot which broke out soon after the election. In 1978 the government adopted a new constitution on the Gaulist model with an elected President, a Prime Minister from Parliament and proportional representation in the house by a complex polling system of voting for political parties as well as candidates. J. R. Jayewardane, who was Prime Minister since the 1977 election became the first President under the new constitution.

Before the 1977 election, the UNP had promised to resolve the growing ethnic conflict. The events that unfolded after the election, however, did just the opposite. According to critics, the main reason for this was the indulgence of Sinhalese extremists within the government in chauvinist activities; even a cabinet minister had been blamed for actively pursuing an extremist agenda. These extremist elements had, no doubt, voiced the grievances perceived by a majority of the Sinhalese. Their tit for tat approach to the conflict, however, was fuel to the separatist war. On many occasions President Jayewardana had come under pressure to remove the extremist elements from his government. He, however, waited till it became too late to do so. When asked by A. J. Wilson, one of his advisors on Tamil matters, as to why he would not dismiss Cyril Mathew, Minister of Industries, Industrial Research and Fisheries and the leader of the extremist group within his government from his cabinet, President Jayewardane's excuse was that "he needed a Sinhalese extremist to neutralize Mrs. Bandaranaike's (SLFP's) anti-Tamil propaganda against his government."[49] This continued dependency on the chauvinist card as a trump in the power game between the two major parties in the country, The UNP and the SLFP, vis-à-vis the declaration of a sacred fight for Tamil Eelam by the separatists, led the country on a war path.

Some of the events that followed had long term and widespread consequences. One such event was the burning down of the Jaffna library at mid-night on May 31, 1981, allegedly by the Police. Many Tamils construed this as a forbidding act of cultural genocide. A. J. Wilson explains, "One such event is the burning of the Public Library in Jaffna with over 90,000 rare volumes and precious manuscripts at mid-night on 31 May 1981. This singular event contained deep portents. For many Tamils it was the beginning of a systematic cultural genocide which has continued up to the present with the destruction or occupation by the military of Tamil schools, colleges and other academic institutions."[50]

Then, in July 1983, LTTE cadres ambushed an army truck in Jaffna, killing 13 Sinhalese soldiers. This triggered a major outbreak of Sinhalese violence against Tamils living in Sinhalese areas, including Colombo, the capital. The communal riots that followed were the biggest in post independent Sri Lanka. Many believed that Sinhalese extremist elements within J. R. Jayewardane's government were behind the scene, leading the riots, which had reportedly claimed over 4000 Tamil lives. In the aftermath of the riots, many Tamils who lived in areas, where Sinhalese were in a majority, retreated to the northern and eastern provinces. Some, especially the educated ones, fled to other countries, mostly to neighbouring India, but also to the West. The effect of these new migrations within and outside the country as a result of Sinhalese violence was primarily two-fold. Firstly, with many Tamils who had lived in Sinhalese areas now moving to the Northern and Eastern provinces, these provinces had started to gain momentum as a some sort of homeland for Tamils in the country. Secondly and more importantly the Tamils who settled in other countries became powerful lobby-groups, internationalizing the Tamil ethnic crisis. Some of these Tamils and the ones who later joined them in other countries began to finance the Tamil movement in Sri Lanka.

According to critics, President Jayewardane had the power to contain the 1983 riots, but miserably failed to do so. He, in fact, they say, had shown very poor leadership and lack of political wisdom and maturity in dealing with the new crisis situation. For example, A. J. Wilson explains that while the riot was still going on, "he appeared on television on 26 July 1983 with the purpose of assuaging the fears and hysteria of the Sinhalese people, but he didn't utter a word of regret to the large number of Tamils who had suffered from Sinhalese thuggery masked by nationalist zeal."[51] Then, he enacted the Sixth Amendment to the Constitution the very next month, requiring Tamil MPs and others in public service to take an oath of allegiance to the unitary state of Sri Lanka. In response to this constitutional change the TULF MPs resigned from

Parliament, creating a temporary vacuum of Tamil representation in the Parliament. The LTTE seized the opportunity and established itself as the main vehicle of Tamil politics in the country. According to critics, TULF leaders treated the Sixth Amendment as an act of blackmail, and, under any event, its timing was suicidal for the government.

This new situation with the LTTE in the centre stage of Tamil ethnic conflict in the country became a defining moment in Sri Lankan politics. The government now had to deal with a militant group outside the parliament in solving the ethnic crisis. Those who sympathised with the Tamil cause in Sri Lanka, both within and outside the country, now had to recognize the LTTE's new role, and work with it for any solution to the ethnic crisis. Meanwhile, Tamil nationalist movements in India started to arm and train the LTTE cadres, and brought an unpleasant complexity to the Indian involvement in the crisis. The Sri Lankan Tamils who fled the country and became strong lobby groups in other countries, especially in Europe, North America, and Australia, started to send substantial financial support to the LTTE, to further strengthen its military power. With such an internationalized base of support, the LTTE was now heading for a full-blown war with the government of Sri Lanka.

The events that followed (some of them described later) show that the tactics used by the LTTE in its separatist struggle were not limited to direct confrontations with the government armed forces in the battlefield. It had also conducted indiscriminate mass killings of civilians and terrorist attacks on the lives of prominent anti-separatist politicians, both Tamil and Sinhalese, outside the battlefield. Between 1983 and 2001, such indiscriminate mass killings had claimed about a thousand innocent lives and injured several thousand others. In these killings, LTTE cadres had simply gunned down innocent people or detonated bombs in crowded places like bus-stands, post offices, hospitals, commuter trains, election rallies, and the like, or driven trucks packed with explosives into crowded buildings. Ranjan Wijeratne was the first Sinhalese politician who succumbed to LTTE terrorist attacks. A car bomb killed him and 18 others on 2 March 1991. He was the Minister of Defense at that time.

In its direct confrontation with the government armed forces, LTTE had fought valiantly, won many victories and proved itself to be an audacious fighting unit. From 1987, it had deployed suicidal bombings as well. Its first suicide bombing killed 39 troops at the Nelliyady army camp in the north of the country. It used the same technique in its later attacks against most of the prominent politicians and government military top brass. Three incidents took place in 1991, 2000 and 2001 demonstrated the level of military sophistication and audacity of the LTTE cadres. In the 1991 incident, LTTE attackers drove a truck packed with explosives into the military Operations Headquarters in Colombo, the capital, killing 21 and wounding 114. On 23 April 2000 the LTTE attackers took control of the Elephant Pass military base in the north, entrapping thousands of government soldiers in the Jaffna peninsula. Then on 24 July 2001 thirteen guerrillas, believed to be LTTE cadres, armed with machine guns and rocket-propelled grenade launchers, carried out a pre-dawn attack on the country's only international airport and the adjoining, biggest military air-base in Colombo. This attack, according to official military sources, destroyed thirteen air craft, including two Kfir jet fighters, one MI-24 Helicopter gun ship and one MIG-27 jet fighter, and led to 18 deaths. After the attack, the Eelam Nation website controlled by the LTTE warned that "If the daring attack on Colombo's civilian international airport was possible, then there is nothing that could prevent the Liberation Tigers of Tamil Eelam from carrying out an attack on the military headquarters and cause serious damage to the city of Colombo without difficulty."[52]

The government's approach to end the separatist war had been mainly two-fold. On the one hand it had extended an olive branch to the LTTE looking for peace talks, and on the other it implemented military and constitutional strategies to defeat the LTTE in the battlefield.

The first negotiations between the government and the LTTE took place in Thimphu, Bhutan, in July and August 1985. In these negotiations, LTTE was an integral part of an umbrella organization, Eelam National Liberation Front (ENLF), which included three other militant organizations: The Eelam People's Revolutionary Liberation Front (EPRLF), The Tamil Eelam Liberation Organization (TELO) and The Eelam Revolutionary Organization of Students (EROS), as well. The People's Liberation Organization of Tamil Eelam (PLOTE) and the Tamil United Liberation Front (TULF), which were outside ENLF, also took part in the negotiations. At the negotiations, Tamil delegates asked the government to agree on four basic principles later called "Thimphu principles," as a foundation for any meaningful solution to the growing ethnic crisis. These principles included: "recognition of

Tamils as a separate nationality; recognition of the traditional homeland of the Tamils and guarantee of its territorial integrity; recognition of the inalienable right of self-determination; and 4. conferment of citizenship on all Tamils who looked upon the island as their country."[53] The government delegation "responded within a legal framework and rejected the principles outright."[54] As there was no possibility for a compromise between the government and the Tamil delegation on the basic principles it had put forward, the Thimphu talks ended in fiasco.

Later, as a follow up to Thimphu talks, President Jayewardane proposed at the 1986 Summit of the South Asian Area for Regional Co-operation (SAARC) in Banglore, India, a three-fold proposal to end the ethnic problem. The main points in this proposal, which was much publicized as 'the Trifurcation Proposal,' were 1. Amparai District where the majority were not Tamils to be separated from the Eastern province and annexed to adjoining Uva Province, 2. The rest of the Eastern Province to have its own Provincial Council, and 3. The Northern province to stand on its own as a separate Province, as before. The LTTE flatly refused to accept this proposal as a means to end the separatist war. In the aftermath of what followed in the battlefield, the government then launched its 'Operation Liberation,' a major army combat against the LTTE. President Jayewardane had reportedly given instructions "to raze Jaffna to the ground, to burn the town and then to rebuild it."[55] The Indian government intervened in this event and first sent by boat some food and other essential supplies to the people affected by the raging war between the government forces and the LTTE on June 3, 1987. The Sri Lankan government refused to allow the supplies into the country. Then on the next day the Indian government sent five aircraft to the island and dropped tonnes of relief supplies to the affected areas from the air, in complete violation of Sri Lankan air space. A month later, the LTTE carried out its first ever suicide bombing.

As the pressure from the government of India mounted for a speedy solution to the escalated war situation in Sri Lanka, the Sri Lankan government showed its willingness to concede on one of the contentious issues discussed at the 1985/6 peace talks, in July 1987. It agreed to provide a temporary merger of the northern and eastern provinces in the country, on condition that a referendum in the eastern province would finally decide whether such a merger should be made permanent. In response to this concession, the LTTE insisted on two pre-conditions for the renewal of peace talks: 1. The withdrawal of Sri Lankan government troops to the positions they occupied before the "Operation Liberation," and 2. All Tamil refugees to be allowed to resettle in their own areas. When the government accepted the two conditions, the LTTE added two more pre-conditions to any peace talks: 1. LTTE was not prepared to return its weapons, and 2. Its opposition to the proposed Eastern Province referendum to make the temporary merger of the northern and eastern provinces permanent.

After reviewing the latest developments, the governments of India and Sri Lanka signed a special agreement, The Indo-Sri Lanka Agreement to Establish Peace and Normalcy in Sri Lanka (see Appendix 4), on 29 July 1987 to end Tamil separatism in Sri Lanka. Rajiv Gandhi, the Prime Minister of India signed the pact on behalf of the government of India, and President Jayewardane signed on behalf of the government of Sri Lanka. The pact required the LTTE to surrender its arms and an Indian Peace Keeping Force (IPKF) to replace the Sri Lankan Security forces in the Northern and Eastern Provinces of the island. The pact also required the Sri Lankan government to set up Provincial Councils to partially decentralize political administration of the island. The government of Sri Lanka started to establish Provincial Councils and IPKF arrived in the island as per the pact. Despite all this, LTTE refused to surrender its arms and, instead, resumed the separatist war, now taking on the Indian troops, IPKF.

R. Premadasa, who served as Prime Minister in President Jayewardane's government, was elected as the next president in 1989. At the same time the parliamentary election of the same year, the ruling party, UNP, managed to retain its majority status in the parliament. President Premadasa had a different approach to the separatist war; as Prime Minister he was never in agreement with President Jayewardane's strategy, involving the Indian government. Soon after becoming President, he opened fresh negotiations with LTTE in May 1989. The negotiations started with the convergence of the interests of both the parties, the government and the LTTE, to get the IPKF out of the country. According to Bradman Weerakoon, Adviser to President Premadasa on international relations, the government has made several gestures to the LTTE during the negotiations. These gestures include "the permission for the LTTE delegates who came to Colombo to have their own armed security, allocation of an entire floor of a five-star hotel in Colombo, a secret supply of money and weapons to the LTTE to fight the IPKF, arrangements for Prabhakaran's wife and children to be brought from abroad and flown to the Wanni and Premadasa conceding the demand to publicly call for the IPKF to be withdrawn."[56] In February 1990, President Premadasa asked IPKF to leave the country. IPKF started to leave the country the very next month, leaving large areas of northern Sri Lanka under LTTE control. After the IPKF left the country, LTTE put forward two demands: 1. the dissolution of the North East Provincial Council and 2. the repeal of the Sixth Amendment to the Constitution. When the government rejected the two demands, the LTTE abandoned the negotiations and once again resumed its separatist war, in June 1990. A year later, as the war raged in the north, a suicide bomber, alleged to be a LTTE cadre, blew up Rajiv Gandhi, the Prime Minister of India, while he was on an election campaign in South India, on 21 May 1991. Two years later another suicide bomber blew up President Premadasa while he was attending a May Day rally in Colombo on 1 May 1993. D. B. Wijetunga, who served as Prime Minister in President Premadasa's government, became the interim president until the next presidential election due in 1994. The next parliamentary election was also due the same year.

At the parliamentary election held on August 16, 1994, there was a change of power in the parliament, from UNP to People's Alliance (PA), a coalition led by the SLFP. The PA itself won only 105 seats out of 225, and, as a result, didn't constitute a majority in the legislature. It, however, became the 'ruling party' in the parliament with the support of the seven MPs of the Sri Lanka Muslim Congress (SLMC) and a Tamil MP of the Upcountry People's Front (UCPF) representing Indian Tamils. Three small Tamil parties in the Northeast also pledged their support to the PA, provided it continued to show genuine interest in solving the ethnic crisis, as promised at the time of the election. PA had given a special undertaking at the election to end the separatist war through talks. The leader of PA, Chandrika Kumaratunge, a daughter of former Prime Ministers, S. W. R. D. Bandaranaike and Mrs. Sirimavo Bandaranaike, became the country's next Prime Minister after the election. The incumbent President, D. B. Wijetunga (UNP), continued in his office until the next presidential election, which was due in three months.

In her new role as Prime Minister, Kumaratunga had two urgent tasks to attend to. One was to initiate a fresh round of peace talks with the LTTE, and the other was to prepare for the incoming presidential election as its PA candidate. She managed to initiate the next round of negotiations with the LTTE on 13 October 1994.

Then while her preparations for the presidential election were still under way, a suicide bomber blew up the main opposition (UNP) presidential candidate, Gamini Dissanayake, on 24 October 1994, 16 days before the presidential election. In the aftermath of the confusion and rage that followed Kumaratunga won the presidential election held on 9 November 1994. After becoming President, she installed her aged mother as the next Prime Minister.

The negotiations with the LTTE initiated by Kumaratunga continued for about six months, but failed to come up with an amicable agreement to end the separatist war, just like in the first two rounds of negotiations led by the former, UNP governments. In the 1994/95 negotiations, there appeared to be a basic difference in the approach of the government and the LTTE. The LTTE wanted the negotiations to proceed in two stages, first the restoration of normalcy and creation of a peaceful environment and after that talks for a peaceful, political solution. The government, however, wanted simultaneous negotiations on all the issues in question. At the end, the LTTE blamed the government for acting in bad faith and resumed its separatist war by bombing two navy boats on 19 April 1995. The government then renewed its military attacks on LTTE under a new banner of "war for peace." While fighting the war, the government asked for national and international support to eradicate terrorism, safeguard democracy in the country, and to liberate Tamils from the dictatorship of LTTE. After seven and a half months of protracted war, Jaffna, the main stronghold of the LTTE in the North, fell to the Sri Lankan army on 2 December 1995. At the height of the war in Jaffna hundreds of thousands of people fled the town without any specific destination, and ended up in refugee camps both within and outside the country. Ever since Jaffna has remained in the hands of the Sri Lankan army.

The recapture of the Jaffna town by the Sri Lankan army was a major military setback for the LTTE. This, however, did not change the aims and objectives of the LTTE in any manner. After regaining momentum in a considerably short period of time, it started to unleash a new wave of violent attacks on the army as well as prominent politicians who came in its way and innocent civilians. On 18 July 1996 it overran a major army camp in Mullaitivu, killing 1200 troopers. On 17 May 1998 an assassin alleged to be a LTTE cadre murdered the mayor of Jaffna who belonged to TULF. In between, LTTE carried out bomb explosions in a Colombo commuter train (24 July 1996), Twin-Tower World Trade Centre (15 October 1997), the Temple of the Tooth in Kandy (25 January

1998), and Colombo's commercial area of Maradana (5 March 1998), killing a total of 141 people and wounding more than 850 others. In response to all this, the Sri Lankan government declared a nation-wide state of emergency on 6 August 1998. Meanwhile the government banned the LTTE following the attack on the Temple of the Tooth in Kandy, the most sacred Buddhist religious place in the country. The government also held local government elections in Jaffna on 29 January 1998, though not seen as free and fair. This was the first time such elections were held in Jaffna since 1983. The elections, however, failed to provide for a viable political process.

Then on 6 September 1998 the LTTE offered to re-commence peace talks, on condition of a third party mediation. The government rejected the offer and continued with the war. So the LTTE continued with its usual attacks both in and outside the battlefield. The politicians targeted in these attacks outside the battlefield over the next two years include a mayor of Jaffna (killed with 11 others on 11 September 1998), Neelan Thiruchelvam, a TULF MP and a key figure in the government sponsored peace efforts (killed on 29 July 1999), President Kumaratunga (survived an assassination attempt with an injured eye on 18 December 1999), Prime Minister Sirimavo Bandaranaike (survived an explosion outside her office killing 13 people and injuring 28 others), C. V. Goonaratne, a senior cabinet minister (killed on 7 June 2000), and M. Baithullah, a Muslim candidate at the 10 October 2000 elections (killed along with 23 others).

In the battlefield the LTTE had significant gains on 23 April 2000; it took control of the Elephant Pass military base in the Jaffna peninsula on this day. This prevented further movement of the government troops by road to the Jaffna peninsula from the south, although Jaffna town still remained under their control. In response to this situation, the government put the country on a war footing on 4 May 2000, assuming new powers under the country's Constitution. Four days later it turned down a truce offer by the LTTE to enable government troops to evacuate from the Jaffna peninsula, and made a stronger commitment to win the war militarily. Meanwhile, President Kumaratunga had been elected for a second term of office at the presidential election held on 21 December 1999.

Later, as the war was still heating up in the battlefield, President Kumaratunga had submitted a power devolution package, said to be modeled on the Indian federal system, to the parliament for discussion in August 2000. Then, within days the government postponed a parliamentary vote on the package due to opposition from the Sinahlese extremist elements in the country.

At the next parliamentary election held on 10 October 2000, the PA won only 107 of the 225 seats in the parliament, but managed to form a coalition with the support of some small Tamil and Muslim parties, securing a slender majority status. Sinhala Urumaya (SU), a newly formed party with a chauvinist agenda, won only one seat. President Kumaratunge appointed Ratnasiri Wickramanayake as the new Prime Minister. The seats in the Tamil areas were shared among Tamil and Muslim parties: TULF 5, National Unity Alliance (NUA) 4, Eelam People's Democratic Party (EPDP) 4 seats, and Tamil Eelam Liberation Organization (TELO) 3 seats.

The newly formed PA led coalition government had the same approach to the separatist war as that of the previous PA government. It was not prepared to open new peace talks, hoping to win the war in the battlefield. Within a month of forming the new government, on 2 November 2000 Eric Solheim, the Norwegian Special Envoy to Sri Lanka, announced that the LTTE was prepared to open fresh peace talks without preconditions. He had personally met the LTTE leader, V. Prabhakaran, a few days before. The government simply rejected the offer. Then on 25 December 2000 LTTE declared a unilateral cease-fire, and called on the Sri Lankan government to match it. The government refused to respond to the cease-fire as well, and launched a series of operations and recaptured areas close to Jaffna town.

Meanwhile, another ethnic issue cropped up in the country. The Sri Lankan Muslim Congress, a critical part of the PA led coalition, asked for a separate administrative district for Kalmunai in the Eastern Province for Muslims. The Muslim Congress also showed its preparedness to reduce the PA coalition to minority status in the parliament by withdrawing its support in the parliament, if this request was not granted. In response to this situation, President Kumaratunga agreed to sign a Memorandum of Understanding with the Muslim Congress agreeing to the creation of a separate administrative district for Kalmunai on 11 June 2001. The government, however, failed to implement this agreement due to widespread protests from both Sinhalese and Tamils. As a result, the Muslim Congress left the governing coalition in July 2001, reducing it to minority status in the parliament. By this time a no-confidence motion against the government brought by the main opposition party, UNP, had been tabled for discussion in the parliament.

In order to save her minority PA government from defeat in a no-confidence vote, President Kumaratunga prorogued the country's legislature with effect from midnight 10 July 2001 until 7 September 2001. Then she tried to get the support of a Marxist party in the opposition, JVP, that had 10 MPs in the parliament, to re-establish majority status for the PA government in the legislature. She managed to get this support in time by the end of the prorogation, but with conditions. On 5 September 2001 the JVP signed a Memorandum of Understanding (MOU) with the PA, the governing coalition under President Kumaratunga's leadership, giving its conditional support for a probationary government for one year. Within weeks of the signing of the MOU between the two parties, President Kumaratunga started to implement its binding conditions. First, on 12 September 2001 she reduced the size of her cabinet from 44 to 20. Then on 24 September 2001 the parliament passed the 17th Amendment to the Constitution with a two-thirds majority to appoint a Constitutional Council and four independent commissions on elections, the judiciary, police and the public service. The appointment of these four special commissions was part of the MOU. This new co-operation between PA and JVP gave a new sense of stability to the PA government. This, however, could not save it from sudden collapse in the days ahead.

The parliament decided to take up the debate of the no-confidence motion against the government proposed by the main opposition party, UNP, on 11 October 2001. Then, in a surprise move, within a day or two, ten government members, including some key cabinet ministers, crossed over to the opposition, ensuring a clear defeat for the government in the no-confidence motion. In response to this new situation, President Kumaratunga dissolved the parliament, elected on 10 October 2000 for a six-year term, on 10 October 2001, preventing the opposition from being a majority on the floor of the legislature.

At the next parliamentary election held in December 2001, neither the UNP nor the PA managed to get a clear majority in the legislature of 225 seats. The UNP, however, became the party with the largest number of seats, 109. The PA got 77 seats, while the JVP, which was prepared to go into a coalition with the PA, got 16 seats. The Tamil and Muslim minority parties in the north and east shared the rest of the seats: Tamil United Liberation Fund (TULF)-15; Sri Lanka Muslim Congress (SLMC)-5; Eelam Peoples Democratic Party (EPDP)-2; and Democratic People's Liberation Front (DPLF)-1. With these election results, the UNP managed to form the next government with the help of the SLMC, under the banner of The United National Front (UNF). The Ceylon Workers' Congress (CWC) of the Indian Tamils in the upcountry also joined the UNF. Ranil Wickremesinghe, the leader of the UNP was sworn in as the next Prime Minister before President Kumaratunga on Tuesday, 11 December 2001, starting a new era of politics in the country with an elected President from the People's Alliance (PA) and a government led by the UNP. The new government had been elected for a six-year term, while President Kumaratunga still had four years of her second six-year term. This was also the first time a Buddhist monk had been elected to the legislature. The Buddhist monk, Baddegama Samitha, was a PA member from the Galle district in the south.

      Soon after the election, the government led by Prime Minister Ranil Wickremesinghe decided to obtain support from the international community to end the separatist war, and to revive the Norwegian intervention as a mediator between the government and the LTTE. The Norwegians were first brought in to play this role by the previous PA government. Then on 19 December 2001, the LTTE announced a month long cease fire to begin at midnight on the Christmas Eve, 24 December 2001, as a goodwill measure during the festive season to "facilitate and promote initiatives towards the peace process."[57] The new government led by the UNP, unlike the PA government in the previous year, matched the cease-fire, and increased its efforts toward peace talks with the LTTE. A few days later, the LTTE also expressed its desire to reopen peace negotiations with Norwegian facilitation. According to a news item appeared in ColomboPage, a Sri Lankan internet newspaper, on 3 January 2002, "LTTE leader Vellupillai Prabhakaran yesterday (meaning 2 January 2002) sent a letter to Norway's Prime Minister Kjell Magne Bondevik calling for Norway's continuous engagement as facilitator. This is the first time that the LTTE leader has sent anyone such a letter. Prabhakaran in his letter complimented the Royal Norwegian government for its impartial and neutral approach in the facilitation process."[58]   Norwegians have since come back to the scene, and are doing everything they can to bring the two parties together for peace negotiations. As a result of Norwegian facilitation, the two parties have first signed a Memorandum of Understanding (MOU) on an open ended cease-fire arrangement on 22 February 2002, pending actual negotiations for a lasting solution to the ethnic crisis. The LTTE, however, appears to have not yet decided to drop its call for a separate state. It treats this as an issue to be discussed during the negotiations for a solution to the ethnic crisis. At the same time, after signing the MOU, the LTTE has put forward four new conditions to be fulfilled prior to the follow up negotiations or peace talks. Some of these conditions have started a new wave of protests and objections from numerous political and interest groups.

One of the conditions that have become contentious is the requirement of the lifting of the ban on the LTTE in the country before the actual peace talks. Prime Minister Wickremesinghe had explained to the parliament on Tuesday, 22 January 2002, that the LTTE wanted the ban lifted, if it were to enter peace talks.[59] The MOU, signed on 22 February 2002, however, did not include any provision for this. It appears that the lifting of the ban on LTTE by the Sri Lankan government would have implications both within and outside the country.

In the international scene, the lifting of the ban on the LTTE in Sri Lanka can be a problem for those countries that have proscribed it within their own jurisdictions. These countries include India, the United States, the United Kingdom, Canada and Australia. According to a Colombo Page online news item, the United States and the United Kingdom have said that "a decision by the Sri Lankan government to get the talks off the ground by lifting the ban on the LTTE would not automatically lead to removing the Tigers (LTTE) from their lists of foreign terrorist organisations."[60] India's position in this regard, however, is much more complex. In addition to the LTTE being a banned terrorist organization, its leader V. Prabhakaran has been identified as a party to the criminal conspiracy to murder Rajiv Gandhi. India's Janatha Party President Subramaniam Swamy had already advised Ranil Wickremesighe on his first visit to India in December 2001 as Sri Lankan Prime Minister, against holding negotiations with the LTTE, saying that it would amount to acting against India.[61] Later, after Prabhakaran appeared at a press conference on 10 April 2002, the Congress party of India and the Tamil Nadu State Government had demanded his extradition to face the consequences of his alleged role in the murder of Rajiv Gandhi. Indian Prime Minister Vajpai himself has said on 11 April 2002 that Prabhakaran should be brought before law and that India would not mediate in the ongoing peace process or lift the proscription of the LTTE.

Within Sri Lanka there is pressure on the government from some of those who oppose separatism not only to maintain the ban on the LTTE, but also not to engage in talks with it unless it lays down arms and give up Eelam. This is primarily due to two reasons. Firstly, a section of the Sinhalese community in the country does not trust that the LTTE is looking for a political solution to end the ethnic crisis, as long as its cadres are armed. For example, a recent release from the Sinhala Veera Vidahana explains why such mistrust exists. It says "all cease-fires to date have ended with the LTTE emerging even stronger .... The LTTE used talks in the past to re-arm and re-group in order to carry out devastating attacks each time ..."[62] In the past the LTTE has also been blamed for killing some prominent politicians during peace negotiations, A. Amirthalingam, the TULF leader, during Premadasa-LTTE negotiations and Gamini Dissanayake, a UNP presidential candidate, during Kumaratunge-LTTE negotiations. Some events reported to have occurred after the December 2001 cease-fire declaration, only confirm these fears in the minds of those who oppose the LTTE. According to a Colombo Page news item of 29 January 2002, the Indo Asian News Service has reported that the LTTE is now on a new recruitment drive. [63] A report in the Lakbima has said that Army intelligence had received information that the LTTE had lectured school principals in the Sampur area in the Trincomalee district that they had reached the last stages of the Eelam war.'[64] According to Udaya Gammanpila, a spokesperson for Sinhala Urumaya, a leading tiger cadre in the LTTE intelligence unit has been arrested while spying in the government controlled Nagar Kovil area in the Jaffna district.

Secondly, some Sinhalese think that the peace process initiated by the government is a mere act of giving in to Tamil racism backed by western nations, and it is detrimental to the nation as a whole. Those who share this view say that the steps so far taken by the government have endangered the lives of the people and affected the sovereignty of the nation. According to a Colombo Page news item of 28 January 2002, Seven organizations have said in a joint release, "The government is pleasing the western nations such as Norway who fully back the Tamil racism."[65] The signatories on the release included Elle Gunawansa, a Buddhist monk; Dinesh Gunawardena, MP; Professor Abaya Ariyasinghe; Dr. Gunadasa Amarasekera; Dr. Nalini de Silva; and Nemsiri Jayatillake.

In the above situation, for any satisfactory progress in the peace initiatives of the government, it has to build a high level of trust with the people of the country as a whole, as much as with the LTTE. At the same time the LTTE must have a genuine interest in finding a political solution to the present ethnic crisis, short of separatism, as its leader, Velupillai Prabhakaran, has indicated in his LTTE heroes' Day speech of Tuesday, 27 November 2001 that his campaign was "neither separatism nor terrorism."[66] In this speech, he had explained, "The Tamil national question, which has assumed the characteristic of a civil war, is essentially a political issue. We still hold a firm belief that this issue can be resolved by peaceful means. If there is genuine will and determination on the part of the Sinhalese leadership, there is a possibility for peace and settlement."[67] In the same speech, he has further said, "We are not enemies of the Sinhalese people nor is our struggle against them. It is because of the oppressive policy of the racist Sinhala politicians that contradictions arose between the Sinhala and Tamil nations, resulting in a war. .... We call upon the Sinhala people to identify and renounce the racist forces committed to militarism and war and to offer justice to the Tamils in order to put an end to this bloody war and to bring about permanent peace."[68]

A detailed chronology of events since 1983 discussed in this chapter is given in Appendix 5.

NOTES

1. K. M. de Silva, 'The Foundation of Sri Lankan History,' Insight Guides: Sri Lanka, (Hong Kong, 1987), p. 33.
2. C. R. de Silva, Sri Lanka: A History, (1st edn., New Delhi, 1987), p 17.
3. Ibid., p. 18.
4. A. Jeyaratnam Wilson, Sri Lankan Tamil Nationalism: Its Origins and Development in the 19th and 20th centuries, (Vancouver, BC, 2000), p.13.
5. K. M. de Silva, p. 33.
6. C. R. de Silva, p. 18.
7. Mahavamsa is the most important of the earliest chronicles of Sri Lanka. It is believed to have been composed by Buddhist monks some time after the fifth century A. D. It traces political and religious history of Sri Lanka from its earliest times to the end of the third century A. D., with some gaps. Modern historians believe that it displays bias and have some reservations to use it as a source material.
8. C. R. de Silva, p. 20.
9. Ravindralal Anthonis, 'Land of Tanks and Jungles,' Insight Guides: Sri Lanka, (Hong Kong, 1987), pp. 27-28.

10. Ibid., p. 27.
11. K. M. de Silva, 'The Classical Era,' Insight Guides: Sri Lanka, (Hong Kong, 1987), p. 35
12. Ibid.
13. Ibid., p. 36.
14. Ibid.
15. C. R. de Silva, p. 27.
16. Buddhist literature treats Sakka as the king of gods. The concept of god in Buddhism is unique. It does not recognise a God of creation. Buddhist literature, however, refers to heavens of gods where one could go after death and stay there temporarily because of accumulated merits on Earth.
17. A. Jeyaratnam Wilson, p. 177.
18. C. R. de Silva, p. 41.
19. C. R. de Silva, p. 41.
20. C. R. de Silva, p. 72.
21. C. R. de Silva, p. 77.
22. S. Arasaratnam, Ceylon, (Englewood Cliffs, New Jersey, 1964), P. 125.
23. Ibid.
24. Ibid., p. 119.
25. Geoffrey Powell, The Kandyan Wars: The British Army in Ceylon, 1803-1818, (London, UK, 1973), p. 283.
26. Ibid.
27. Ibid., pp. 823-285.
28. K. M. de Silva, A History of Sri Lanka, (London, 1981), pp.231-235.
29. Ibid., p. 231.
30. Ibid., p. 262.
31. Michael Roberts & L. A. Wickramaratne, 'Land Problems and Policies, c.1832 to c.1900', History of Ceylon, Volume Three, (University of Ceylon, Peradeniya, 1973), p. 122.
32. K. M. de Silva, A History of Sri Lanka, p. 281.
33. K. M. de Silva, 'The Legislative Council in the Nineteenth Century', History of Ceylon, Volume Three, (University of Ceylon, Peradeniya, 1973), pp. 248.
34. Ibid., pp. 243-244.
35. H. L. Seneviratne, The Work of Kings: The New Buddhism in Sri Lanka, (Chicago, 1999), pp. xi-xii.
36. Ibid., p. 20.

37. K. M. de Silva, 'The History and Politics of the Transfer of Power', History of Ceylon, Volume Three, (University of Ceylon, Peradeniya, 1973), p. 494.
38. Ibid., p. 493.
39. K. N. O. Dharmadasa, 'Language Conflict in Sri Lanka', Sri Lanka Journal of Social Sciences, Vol.4, No.2, December 1981, pp. 48-49.
40. A. Jeyaratnam Wilson, p. 77.
41. K. M. de Silva, 'The History and Politics of the Transfer of Power', History of Ceylon, Volume Three, P. 533.
42. H. L. Seneviratne, p. 304.
43. Ibid.
44. K. M. de Silva, 'University Admissions and Ethnic Tensions in Sri Lanka: 1977-82,' Robert B. Goldmann and A. Jeyeratnam Wilson (ed.), From Independence to Statehood (London, 1984), pp.97-107; the particular quotation occurs in Note 3, p. 107.
45. A. Jeyaratnam Wilson, p. 105.
46. A. Jeyaratnam Wilson, p. 107.
47. A. Jeyaratnam Wilson, p. 107
48. A. Jeyaratnam Wilson, p. 110.
49. A. Jeyaratnam Wilson, p. 143.
50. A. Jeyaratnam Wilson, p. 160.
51. A. Jeyaratnam Wilson, pp.113-114.
52. Sri Lanka News – Lanka Page [Homepage of SriLankaPage Information], [Online]. (2001, July 28-last update). Available: http://www.lankapage.com/ [2001, July 28].
53. V. Suryanarayan. (2002, January 6). The Tigers' Soft Image. The Hindu [Online], Volume 19, 40 paragraphs. Available: http://www.flonnet.com/fl1901/19010470.htm [2002, February 7].
54. Ibid.
55. A. Jeyaratnam Wilson, p.151.
56. V. Suryanarayan, op.cit.
57. Sri Lanka News – Lanka Page [Homepage of SriLankaPage Information], [Online]. (2001, December 19-last update). Available: http://www.lankapage.com/ [2001, December 19].
58. Sri Lanka News – Colombo Page [Homepage of ColomboPage Sri Lankan Internet Newspaper], [Online]. (2002, January 3). Available: http://www.colombopage.com/ [2002, January 3].

59. Sri Lanka News – Colombo Page [Homepage of ColomboPage Sri Lankan Internet Newspaper], [Online]. (2002, January 22-last update). Available: http://www.lankapage.com/ [2002, January 22].

60. Sri Lanka News – Colombo Page [Homepage of ColomboPage Sri Lankan Internet Newspaper], [Online]. (2002, January 28-last update). Available: http://www.colombopage.com/ [2002, January 28].

61. The Hindu News Update Service [Homepage of The Hindu], [Online]. (2001, December 23). Available: http://www.hinduonnet.com/thehindu/holnus/02231803.htm [2001, December 24].

62. Sri Lanka News – Colombo Page [Homepage of ColomboPage Sri Lankan Internet Newspaper], [Online]. (2002, January 31-last update). Available: http://www.colombopage.com/ [2002, January 31].

63. Sri Lanka News – Colombo Page [Homepage of ColomboPage Sri Lankan Internet Newspaper], [Online]. (2002, January 29-last update). Available: http://www.colombopage.com/ [2002, January 29].

64. Sri Lanka News – Colombo Page [Homepage of ColomboPage Sri Lankan Internet Newspaper], [Online]. (2002, January 24-last update). Available: http://www.colombopage.com/ [2002, January 24].

65. Sri Lanka News – Colombo Page [Homepage of ColomboPage Sri Lankan Internet Newspaper], [Online]. (2002, January 28-last update). Available: http://www.colombopage.com/ [2002, January 28].

66. Sri Lanka News – Colombo Page [Homepage of ColomboPage Sri Lankan Internet Newspaper], [Online]. (2001, November 27-last update). Available: http://www.colombopage.com/ [2001, November 27].

67. V. Suryanarayan. (2002, January 6). The Tigers' Soft Image. The Hindu [Online], Volume 19, 40 paragraphs. Available: http://www.flonnet.com/fl1901/19010470.htm [2002, February 7].

68. Ibid.

CHAPTER 3: PRESENT PARANOIA

Unwinnable War

As stated earlier, the separatist war and related terrorist activities in Sri Lanka have already claimed more than 65,000 lives. In addition, they have uprooted more than 670,000 Sri Lankans from their homes and forced them to live with the trauma that displacement brings. Sri Lanka has become one of the world's major sources of refugees in the world. A vast majority of those displaced are Tamils. Among others displaced, there are thousands of Sinhalese and Muslims who have become the victims of the ethnic cleansing pursued by the LTTE. In an issue paper published by the United States Committee for Refugees in October 1991, Sri Lanka had been characterized as an "Island of Refugees."[1] In his article entitled "Land of the Displaced" published in June 2001, V. Suryanarayan estimates the number of people affected by the prolonged conflict in Sri Lanka to be 679,214, belonging to 187,369 families.[2] The same article gives a breakdown of this massive human displacement, "According to the Commissioner-General of Essential Services, 171,233 persons belonging to 40,750 families stay in 348 welfare centres; 485,405 persons belonging to 141,522 families stay with friends and relatives; and 22,576 persons belonging to 5,097 families are non-displaced but are economically affected. The exact ethnic breakdown is not available, but it is estimated that 78 per cent of the displaced are Tamils, 13 per cent Muslims, and eight per cent Sinhalese."[3]

The preceding chapter showed how the government of Sri Lanka has so far tried to bring about a solution to the separatist war through military and non-military (cease-fires and peace talks) means. It is an undisputed fact that the government has the financial and military superiority. It spends a colossal sum of money every year on the war effort, which otherwise could have been directed to development, and deploys more than 100,000 troops in the battlefield. It makes substantial gains by recapturing strategic areas that have been under LTTE control from time to time. But no sooner does this happen in one place, then the LTTE claims gains in a counter attack elsewhere, reversing the government's gains. According to analysts, the number of troops on the LTTE side is not even one-fourth of that of the government. Despite this obvious shortcoming, the LTTE has demonstrated on many occasions that its cadres can take on the government army and make substantial military gains. In 1987, they daringly challenged the Indian army brought into the country for peace keeping by the Sri Lankan government. LTTE cadres have always fought ferociously on the battlefield with no intention to return defeated. Their only goal is to fight or die for their cause. They always carry a cyanide capsule hung around their neck. They swallow it and die, if ever captured by government troops. They also have secret, suicide bombers who carry explosives wrapped around their body. By detonating the explosives, they take the lives of their targets, usually high level politicians who are perceived as opponents or dilutors of their cause, along with those who happened to be in their proximity - while sacrificing their own lives.

Critics believe that neither the government nor the LTTE can bring a military closure to the separatist war. Even if the government forces recapture every inch of the land now under LTTE control, the war will not end, as it would continue to remain an area of contention between the two parties. On the other hand, if the LTTE succeeds in bringing the entire north and east under their control, the government forces are not going to give up. So the war will continue from one battle to another with claims of military gains on both sides. This also clearly shows that the war itself cannot and will not bring about a lasting solution to the present crisis. A lasting solution to the crisis can come about only by addressing the root cause of the war.

Root Cause

Going by the sequence of events that led to the separate war, it is very clear that the root cause of the war is the lack of equal opportunities for the Tamil minority in the country. The solution would have been to treat the needs and aspirations of Tamils and other minorities in the country the same way as those of the majority Sinhalese. But this is not what happened in the country after independence; what did happen was that slowly and systematically the rights and freedoms of its minorities, especially Tamils, were taken away, finally reducing them to second class status. Post-independent governments had refused to accept and recognize the language and religion of Tamils on par with those of the Sinhalese, passed laws restricting the intake of Tamil youth to universities, and continued to indulge in divisive ethnic politics, alienating Tamils from the governing process of the country.

No one in the country publicly objected to the concept of equal opportunities at any time. The majority Sinhalese had first made a cry to correct an imbalance of opportunities in the country in favour of Tamils that had existed at the time of independence. Then Tamils had disproportionately occupied the positions in the public service, professions and higher learning institutions of the country. This was a result of an imbalance in the educational opportunities that existed in the country during colonial times, with a disproportionately larger number of secondary schools of western education concentrated in the north. Now after a few decades of post independent rule by governments lead by Sinhalese leaders, Tamils are complaining of an imbalance of opportunities and power sharing in favour of the Sinhalese. Thus, the tables appear to have turned around.

Since independence, the people of the country have elected seven governments within the two-party system that has evolved, in 1956, 1960, 1965, 1970, 1977, 1994 and 2001. Before coming to power, the leaders of all these governments promised to correct the inequalities, injustices and prejudices that existed in the country based on language and ethnicity. But what they claim to have done to achieve that noble goal only brought negative results. This situation has changed the dynamics of the cries for equality in the country from peaceful debates among the leaders of different ethnic groups in its parliament at the time of independence, to the present bloody civil war between the government and Tamil youth. Let us now try to examine what may have led to this dreadful situation.

Colonial Inheritance

In the first place the 1948 independence was not a total transfer of political power from the colonialists to the people of Sri Lanka. Instead, it was only a legislative reform with the transfer of some political power, not sovereign power, in the form of a dominion status to Sri Lanka. The beginning of the demise of the British Empire commenced soon after World War 11 brought about this legislative reform. First the colonialists had to grant independence to India in response to its freedom struggles, both non-violent and violent. In the wake of this situation, the colonialists decided to transfer some political powers to Sri Lanka. There were no freedom struggles in Sri Lanka after those staged in the Kandyan areas in the nineteenth century. What went on in the first half of the twentieth century were only negotiations, not for independence but for legislative reforms, by the English educated Sinhalese and Tamil élite whose economic interests had become closely connected with those of the British.

It was the Colonial Office in London that finally decided the form of government Sri Lanka was to have at "independence." The Soulbury Constitution [4] of 1947 laid out the framework for this new form of government. This constitution totally ignored the basic concepts of equality, fundamental human rights and even citizenship. Thereby it left the doors open for inequality, discrimination and disenfranchisement and eventual discord over caste, race, language, religion, and the like. The élite who received "independence" were content to stand as the new rulers in place of their colonial masters and made no significant effort at national consolidation and the integration of all the peoples of the country as one nation. As a consequence, the then existing divisions, inequalities, injustices and prejudices became the bedrock of "independent" Sri Lanka, and were perpetrated by the policies of the governments that followed.

National Disintegration

The nature and extent of political groupings among the 95 elected members of the 1947 parliament was a mirror image of the divisions among the people of the country at the time of independence. 61 of the 95 elected members, including some Tamils, represented a full brand of political ideological differences, from conservatism to communism. Yet there were 34 members who had chosen not to be part of the ideologically divisive politics. Twelve members of these 34 had been elected purely on ethnic grounds: six from the Tamil Congress representing Sri Lankan Tamils in the north and the east and the other six from the Ceylon Indian Congress representing the Indian Tamils in the hill country. Those who were not swayed by any of the political parties elected the remaining 22. With members elected on universal franchise (established in 1931), this election helped bring onto the centre stage of governance the diverse concerns and political views of all Sri Lankans at this crucial time of transfer of power from colonialists to natives. This was a blessing and a great opportunity for the country to move from there to an independent system of government fit for all Sri Lankans through a democratic process. But this simply didn't happen.

The 1947 Soulbury Constitution, though inadequate to bring about integration of all the peoples of the country under Sri Lankan nationalism, had some measures to prevent discrimination against any particular group or groups of people. The requirement of two-thirds majority in the parliament for passing laws, discriminating any person or persons on the basis of religion, race or language, is one such important measure. In addition, it required the establishment of a second chamber, the Senate, of 30 members, 15 elected by the parliament and the other 15 nominated by the Governor General to represent minority interests. The leaders of independent Sri Lanka, however, appeared to have ignored the strategic importance of such measures, and chose a political path, further worsening the already existing ethnic and racial disunity in the country. The first priority of these leaders should have been to build consensus among all the diverse parties both within and outside parliament on a new, independent constitution for the country. By any stretch of imagination, this was not easy. But this was what was required at that time. According to the Soulbury constitution, however, any amendment to the constitution was also possible only with a two-thirds majority in the parliament. But this would not have been impossible, as all the concerned parties would have benefited by such a move. Instead of tackling this difficult task of laying a proper foundation for independent Sri Lanka, the leaders at the time chose to resort to simple majoritarianism in deciding the new nation's future. They were able to do so, as the existing constitutional provisions were totally inadequate for protecting minority rights.

Non-secularism

No doubt, the commitment to a secular government of the first Prime Minister of "independent" Sri Lanka, D. S. Senanayake, and the change in the stance of the Tamil Congress and its leader, G. G. Ponnambalam, on the issue of minorities from "fifty-fifty representation" to "responsive cooperation" have played a positive role towards national consolidation. This was, however, short lived with the untimely death of Prime Minister Senanayake in 1952, and the sudden removal of the TC leader from the cabinet in 1953 by a subsequent Prime Minister, Sir John Kotelawela, for no apparent reason. Some believe that the removal of the TC leader from the cabinet was due to a personality clash between him and the prime minister, and had nothing to do with their individual political beliefs. This act of removal of the TC leader from the cabinet, however, sent a strong message to minorities that the strategy of responsive cooperation as pursued by TC would not bring about a solution to their problems. According to critics, this single event helped boost the image of the Federal Party as the dominant voice of the Tamil minority. Meanwhile, Prime Ministers and Presidents who ruled the country after D. S. Senanayake were not committed to secularism as a means to national consolidation and integration of all the peoples of the country.

The biggest blow to national consolidation and integration came from the policies of S. W. R. D. Bandaranaike, who became the Leader of Opposition in 1952 and Prime Minister in 1956. He never showed any commitment to secularism. On the contrary, he openly mixed up his power and politics with religion. He turned the genuine aspirations of the majority Sinhalese Buddhists of the country for the revival of their language and religion from the bonds of colonialism to a divisive instrument of political power against similar aspirations of its minority Tamil community. In preparing for the 1956 general election, his party, the SLFP, brought Buddhist monks to the centre stage of post-independent party-politics, made a no-contest pact with Marxist parties, and promised to make Sinhala the only official language in 24 hours as stated earlier.

At the time of independence, it was a natural aspiration of the Sinhalese Buddhists to free their language and religion from the bonds of colonialism. This was in no way a challenge to other languages and religions in the country. Understandably, Tamil Hindus too had similar aspirations. Thus, both groups simply wanted to replace English with their indigenous languages, and safeguard their religious freedom from further interference by foreign domination. Others in the country, including Muslims, Burghers (or Eurasians), and Veddhas, simply looked forward to a free and democratic society where their languages and religions would be equally respected, as those of the Sinhalese Buddhists and Hindu Tamils. The biggest challenge the national leaders faced was to pave way to a new, independent Sri Lankan nation where such natural aspirations of all its peoples could be satisfactorily met under a centralized administrative system. In this historic challenge, the national leaders faced two major obstacles. One major obstacle was the concept of Sinhalese-Buddhist nationalism disseminated in the minds of the Sinhalese Buddhists by the Sinhalese chauvinist forces in the country from the time of Anagarika Dharmapala. The other major obstacle was the differences and prejudices on the basis of language among the very leaders in the national political arena of the country that had already sharpened under their common colonial masters. Despite these obstacles Prime Minister Senanayake and TC leader G. G. Ponnambalam tried to work together in the best interests of the country. Yet, the country as a whole failed to lay down a meaningful foundation for an independent Sri Lankan nation fit for its entire people.

Unreal Expectations

With their unrealistic demands in the past, Tamil leaders had given a contorted twist to the language politics of Tamils in early times. In fact, as stated before, both Sinhalese and Tamil leaders in the late nineteenth and early twentieth centuries, except A. E. Goonasinghe, were against the introduction of universal franchise. They wanted to limit the franchise to the wealthy and the English educated. This was on a baseless presumption that those not wealthy and not English educated, including those well-educated in a vernacular language, Sinhalese or Tamil, were not suitable to be given the responsibility of voting. In addition, Tamil leaders at the time wanted some form of equal representation in the legislature even with territorial representation. The fifty-fifty representation demand of TC was designed to achieve this objective. By any stretch of imagination these were not realistic expectations. It was very clear to everyone that the forces of universal franchise and territorial representation would eventually triumph, and Tamils would be a linguistic minority in a unitary Sri Lanka. What Sinhalese and Tamil leaders should have thought about was not a method of implementing fifty-fifty representation in the parliament, but a system of government that could ensure equal opportunities for all peoples in the country across language or any other social or cultural distinction. The Kandyans' proposal for a federal system of government at the Royal Commissions of 1927 and 1947-7 had been designed to address this issue. But, as stated in an earlier chapter, neither the elite leaders of Tamils nor those of the Low Country Sinhalese supported that proposal. By not supporting the proposal, the leaders of these two communities appear to have been more interested in maintaining the status quo rather than building a new, independent society on the foundations of equality and equal opportunities for all the peoples, who had earlier lived in three distinct native kingdoms.

Marxists' Role

The role played by the Marxist parties, including the LSSP and CP, by entering into political alliances with the SLFP and supporting its chauvinist policies from time to time had also been a contributory factor to the ethnic crisis. These Marxist parties started their politics in the early thirties and forties with traditional Marxist revolutionary slogans of equality and class struggles. Their first language policy had been to recognize both Sinhalese and Tamil as national languages on an equal footing. This situation later changed as they entered into political alliance with the SLFP to defeat the conservative UNP government. First Philip Gunawardane and his group within the LSSP embraced the 'Sinhala Only' policy of the SLFP when the Marxist parties entered into a no-contest pact with the SLFP at the 1956 election. Then the rest of the Marxists followed suit when they formed a coalition with the SLFP in 1964.

The governments of the political alliances of the SLFP and the Marxist parties had many liberal and socialist policies drawn from the individual parties involved. But why the Marxist parties agreed to accept a language policy of 'Sinhala Only' was a mystery. Then again the same Marxist groups were willing parties to the new constitution adopted in 1972, enshrining Sinhalese language and Buddhism with special references. This embrace of the chauvinist policies of the SLFP by the Marxist parties reduced their traditional support. It was a complete loss of face for these parties in the Tamil areas, as they no longer stood for the rights of the Tamil minority. In the Sinhalese areas, a new group of more radical Marxists emerged in the sixties under the banner of Janatha Vimukthi Peramuna (JVP). It staged a bloody rebellion in 1971 to topple the then government jointly run by SLFP, LSSP and CP. Ironically, the top leaders of all these Marxist parties that played a role in the centre stage of the country's politics were Sinhalese, except for Peter Kienamon, a Burgher, who led CP (Moscow) wing and Shanmugadasan, a Tamil, who led CP (Peking) wing. At first all the Marxist parties, except JVP, had a notable number of Tamils in their high-ranking positions. But this situation changed once these parties opted to work with the SLFP. The JVP in particular took into account a concept of potential Indian expansionism in framing its policies right from its very beginning, and this may have distanced many Tamils from its leadership because of their closer common linguistic and religious bonding with the people of South India.

Today, the JVP is vehemently against any form of devolution of power to Tamil minority in the north and east.

Racism Among Leaders

The lack of political parties with policies and platforms of national perspective and the lack of political leaders elected on merit rather than on language, religion, or family connections have also remained a significant drawback in the post-independent era. In the early twentieth century the Sri Lankan leaders in the country displayed their ability to stand above their linguistic, religious and ethnic differences in national politics. The election of Sir Ponnambalam Arunachalam, a Tamil, as the first President of the Ceylon National Congress, where Sinhalese were in a significant majority in 1919 clearly testifies to this. Everyone thought that he was the best-suited person for that position at the time, and the majority Sinhalese within the CNC accepted his leadership without protest. This situation, however, later changed in the early thirties. By the time of independence in 1948 the CNC had transformed into the United National Party (UNP), with only Sinhalese in its top ranks. Ever since the UNP has always remained that way, with some notable exceptions. SLFP never had any Tamils in its highest ranks. The Marxist parties were no different, with only rare exceptions. In short all the political parties that aspired to form government had only Sinhalese in their highest ranks. Only the parties formed to represent Tamils' interests had Tamil leaders. This alienation of Tamils from the mainstream politics of the country contributed to further polarization of its people on the basis of language. In the absence of Tamils among their own top ranks, both the UNP and SLFP chose to appoint one or more Tamils to the cabinet in their governments as a gesture of goodwill towards the Tamil minority. There were, indeed, other occasions where the governments led by both the UNP and SLFP gave cabinet positions to the members of Tamil minority parties that had coalesced with them on specific agreements on minority issues.

The system of government established by the Soulbury constitution for independent Sri Lanka had its own limitations to bring the Tamil and Sinhalese leaders together and reduce their differences. It, however, had some in-built features to consolidate and integrate all the peoples of the country as one, Sri Lankan nation. This was possible only if the leaders at the time had the courage to put aside all their differences and to start working together with a new vision for the country, accepting the birth rights of all its peoples on an equal footing. This didn't happen, especially in the case of the major parties that emerged; instead, the leaders at the time chose to build political parties on the basis of their ethnic differences. If they did form political parties with genuine national platforms, they could have ended up with leaders from all linguistic, religious and ethnic communities. In such a situation, Sri Lankans would not have cared for a person's language, religion or ethnicity in electing one as a leader of a national political party or of the country as Prime Minister or President. It is never too late for Sri Lankans to learn from the rest of the world in this regard. Canada offers a good example. It has two main languages, English and French. Only 25 percent of the population is French speaking, but it has had Prime Ministers from both the linguistic communities. Elliott Trudeau and Jean Chretian are two French speaking Canadian Prime Ministers. Elliot Trudeau was Prime Minister from 1968 to 1979 and from 1980 to 1984, and had led his party to landslide victories at general elections. Jean Chretian too had similar landslide victories at general elections held in 1996 and 2000. Then in the 2000 election, the Progressive Conservative Party of Canada led by Joe Clark, a former Prime Minister and a English speaking Canadian from the west of the country, could retain only his seat in the entire west, but got many seats from the east of the country. In Tanzania, Africa, Julius Neyerere, a Christian, was repeatedly elected by popular vote as the leader of its governing TANU party and President of that country, although Muslims were the significant majority. The people of this country wanted him back as President, even after he voluntarily installed his second in command, Rashidi Kawawa, a Muslim, as president.

At the time of independence, Sri Lanka had some political parties that appeared to have stood above the differences on language, religion or ethnicity, at least in principle. The UNP and the two Marxist parties, the LSSP and CP, had such a stand. The top leaders and the high-ranking officials of every one of them were, however, not mixed enough across the borders of language, religion and ethnicity. The main reason for this may have been the continued dominance of Tamil language politics in Tamil areas under the leadership of first TC, and later the FP. If, however, the UNP and the Marxist parties guarded and retained their platforms of national perspective and continued with their efforts to have more and more Tamil speaking people among their rank and file, the chauvinist politics of the country may have had a natural death. This, however, was not what actually happened. The embrace of Sinhalese-Buddhist nationalism and 'Sinhala Only' policies by the SLFP before the 1956 election brought in a recipe for a complete U-turn of the country's politics to the medieval, Sinhalese-Tamil conflicts. The real effects of the SLFP on the country's politics were mainly two-fold. On the one hand it helped further strengthen the cause of the communal politics of the TC and FP among the Tamil-speaking people of the country. On the other hand, it adulterated the national policies of the UNP and the Marxist parties, subjugating them to the forces of chauvinism, through a process of an UNP-SLFP seesawing power game. Every time the SLFP formed a government, the UNP became the main opposition party in the parliament, and every time the UNP formed a government the SLFP became the main opposition. Only once was there an exception to this mastery, when the Federal Party became the main opposition party in 1977. The Marxist parties have been in coalition governments with the SLFP. While in government, both the major parties, the SLFP and the UNP, tried to implement measures to correct the wrongs done by their own discriminative policies against minorities, especially Tamils. However, at all such occasions, the opposition party waiting to form the next government incited the Sinhalese majority against the government in power, saying that such measures would eventually lead to divide the country. Thus both the major parties had been well and truly caught up in a chauvinist system of politics they could not get out of, even if any chose to do so. This finally led to the present situation with no major political party in the country with national policies, respecting all its citizens on an equal footing. No major party equally represents the interests of all the peoples of the country any more. Those led by Sinhalese leaders represent the interests of Sinhalese. Those led by Tamil leaders represent the interests of Tamils, and those led by Muslim leaders represent the interests of Muslims. No party or leader in government stands for equal rights and freedoms for all its citizens, across the borders of language, religion and ethnicity. As a result, the parliament where these party leaders debate and take decisions on majoritarianism has become an instrument of further aggravation of the prejudices and differences among the different linguistic, religious and ethnic groups of the country. In this situation, the Sinhalese and Tamil leaders of the country no longer appear to have any desire to work together on a common national platform.

Escalation of Mistrust

The non-implementation of the BC Pact of 1957 and the blatant shortcomings of the District Development Councils (DDCs) implemented under the DC Pact of 1965 lead to further deterioration of the relationship between the central government headed by Sinhalese leaders and the Tamil minority in the country. The District Development Councils Act, No. 35 of 1980, was not an instrument of devolution of real power to regions. In fact, it neither transferred any legislative powers to regions, nor included provisions on colonization settlements. As if all this was not enough, most of the members of the DDCs, such as members of parliament, appointed members of the house of representative, and mayors, were not electorally responsible to the people they were expected to serve at District level. The District Ministers who acted as the Chairperson of the DDCs didn't have to be from the same District. The Executive Committee of the DDC was to consist of a District Minister (Chairperson) and two members appointed by the President of the country in consultation with the District Minister. The DDCs had to raise the needed funds from taxes and rates, but subject to the prior approval of the parliament, meaning the central government. These arrangements put DDCs and their operations under direct control of the central government. Thus the implementation of the DDCs didn't result in real devolution of power or autonomy. Inadequate funds and direct and indirect control by the central government failed the DDCs, in their attempt to achieve their intended purpose.

In 1978, the government brought about some constitutional changes creating the office of an Executive President. According to the changes, the people should elect the President by popular vote. The people generally believed that the person so elected as President by the popular vote would represent all the peoples of the country, across the barriers of language, religion and ethnicity. Critics say, however, that this was good in theory, but not in practice. In practice, one could get elected as Executive President by popular vote without having to earn a single vote from the linguistic minorities in the country. The Executive Presidential system so introduced did not, therefore, solve the growing linguistic and ethnic crisis. The system needs strategic, structural adjustments with adequate checks and balances to make sure that the elected Executive President has, in fact, obtained adequate support from all the regions of the country. It is not uncommon to see such checks and balances in the constitutions of other countries of executive presidential model. The Electoral College system of electing Executive President in the American republican constitution is a case in point. In the 2000 presidential election, Al Gore, the Democratic Party candidate won the popular vote in the USA by more than half-a-million ballots, but lost in the electoral college, making his Republican Party opponent, George Bush, the new President. Sri Lankans should learn from this and other similar experiences in the world and try to evolve a suitable system.

Provincial Councils established in 1988 following the Thirteenth Amendment to the country's constitution also failed to give the degree of self-determination and autonomy expected by the regions. This constitutional amendment and the provincial councils came about as a means to resolving the worsening ethnic crisis, after protracted negotiations between the government of Sri Lanka and Tamil militant groups, with India playing a mediating role. These negotiations ended up in the form of an Indo-Lanka agreement signed between Rajiv Gandhi, Prime Minister of India, and J. R. Jayawardane, President and the Head of State of Sri Lanka, in July 1987. The agreement provided for the devolution of power to the provinces in Sri Lanka as a way to resolve the ethnic crisis. All parties involved in the negotiations expected that such devolution of power would result in popular participation in the country's governance and establish a degree of self-determination and autonomy for the provinces, in a manner acceptable to all the parties concerned. People also expected that such a move would help the country uplift its rural communities with more resources being allocated to them and by facilitating a more equitable and balanced development within the country.

The Provincial Councils established with such expectations, however, failed to bring about the expected results. The Thirteenth Amendment had three separate lists of subject areas of government, one assigned to the central government, one to the provinces, and the other to both the central government and the provinces. During the time of implementation, however, the central government did not want to part with authority and responsibility on the provincial subjects, notably some in extremely sensitive areas such as public security (law and order) and the control over state land. The President himself appointed the police chiefs of the provinces, Deputy Inspector Generals (DIGs), in consultation with the provincial Chief Ministers. The DIGs were responsible to the Inspector General of Police (IGP), the head of the police service of the central government. A three-member Provincial Commission handled Police recruitment matters in a province. This Commission consisted of the DIG in charge of the province and two nominees, one of the central Public Service Commission and the other of the Chief Minister of the province. All this didn't result in transferring authority and responsibility in public security to the provinces as envisaged by the Thirteenth Amendment.

The Provinces did not obtain effective control over state land, although land use and settlement came under provincial jurisdiction. The real power to execute grants and disposition of state lands and immovable property continued to remain with the President, at the central level. This failed to alleviate the fears of Tamil people in the northern and eastern provinces on future colonization schemes threatening the existing demographic composition of their areas. Indian Tamils concentrated in the central highlands also realized that the provincial councils in their areas didn't have the power or influence to make a meaningful difference to their lives in the plantation sector.

Having higher education as a subject in the concurrent list also raised questions among Tamils, especially those who lived in the northern and eastern provinces. Tamils were generally suspicious of the intention of the central government to have control over higher education, because of its past record of discrimination towards Tamil students in university admissions. Another major contentious issue was the continuation of the authority and responsibility on "national policy on all subjects and functions" in the hands of the central government. This simply meant that executive power had not fully devolved to provinces in any subject area.

Despite these shortcomings, the Provincial Councils obtained power to enact statutes. The process of making the provincial statutes, however, remained under the control of the central government. The Governor of the province, appointed by President, had to assent the bills passed by the Provincial Council. The Governor had the power to refuse to give his or her assent to a bill passed by the Council. In that event the Governor would have to return the bill to the Council for its reconsideration. If the Council passes the bill for a second time without any change, the Governor could forward it to President. The President in turn could refer it to the Supreme Court to determine whether it is at variance with the country's constitution. If the Supreme Court finds that the bill is, in fact, in variance with the provisions of the country's constitution, the Governor could still refuse to assent the bill. This central control of the legislative powers of the provinces has lead to further loss of faith of the people, especially the Tamils in the north and the east, in the country's political system and leadership.

Adding a New Problem

Temporary unification of the eastern and northern provinces under one Provincial Council pursuant to the July 1987 Indo-Lanka Agreement brought in a new controversial factor into the ethnic divide. The people of the eastern province have the opportunity to finally accept or reject the merger of the two provinces through a referendum. At first, the government wanted to conduct this referendum within six months of the temporary merger. But this has not happened. The demand for the merger had come from Tamils in the northern and eastern provinces, as they treated the two provinces as their homeland. But Muslims in the area wish to safeguard their own identity by special accommodation, even in a merged provincial set-up. The eastern province has a much higher percentage of Muslim population than in the northern province. The following table shows the 1981 census figures representing the percentages of population of different ethnic and linguistic communities living in these two and other provinces, broken down to district level:

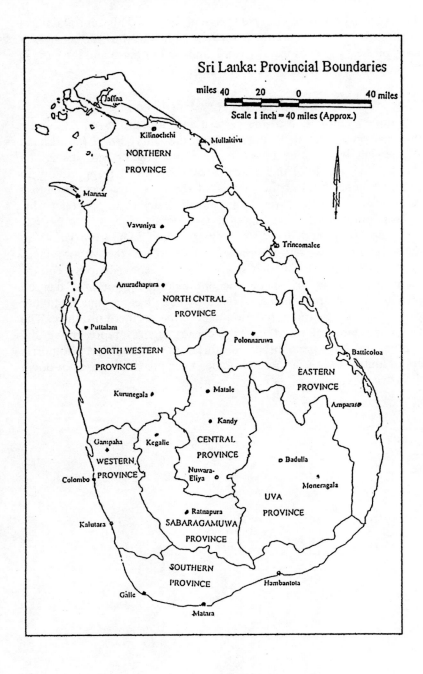

Sri Lanka: Provincial Boundaries

miles 40   20   0   40 miles

Scale 1 inch = 40 miles (Approx.)

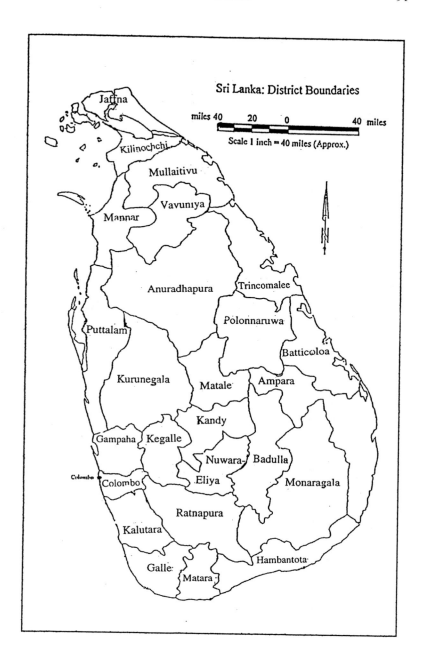

Sri Lanka: District Boundaries

Table 1
Sri Lanka: Population Distribution

Province	District	Sinha-lese	Sri Lank-an Tamils	Indian Tamils	Musl-ims	Othe-rs
Northern	Jaffna	0.8	95.2	2.4	1.6	0
	Kilinochchi	0.8	95.2	2.4	1.6	0
	Mullaitivu	5.2	75.4	14.5	4.7	0.1
	Mannar	8.2	51.3	13.0	26.1	1.4
	Vavuniya	16.6	56.8	19.6	6.8	0.2
Eastern	Trincomalee	33.4	34.3	2.1	29.3	0.9
	Batticoloa	3.4	70.8	1.2	23.9	0.7
	Amparai	37.8	20.0	0.4	41.5	0.3
North Central	Anuradhapu-ra	91.1	1.4	0.1	7.1	0.2
	Polonnaru-wa	91.4	2.0	0	6.4	0.2
North West	Puttalam	82.6	6.6	0.5	9.9	0.4
	Kurunegala	92.9	1.2	0.5	5.0	0.2
Central	Matale	79.9	5.8	7.0	7.0	0.5
	Kandy	74.3	5.0	9.4	10.5	0.8
	Nuwara-Eliya	42.1	12.7	42.7	2.0	0.5
Sabarag-amuwa	Kegalle	85.9	2.2	6.7	5.0	0.1
	Ratnapura	85.0	2.4	10.6	1.7	0.3
Uva	Monaragala	92.7	2.0	3.2	1.9	0.2
	Badulla	69.1	5.9	20.2	4.2	0.7
Western	Gampaha	92.0	3.5	0.4	2.7	1.4
	Colombo	77.6	10.0	1.2	8.3	2.0
	Kalutara	87.2	1.2	4.1	7.4	0.3
Southern	Galle	94.5	0.9	1.4	3.2	0.1
	Matara	94.5	0.7	2.2	2.5	0
	Hambantota	97.1	0.6	0.1	1.2	1.0

Source: Department of Census and Statistics, an abstract from 'Table 20 – Percentage distribution of population of Sri Lanka by ethnic group and district – Census 1981,' Statistical Abstract of the Democratic Socialist Republic of Sri Lanka 1992, (Colombo, Sri Lanka, 1993), p.48.

The new situation that has come about as a result of the temporary merger of the two provinces has strained the relationship between Tamils and Muslims living in the area. At the beginning of 2001, President Chandrika Kumaratunga agreed to a demand by the Muslim leaders of the Amparai District to create a separate administrative district for minority Muslims by merging three exclusively Muslim electorates in the region. This, however, has so far not materialized due to pressure from Tamils and Sinhalese. All this has made it more difficult to find a lasting solution to the ethnic crisis than ever before.

Democracy Betrayed

The model of democracy defended and pursued by post independent leaders of the country has been, perhaps, the biggest single factor towards the present crisis situation. Historically, as explained in the previous chapter, native, regional chieftains or monarchs ruled the country. Only a handful of monarchs claimed their reign over the whole country. Some South Indian monarchs too came and ruled some parts of the country from time to time. Then there was colonial rule for about 450 years, until independence in 1948. At the time of independence, there were no monarchial claims to the country. The colonialists had either executed or exiled the last surviving members of the native royal families. The departing colonialists, the British, had established a Westminster style democratic system of government in the country just before independence. The people of the country as such had not experienced democracy under monarchial or colonial rule, except for universal franchise gained in 1931. The people thought that their post-independent leaders would bring them into an era of full-blown democracy under the new system of government established at the time of independence. These leaders completely changed the constitution of the country, not once but twice, in their efforts to improve their democratic rule. By these constitutional changes, they also changed the name of the country from Ceylon to the

Democratic Socialist Republic of Sri Lanka. But after fifty years of their post-independent "democratic" rule, the country has ended up in political upheaval with no apparent solution. There are two main reasons for the failure of democracy in Sri Lanka.

The first is the continued attempts by post-independent leaders to build some form of dynastic-type rule in the country. A close look at the main players in the political arena over the last fifty years clearly shows that the country's destiny has been in the hands of the members of the same few families. These few elitist families control the affairs of both the major political parties, the SLFP and the UNP, which have exchanged the ruling power of the country between them. The lines of succession of the top leadership of these two major political parties in the country nakedly testify to this blatant state of affairs. On the UNP side, when Prime Minister D. S. Senanayake's rule ended in 1952, his son, Dudley Senanayake, succeeded. When Dudley Senanayake's rule ended in 1953, his uncle, Sir john Kotelawela, succeeded. When Sir John Kotalawela's rule ended, Dudley Senanayake succeeded for the second time. When Dudley Senanayake finally died, another in the same family circles, J. R. Jayawardena, succeeded. When J. R. Jayawardena's rule ended, his nephew, Ranil Wickremesinghe, succeeded, after a short period of R. Premadasa and D. B. Wijetunga, the only two leaders who broke the dynastic rule. On the SLFP side, when Prime Minister S. W. R. D. Bandaranaike's rule ended in 1959, his wife, Sirimavo Bandaranaike, succeeded - after a short interim government led by W. Dahanayake. When Sirimavo Bandaranaike's rule ended, their daughter, Chandrika Kumaratunga, succeeded. President, Chandrika Kumaratunga had even installed her aging mother as Prime Minister, and appointed a number of her closest relatives to key cabinet positions in her government, disregarding non-relatives of higher caliber and competence. On 10 November 2001, a UNP spokesperson, Karunasena Kodituwakku, summed up the latest dynastic struggles of the Bandaranaike family, "Since President Kumaratunga could not be President three times (according to existing constitution), she would like a Bandaranaike heir to the throne. She could be (now) planning to install her brother at the (SLFP) party helm until such time her children were able to come to politics."[5] This way of dynastic rule and divisive policies of these leaders have resulted in the alienation of not only Tamils, but also the majority Sinhalese from the real decision making process at its highest level. Through their constitutional changes, these leaders have renamed the country as a Democratic Socialist

Republic and declared on paper that sovereignty belongs entirely to the people. These leaders, however, have continued to rule the country mainly on their dynastic strengths. Their actions have changed the meaning of democracy from the rule of the people, by the people, and for the people, to the rule of the people, by a few dynastic-type families, for the benefit of themselves, their kith and kin, stooges and sycophants.

Some argue that the continued retention of the leadership of the country in the hands of a few dynastic families is not due to any conspiracy that they have committed. Instead, they say, it has come about because of the charisma of the members of these families and their ability to win elections. Even if that is so, the people of Sri Lanka must at least now realize that there are more important leadership qualities to look for in a leader, rather than charisma and ability to win. What the country now needs is not dynastic-type leaders of charisma and ability to win, but statesmen who can stand above the linguistic, religious and cultural differences of the present multiethnic society and have the wisdom and knowledgability to solve its burning problems.

The members of the dynastic-type families, however, behave in the country as if they have a birth right to rule, and expect the rest of the people in the country to look up to them for future leaders. These families use their power and prestige to take control of all other political organizations and movements in the country of the men and women not connected to them by close family ties. Those organizations and movements that refuse to join them never get a place in the political arena, as the ruling power always remains between their two major parties.

The author has learnt this satanic fact through his own experience as well. In October 1979, he co-founded a new, democratic political party in the country by the name of Podujana Party (PP). Its top three leaders came from three different regions of the country: one from the south, one from the north, and the other from the centre. The party's saffron colour banner had a face of a newly born baby, a chaplet of rice plants with rice seeds consecrating the baby's face and an inscription, "One Lanka – One Nation, One Nation – One Family." The co-founders of the new party had invited representatives from the media to their first press conference they held in the heart of the capital, Colombo, with the fanfare that befitted such an event. But the media down played it, except for a few independent newspapers. The state controlled Sinhalese newspaper with the biggest circulation did not stop by downplaying it. It took a further step by carrying a headline in its next day's edition misquoting a statement made by the President of the country at the time, J. R. Jayawardane. The headline read that his governing party, UNP, had now become a podujana party, meaning a party of all the peoples of the country. After active engagement in propagating the PP in the country, its co-founders applied for registration under the Election Act to qualify for the status of a registered political party. They did this on two occasions, both times with no success. On inquiry, the government refused to give reasons for turning down their application on both occasions. As the new party gained momentum in the country, three old parliamentarians also joined its ranks as card-carrying members. This raised the image of the party to a new dimension, as having two or more past parliamentarians would automatically qualify for registration under the provisions of the Election Act at the time. The author, in his capacity as the leader of the new party, informed President Jayawardane that his administration had no choice but to register his new party the next time because of this new situation. By the next time, however, the government had amended the Election Act, removing the related provisions. Despite these drawbacks, the new party continued with its efforts in preparing for the general election scheduled for 1983, with potential candidates for most of the electoral districts in the country. Meanwhile, R. Premadasa, the Prime Minister at the time, called the author and offered him a place in the legislature as a member of the then ruling party, UNP, which he declined. Earlier while Premadasa was Minister of Local Government, he had invited the author to accept UNP nomination for the Nuwara Eliya seat in central Sri Lanka in 1970. The writer simply rejected this invitation as well, as he was never attracted to the UNP or the SLFP, primarily because of their chauvinist and dynastic nature. Instead, he chose to build a new political party as a vehicle for those who aspire to build a new society based on genuine democracy and equal rights and freedoms for all their fellow beings. All the Podujana Party candidates who were preparing for the 1983 election were ready to appear as independent candidates at the election, but on a common national platform of the Party, in the event it failed to get registered status by then. This failed again, as President Jayawardane postponed the 1983 general election by six years by an undemocratic strategy of a referendum to extend the term of the incumbent parliament. Once President Jayawardane challenged the nation for any new leadership from among the people, if there was a way to run the country better than how his UNP was doing or how his major opponents in the SLFP or the Marxist parties could do. But when a new political party emerged to face the challenge, he manipulated the ruling system in the country, preventing the new party from playing its intended democratic role.

Secondly, with their chauvinist policies, the two major political parties in the country, the SLFP and the UNP, have simplified the way of implementing democracy in the country to rule by simple majoritarianism in the legislature. Democratic institutions all over the world, no doubt, take decisions on the basis of majoritarianism, with a weighted degree of majority in each case, depending on the nature and sensitivity of the issue in question. For example, a parliament may require a 51 percent simple majority to pass a law in education or commerce, but a two-thirds majority to pass a constitutional amendment. Such a system, however, could serve its democratic purpose, only if those who voted on any given issue did so, agreeing with reason that it was conducive to the good and benefit of all. This is especially important for democracies of non-homogeneous societies like Sri Lanka. Otherwise, there will not be adequate security for minority rights in such societies. This was, in fact, what was happening in Sri Lanka ever since independence. The members of the Sinhalese linguistic majority in the country have passed laws for the benefit of their kind, the Sinhalese, ignoring how such laws would affect the Tamil minority in the country. Such laws have, among other things, defranchised and removed the citizenship of most of the Indian Tamils living in the upcountry, enshrined Buddhism in the constitution with special esteem and state protection, made Sinhalese the only official language in the country, restricted Tamil youth with necessary qualifying marks from entering universities, and imposed similar restrictions in the recruitment and career advancement of the public service personnel. Thus, the majority rule in post-independent Sri Lanka, under the name of democracy, has mostly worked for the benefit of the Sinhalese majority disadvantaging the Tamil minority. The government of Sri Lanka appears to have assumed authority over the rights of the individual, with no assurance to protect its entire people. This should not have happened in a genuine democracy.

Freedom of speech is entrenched and retained in the country's constitution that the post-independent governments have adopted. People in the country, however, do not and cannot enjoy that freedom, because of special laws limiting that freedom,

prolonged state of emergency, and threats of intimidation. The
media's role is under strict control too. The people in the country
have lost trust and confidence in democracy and elections. The
Supreme Court of the country has also said organized violence,
intimidation and vote rigging have openly taken place at some
recent elections. The rulers of the country risk the lives of their
innocent subjects for the sake of their own success. Kurunegala
Bishop Kumara Ilangasinghe summed up his feelings on the
ongoing state of affairs in the country at the ordination and
installation of the 14th Anglican Bishop of Colombo, Duleep de
Chikera, in 2000, "Many of those who matter seem to be having
confidence in violence to achieve their ends. Corruption, dishonesty
and injustice are rampant. .... The underworld has been active
quite openly with definite support and nurture of those who matter.
.... Today life is denied in many aspects of our society. The fruit
that we need to beat is to affirm the life in the midst of death."[6] At
the same congregation, he also had cited the case of a king who had
promised a devil called Alawaka a human being daily to save his
own life, and said, "The king should not have entered into an
agreement with the devil to offer his subjects and instead fought
with him."[7]

Unbuddhist Influence of Some Buddhist Monks

The Buddhist monks' role in the country, especially after it gained
independence from colonial rule in 1948, has been another
significant factor in its ever-worsening ethnic crisis. Historically one
became a Buddhist monk to follow a spiritual path leading to
Nibbana or Nirvana, a state of liberation and spiritual illumination
beyond pleasure or pain. According to the teachings of the Buddha,
pain and suffering cannot be avoided so long as one is subject to
worldly desires, and only through meditation and a strict moral
conduct one could finally reach Nibbana. The Buddha had
specifically circumscribed a code of conduct (Vinaya) toward this
end, for both the Sangha and the laity. According to this code of
conduct, the laity should undertake to observe a minimum of five
precepts (Puncha Sila), and abstain from killing, stealing, sexual
misconduct, lying, and intoxicants. The next level of moral conduct
has eight precepts (Ata Sil), adding three more to the first five.
These three include abstinence from enjoying music, dances, and
cosmic shows, abstinence from extravagance, and avoidance of
solid foods in evenings and nights. Buddhist laypersons, both young

and old, had continued with a tradition to observe the eight precepts on some selected days, especially on Poya days. The code of conduct expected of Buddhist monks starts at a higher level of moral conduct, and ends up with ten million precepts at its highest level, after higher ordination. From the earliest times some monks had chosen to live in monasteries in villages, while others had lived in forests. All the monks, however, irrespective of where they lived, had adhered to the same code of conduct.

As a result, historically Buddhist monks in general had a much higher level of moral conduct and insight when compared to the rest of the society. It is, therefore, understandable that the rest of the society, including the monarchial rulers, had held the Buddhist monks in highest esteem, with profound admiration and reverence. Through this special admiration and reverence, the laity at the time had sought guidance and advice from Buddhist monks, especially from those who lived in village monasteries, not only on the teachings of the Buddha, but also on their mundane problems. The monarchial rulers at the time were not an exception in this regard. They too had consulted Buddhist monks on problems they faced in ruling their territories. The advice the monks had given to the laity, including the monarchial rulers, at the time was consistent with the Buddha's teachings. In their advice to monarchs, the monks always wanted them to be righteous before the masses and to show fairness and equity in all their dealings. The basic principles of ruling, advocated by the Buddhist monks, included dana, [8] seela, [9] parithyaga, [10] fearlessness in duty, compassion, simple living, un-revengefulness, non violence, nation before self, and patience. Giving such advice to the laity and teaching and propagating the Buddhist doctrine, the Dhamma, however, had remained a secondary part of the monks' role. Their primary role had been to follow the spiritual path of strict moral conduct and meditation leading to Nibbana.

The early Sri Lankan society was not as demographically diverse as today. By and large all Sri Lankans spoke one language, Sinhalese, and practiced one religion, Buddhism. In this situation, Sri Lankan nationalism and Sinhalese-Buddhist nationalism were one and the same thing. This form of nationalism at the time helped unite the people in the country against foreign invasions by non-Buddhist forces. It is possible that at times of such invasions, even some Buddhist monks had become nationalistic activists as early chronicles depict. On the whole, the Buddhist monks' role at the time had always helped local rulers to do what was righteous and bring about unity among the people at times of national crises.

The significance of this role of Buddhist monks later changed under non-Buddhist foreign rulers. First there were spells of partial rule by South Indian Hindu rulers till about the middle of the thirteenth century. Then came rule of the maritime regions by three European powers of Christian faith, the Portuguese, the Dutch and the British, for about four centuries. Finally, one of the three European powers, the British, ruled the whole country for another 133 years from 1815 to 1948. Under these non-Buddhist foreign rulers, Buddhism and Buddhist monks had suffered in many ways. These rulers destroyed Buddhist temples and monasteries, and humiliated and ignored the Buddhist way of life and values. The rulers no longer consulted Buddhist monks on matters affecting the country and its people. New religions and their missionary activities thrived in the country at the expense of Buddhism. Some Buddhists embraced these new religions, especially during the period of European rulers. Christian missionaries of this time had been successful in converting Buddhists to Christianity in significant numbers. Many non-Buddhists also arrived in the country from outside and settled. There were influxes of people of Hindu faith particularly during the periods of South Indian rulers. Most of them were Tamil speaking. What happened during the periods of partial and total foreign rule of the country had slowly and surely transformed its demographic composition from a predominant Sinhalese-Buddhist society to a plural one of many ethnic groups, languages and religions.

During this demographic transition, the Buddhist monks did what was possible to preserve Buddhism and Sinhalese-Buddhist civilization, while trying to pursue their main goal of spiritual advancement. Their efforts to preserve Buddhism and Buddhist civilization were multi-faceted. Their primary goal in these efforts was to educate the masses on the importance of preserving and reviving Buddhism and their indigenous Sinhalese-Buddhist culture and civilization. All the Buddhist monks in the country during this transition period did contribute toward this end. Some took a further step and played a direct role in trying to defend the country from non-Buddhist foreign aggression. For example, the Buddhist monks at the famous Dambulla Buddhist temple (Dambulla Raja Maha Vihara) in central Sri Lanka played such a role on two main occasions, one before European colonialism and the other during the time of the British. H. L. Seneviratne gives an account of the narration of related incidents by Inamaluve Sumangala, an incumbent monk of this temple, "Dambulla is associated with struggles of liberation against foreign invaders, and it has acted as a catalyst in launching (mass) movements to repel them. Inamaluve gives examples: the monk Tissa of Dambulla gave refuge to the fleeing King Valagamba when he was attacked by South Indian invaders, fed him the pindapatha (begged) food and reunited him with his dissenting ministers. Armies were organized and a struggle launched to regain the country from Dravida rule. Centuries later, the rebellion of 1848, known as the Matale Revolt, was launched at Dambulla (where Gongalegoda Banda was crowned as the last Sinhalese king) in an attempt to free the nation from the British."[11]

Meanwhile, what occurred in Kandy on March 2, 1815, was yet another noteworthy incident in this regard. On this day, the British arranged to ceremoniously raise their Union Jack flag for the very first time on the Kandyan soil. As the British started to raise the flag, a Buddhist monk, Wariyapola Sumangala, scurried in from behind the audience and disrupted the ceremony, by pulling down the flag and stomping over it in front of all those who were present. Then, in the late nineteenth and early twentieth centuries Buddhist monks made many fearless freedom-speeches and writings. These speeches and writings inspired the natives with nationalistic feelings and passion. The book of patriotic poems written by S. Mahinda, a Tibetan Buddhist monk who lived in the country in the early twentieth century, was one of such famous writings that helped create a new passion for independence from colonial rulers among the natives, especially at grass roots level. This and other similar writings of Buddhist monks helped create an urge for the revival of Buddhism and Sinhalese-Buddhist civilization as well as political independence among the laity and the Sangha alike. On the whole it is fair to say that struggles for moral and cultural emancipation and national liberation had characterized the role of the Buddhist monks in the country during the colonial era. Until the early twentieth century, these struggles did not have any direct entanglement with the need to evolve a form of self-rule in the country fit for all the linguistic, religious and ethnic groups now living in it. Then from the early twentieth century, Anagarika Dharmapala (1864 – 1933), a reformist dominated the Sinhalese-Buddhist revival movement. He had given a political nuance to the Sangha's liberation-efforts, conceptualizing Sri Lankan nationalism as Sinhalese-Buddhist nationalism, as was the case thousands of years back. In doing so, he completely disregarded the extent of the linguistic, religious and ethnic diversity of the contemporary society. He also redefined the main role of the Buddhist monk to be social activism in order to get their active participation in propagating his mission. Many contemporary monks embraced this call for a new mission in their lives, and passed it on to their future generations. The subsequent writings of Buddhist monks resounded the thoughts of Dharmapala in this regard. The Heritage by Walpola Rahula published in 1946 in particular became an immense driving force at the time of independence for the Buddhist modernist activities started by Dharmapala.

After independence, Buddhist monks continued with their demand for Sinhalese-Buddhist nationalism. But the political leaders of the time were busy trying to find a way of governance fit for all the linguistic, religious and ethnic groups, under a new form of nationalism acceptable to all Sri Lankans, and not Sinhalese-Buddhist nationalism as advocated by the monks. A prominent politician, S. W. R. D. Bandaranaike, however, had a second thought on his commitment to Sri Lankan nationalism as other national leaders at the time had by becoming the saviour of the Buddhist monks' course of Sinhalese-Buddhist nationalism. Whether this was a genuine change of his beliefs on the concept of Sri Lankan nationalism or a mere act of political expediency for the sake of a short cut to power is not known. After coming to power at the 1956 general election on a Sinhalese-Buddhist nationalistic Dharmapala-style platform, he started to implement policies of Sinhalese-Buddhist nationalism, not honouring the genuine, natural interests of the non-Sinhalese and non-Buddhists in the country. After an assassin gunned him down in 1959, his wife, Sirimavo Bandaranaike, took over the reign and continued to pursue the same policies. These policies in time came in direct conflict with the genuine aspirations of the non-Sinhalese and non-Buddhist communities of the country, finally causing a bloody ethnic, civil war.

Since 1956, as already explained, there had been many efforts made by governments to correct the wrongs committed by Sinhalese-Buddhist nationalist policies to the non-Sinhalese and non-Buddhist minorities. The Bandaranaike – Chelvanayagam Pact of 1957, the Dudley Senanayake - Chelvanayagam Pact of 1965 and the devolution package tabled in the country's legislature by President Kumaratunga in 2000 were significant among such corrective measures. The Sangha, the Buddhist monks of the country, however, had derailed all these and other measures toward the correction of the wrongs done to the minorities. By any standards, Buddhist monks are neither meant to be nor have become experts in political science or constitutional matters. But it is the power of their social and political activism in the country that has now become one of the biggest threats to any political solution to the ever-worsening ethnic crisis. Critics believe that only a small minority of the Buddhist monks in the country protest against such government conciliatory measures. Still, the fact remains that those who do protest have the power to derail any measure by the government to correct the wrongs done to minorities.

Some people continue to argue that the change in the role of Buddhist monks to the current level of social and political activism has re-established their role in early history. This is very much a moot point. What is clear to all is, however, the change in the commitment of monks to the spiritual path of strict moral conduct and meditation expected of them as taught by the Buddha. As a result of this change, we have now reached a point where there is hardly any difference that exits between the Sangha and the laity in terms of moral conduct or insight. There were numerous factors that contributed to this change. During the periods of foreign rule, monks had to devote lots of their time and energy, which otherwise would have been directed to their primary goal of spiritual liberation, to combat the forces of oppression and destruction of Buddhism and the Buddhist civilization. Then from about the beginning of the twentieth century, the monks worked as social activists heeding to a call from Anagarika Dharmapala, who was neither a complete monk nor a complete layperson. Thereafter, from the middle of the twentieth century, the monks became political activists under the leadership of S. W. R. D. Bandaranaike. As these changes occurred, the monks tried to justify their changing role and priorities. The Heritage written by Walpola Rahula, a Buddhist monk, and published in 1946 and Vartamana Bhiksu Parapura (VBP) written by Horatapala Palita, another Buddhist monk, and published in 1970 are two classic examples in this regard. H. L. Seneviratne explains that in the new definitions suggested by these recent books authored by monks, the vinaya rules articulated by the Buddha for a strict moral conduct leading to Nibbana "are a product of time and place and thus have no universal and timeless validity. That is these rules are cultural and enjoy no autonomy. Since morality in relation to the realization of ultimate truth has by definition to be universal in validity, and therefore, autonomous, this amounts to a denial of a moral base and meaning to vinaya."[12]

The net result of all these and other changes to the role of Buddhist monks over the last decades and centuries is what we now witness in the country.

Today, many Buddhist monks have abandoned their traditional bonds with their rural communities. They have put to the back burner their primary goal of following a spiritual path to attain Nibbana, and are preoccupied with mundane matters. They engage in all kinds of activities, and seek successes in gaining comfort, indulgence, wealth, fame, and power, like the laity. Some have become the tools of prominent politicians and indulge in divisive party-politics. Some manage real estate and other types of businesses. The government has charged some of those who run businesses with allegations of embezzlement. Some have become well known by being doctors, astrologers, land developers, money lenders, environmental activists, marriage registrars, novelists, song-writers, painters, vendors of exorcism, and the like. Some uphold and perpetrate the caste system that had been implanted among the Sinhalese through the influence of Hinduism, refuse ordination for women, and indulge in divisive, communal politics. Most of the monks today openly support the ethnic war, and have very little to offer to end it. One monk, Elle Gunawansa, engages in writing military and warlike songs that instigate the people to kill. In one of his songs, this monk tells the soldier fighting the ethnic war that he shouldn't re-sheath the sword he has drawn out unless it is smeared with blood, and that he will reach Nibbana for fighting the enemy. [13] The monks in the country today have divided themselves into three sects or nikayas: Siam, Amarapura and Ramanna. It is an open secret that some monks, especially in the Siam nikaya, openly uphold and practice the moribund caste system, in which one becomes superior or inferior to another purely based on birth. In general, the monks want to see only those who were born to castes perceived as the highest in the topmost political positions, such as President or Prime Minister. According to critics, Sri Lanka is the only country in the world where one could see Buddhists practice a caste system. Robert Zimmermann explains this, "Sri Lanka is unique in that the Sinhalese are the only Buddhists in the world who accept the caste system."[14] As he sees, "both the Sinhalese and Tamil societies are organized according to the caste system. A caste governs a group of families and its specific relationships with other groups of families in the same area. .. Caste influences a person's life from the smallest details to the most important issues. Each caste is traditionally associated with a

specific trade or occupation so that those belonging to a certain
caste usually follow the occupation of that caste, for example
farming."[15] The validity of such a caste system among the Sinhalese
has lessened considerably over the years due to the influence of
westernization, urbanization and modernization, but has not
completely disappeared.

Critics of Buddhist monks in Sri Lanka point out that there
is very little anyone can learn about Buddhism from the modern life
style of Sri Lankan Buddhist monks. In this regard, a recent
experience of a German researcher on Buddhism who went to Sri
Lanka to see for himself Buddhism in action, and, in particular, the
life on the "Middle Path" professed by the Buddha, is extremely
noteworthy. He says that he saw more Buddhism among the poor in
the country than among the Buddhist monks and the rich, especially
in the big cities. According to him only the poor in the country lead
a life of the Middle Path taught by the Buddha, but this was perhaps
not because of any religious conviction but because of poverty.
Buddhist monks and the rich on the other hand had neither
conviction nor any reckonable commitment to a life of the Middle
Path.

The writer himself once experienced the extent of political
activism among Buddhist monks during the current ethnic crisis.
The writer and his family visited Dimbulagala Rajamahaviharaya in
Polonnaruwa in North-central Sri Lanka on a Poya Day in 1984.
When they entered the temple, its chief priest was delivering a
sermon to those who had gathered. The writer and his wife joined
the congregation and settled for the sermon with the fullest possible
attention, all seated on the floor, cross-legged, with their two
daughters, 12 and 10 years old, on either side. The high priest
continued with his sermon in Sinhalese, a language his children
understood, although they had spent most of their lives outside the
country. For a while, everything went very well. Everybody around
the writer, including the two children, was engrossed in the sermon.
The sermon was about the Buddha's personal qualities:
compassionate, tolerant, exalted, omniscient, endowed with
knowledge and virtue, knower of the universe, supreme trainer of
persons, teacher of gods and humans, enlightened and holy, ...
Then all of a sudden the high priest changed the topic to the
potential threat of Tamil minority to Sinhalese Buddhist colonists
who settled in the northeast part of the country. With the change of
the topic, he also roughened up his voice with anger and hatred and
started to indulge in divisive, chauvinist politics. The 12-year

daughter of the writer felt very uneasy at this turn of events, and started to nudge the writer suggesting they leave. The writer tried to calm her down and asked her to be patient till the priest finished the sermon. After staying calm for another few minutes, she suddenly sprang up to her feet and shouted with the top of her voice "the Buddha didn't preach hatred or violence. So, why is this priest talking like this." By the time the writer got up to reach her to silence her, four hefty men approached them, beckoning them to leave. The priest continued with his sermon regardless. The writer had no option but to leave with his family before a brawl broke out in the crowd. Thus even a child of 12 years was challenging the monks' order in the country.

The change in the extent of the commitment of the Buddhist monks to the spiritual path of strict moral conduct and meditation expected of them according to the Buddha's teachings, has come under heavy criticism. This criticism has come from the laity as well as some members of the Sangha. Even Anagarika Dharmapala who redefined the monks' role to include social activism never expected the monks to abandon the Sangha vinaya and engage in immoral activities. He had specifically criticized the monks who engaged in borrowing or lending money and the practice of medicine and astrology. He felt through the practice of medicine or astrology, monks got too involved with the laity in an improper manner. According to experts, Dharmapala had expressed his disapproval of what he saw around him. H. L. Seneviratne quotes what Dharmapala had once said, "the monks who accept gold and silver are impure. .... In Lanka now adharma (non-righteousness) has come to power. Immoral monks are too many."[16]

Later there were many other laypersons that openly criticized the changing role of the Buddhist monks. Most of these critics were Buddhist scholars and intellectuals. The list of names of these critics is long. It includes well-known people like D. Amarasiri Weeraratne, Edwin Kotalavala, Lucien Rajakarunanayake, Sunil Ariyaratne, Uvindu Kurukulasuriya, and Regi Siriwardane. The book entitled **Buddhism Betrayed?** by S. J. Tambiah, a non-Buddhist strong critic, in particular had become a thorn in the eye for the Sangha. In the first place the Buddhist monks were not prepared to acknowledge such a strong criticism from a non-Buddhist. They labeled Tambiah as an enemy of Buddhism. A Sinhalese newspaper, Ravaya, however, translated and published one chapter of the book, and said that it was doing so to enable the public to decide for themselves whether Tambiah was an enemy of Buddhism as claimed by the Sangha or a better Buddhist than those who claimed to be the defenders of Buddhism. Later, the government gave in to the monks and banned the book.

The first strong critics of the Sangha came from the members of a movement called Vinayawardhana. This movement first appeared in the 1940s. They showed their utter disappointment and disapproval of the Buddhist monks' changing role in the country, and called for a strict return to vinaya, the code of monastic discipline as taught by the Buddha. Some of these monks left their traditional temples to live in forest hermitages. The writings of the members of the Vinayawardhana at the time asked many questions regarding the changing role of the Buddhist monk in the country. Henpitagedara Gunavasa's **What is the Heritage of the Bhikku?** and Tambugala Aanada's **Dharmavinayalokaya** (The Light of the Doctrine and Discipline) are two such important works. Later a number of young Buddhist monks have written and published works of numerous types toward the same end. These new writings have appeared in both non-fiction and fiction styles, and include Ko Ananda's novel, **He Siddhartha nam veyi** (His name is Siddhartha), published in 1978, and Bo Nandissara's novel, **Loku hamuduruvan vetatayi** (To the Chief Monk).

In early history there were also times of change in the monks' role, drifting away from the Sangha vinaya, the code of monastic discipline. During such times of crises, the laity, including the country's monarchial rulers, expressed their displeasure towards the corrupt monks in no uncertain terms. Vikramabahu 1 (1111 – 32), Parakrambahu 1 (1153 – 86), and Nissankamalla (1187 – 96) who ruled from Polonnaruwa are known for their attempts of purification of the Buddhist monks' Order. According to C. R. de Silva, Vikramabahu 1 was hostile to the elements of the sangha and had turned corrupt monks out of their viharas.[17] Parakramabahu's "patronage of the Sangha and the rebuilding of temples and stupas was accompanied by a purification of the Order. An inscription at Gal Vihara states that the king with the advice of Mahakassapa, Chief priest of the Dimbulagala Vihara, expelled many hundreds of monks and united the three groups into a single nikaya."[18] Nissankamalla, "was a great patron of the Sangha and expelled corrupt bhikkus."[19]

Later, in the eighteenth century there appeared to have been the worst of all times, with Buddhism and Buddhist monks facing "extinction" in the island. Kirthi Sri Rajasinghe, the king of the Kandyan kingdom at the time, invited two embassies and chapters of monks from Thailand, first under Venerable Upali Thero in 1753 and later under Venerable Varanyanamuni in 1756, to re-establish the Buddhist order in Sri Lanka. This, in fact, was the origin of Siam Nikaya, the first of the present three main Nikayas among Buddhist monks in Sri Lanka. Later, some monks who were not fully satisfied with the Siam nikaya monkhood were ordained in the Burmese city of Aamarapura. These monks founded a new nikaya called Amarapura nikaya, in 1803. Monks belonging to both these nikayas by and large lived in village monasteries. Then in 1862, monks who preferred to live away from the worldly life headed by a forest monk, Pannananda, went to Burma for re-ordination, and founded the third nikaya, Ramanna Nikaya. Some of these historical events show that the monarchs of the country had the ability to take some form of corrective steps in situations where the monks had abandoned the Sangha vinaya in a significant way. At the same time some others show that some leaderships had emerged from within the Sangha from time to time in the search of ways and means to correct them.

In the present political set up, no President or Prime Minister has the will or the power to do what early monarchs did to correct the Sangha. If one tries to do what early monarchs did, it would become a point of contention among the different political parties in the country. The monks affected by such a move will work for an opposition party in preference to the one that rules. Under any event the author does not suggest that government should have any control over the practice of any religion, in the present-day context. A new leadership from within the Sangha, however, can effectively change the Sangha Order. The Sangha, especially their young and educated members, should take it upon themselves to challenge and rediscover their role as Buddhist monks, and to determine how best the Sangha can make a positive contribution to the ongoing efforts to solve the ethnic crisis.

The potential for such a new leadership from among the Sangha is very real, especially when one thinks of the much bigger undertakings the Buddhist monks of Sri Lanka had accomplished in the past, from the time of Mahavihara (The Great Monastery) in 240 BC. They started Bhikku and Bhikkuni Sangha sectors for men and women, wrote down the Pali Tripitaka (Buddha's teachings) for the first time on palm leaves in 100 AD and spread both Theravada and Mahayana throughout Southeast Asia. They also introduced the Sangha order of nuns into China in 433 AD, translated Buddha's teachings into western languages, and initiated and founded the

World Fellowship of Buddhists. Sri Lanka had always been the centre of Theravada Buddhism in the world.

At times of decline of Buddhism in Sri Lanka, Buddhist monks in other countries came to play a role in preserving Buddhism. This helped Sri Lanka maintain its excellent service to Buddhism and status as the country with the longest continuous Buddhist record in the world. The contribution of Venerable Buddhaghosa, a Buddhist monk believed to be a South Indian Tamil, in the early history was extremely significant in this regard. He assembled the various Sinhalese commentaries on the Buddhist canon – drawing primarily on the Maha Atthakatha (Great Commentary) preserved at the Mahavihara – and translated his work into Pali in 425 AD. This made Sinhalese Buddhist scholarship available to the entire Theravada world. As the main part of the work, he composed the Visaddhimagga -The Path of Purity – which eventually became the classic Sri Lankan textbook on the teachings of the Buddha. In 1070 AD, after the Bhikku and Bhikhuni communities died out following Chola invasions from South India, Buddhist monks from Pagan in Burma arrived in the island, and reinstated the Theravada ordination line in Sri Lanka. Later, Buddhist monks arrived from Kancipuram, India, in 1236 in a similar situation to revive the Theravada ordination line. Then in 1753, the king of Siam (Thailand) sent Buddhist monks from that country to Kandy.

One of the questions commonly asked in many Buddhist forums today is that should not Buddhist monks stay out of politics in the first place? As said before, one becomes a Buddhist monk to follow a spiritual path leading to Nibbana or Nirvana, a state of liberation and spiritual illumination beyond pleasure or pain. According to the teachings of the Buddha, pain and suffering cannot be avoided so long as one is subject to worldly desires, and only through meditation and a strict moral conduct one can finally reach Nibbana. Politics, on the other hand, is a path of materialism trying to satisfy people's worldly desires. This clearly shows that the path of liberation of Buddhist monks has no place in politics. In their spiritual journey, however, all monks are never at the same place at any given time; some could be at its very beginning, while others at different advanced stages. It is, therefore, not possible to expect the same kind of response from the entire Buddhist clergy to political appeals in the country. It is important to note here that all the Buddhist monks in the country did not respond to S. W. R. D. Bandaranaike's or Dharmapala's chauvinist appeals in the same way. Once the writer asked some specific questions from two Canadian Buddhist monks: Ajahn Sona and Thitapunno, about the basic principles of the Sangha vinaya as far as the present involvement of Buddhist monks in politics and the essential qualities for a good leader according to the teachings of the Buddha. Ajahn Sona is the incumbent Abbot of the Birken Forest Monastery in Princeton, Canada. Chitapunno was a monk resident at the same monastery. The Appendix 6 contains the specific questions I asked them and their answers to the questions, and will be of interest to the reader.

Although the Sangha vinaya has no place for politics, the Buddhist monks in the country can be part of the solution to the current ethnic crisis by being true followers of the Buddha. According to the teachings of the Buddha, no one particular community could be considered as superior or inferior to another, on the basis of language, religion, ethnicity, or strength in number. All are born free and equal as human beings. One gets a linguistic identity from the parents. In other words, one belongs to a particular language group because of his or her birth, and no other reason. The Buddha had specifically preached that no one becomes great by birth, but by action. This is a philosophy that challenged the very basic tenets of Hinduism, whereby one becomes superior or inferior to another purely on the basis of birth. Buddhism requires people to think independently, free from any outside influence, and decide for themselves. It is a self-made religion. The stratification of the society into different castes based on birth is a manifestation of Hinduism. The Buddha (623 – 543 BC) had publicly opposed such social stratification. The beneficiaries of the system, however, had always tried to maintain it. Despite this, India had once embraced Buddhism and remained mostly Buddhist for more than a thousand years. In time, however, it has gone back to its old days of Hinduism. This may have been possible due to the lack of missionary movements in Buddhism in the centuries that followed. Despite this, however, in recent times there is another wave of religious change in India with more and more people converting back to Buddhism. There were some mass conversions, especially among those belonging to castes considered low by Hindu principles. The biggest ever mass conversion from Hinduism to Buddhism in India occurred on 14 October 1956. G. S. Thind gives a vivid description of this mass conversion in his **Our Indian Subcontinent Heritage**, 2000. According to him, on this day five-hundred thousand Hindus in India gathered at one place, Deekshana

Bhoomi, and got converted to Buddhism, along with Dr. B. R. Ambedkar, a well known leader of the down trodden of that country. [20] Some academics believe that the number of people who converted to Buddhism on this day was one million. Dr. Malalasekara, President of the Fourth Conference of the World Fellowship of Buddhists at Kathmandu, Nepal, held on November 15, 1956, had described this mass conversion to Buddhism as the greatest ever-religious conversion in the world. [21] G. S. Thind predicts that within the first half of the twenty-first century another 400 million or more Indians would follow suit. [22] There is evidence to suggest that this process has already begun. According to a Reuters report[23] an estimated 20,000 people converted to Buddhism at the Ram Lila grounds in the heart of capital New Delhi on 4 November 2001. The organizers of the event had first expected about one million Hindus to convert to Buddhism on this particular day. The Police, however, had asked the organizers to scale down the event as a precaution against possible religious clashes. According to the Buddhist monk who conducted the conversion ceremony, Venerable Rahul Dev Bodhi, a similar event would occur every month till April 2002.

What motivates all these converts is the power of the Buddhist principle of equality of humans irrespective of birth. In the words of one of the converts of the 4 November 2001 event, Harish Khare, a 36-year government employee who had traveled from the Western State of Maharashtra for his conversion, "The message of Buddhism is that all human beings are equal."[24] This principle understandably embraces the basic values of compassion, tolerance, pluralism, non-violence, and peace and harmony. These values have unlimited power to bring together different groups of people in any nation, however different they are, and to allow them all to live in peace and harmony. These values can unite people not only across the borders of language, religion, and ethnicity, but also across the boundaries of nations making the world a better and safer place to live in. The world once witnessed this power at its best during the time of Asoka Empire in India. H. L. Seneviratne explains, "..What is undeniable is that there is no evidence of any other religious source than Buddhism that encouraged tolerance, pluralism, nonviolence, and so forth in the Asokan (mega-empire) system. Tambiah has graphically described how the Buddhist conception of chakkavatti kingship became the model for the pluralistic ordering of relations between the emperor and the rulers of the kingdoms that constituted Asoka's centre-oriented but non-centralized mega-empire."[25]

Going by the above, if the Buddhist monks in Sri Lanka today are truly Buddhist, they should not have any problem, philosophical or otherwise, in accepting and treating those who belong to languages, religions or ethnicity other than theirs, as their equals. In forming any opinion on the current ethnic crisis in the country, the monks should refrain from just believing what has been said and done by others, and accept only what agrees with reason and what is conducive to the good and benefit of one and all. This is, in fact, what the Buddha wanted all his disciples to do. According to Kalama Sutta (Anguttara Nikaya, Vol 1, 183-193 P.T.S. Ed), the Buddha had specifically said, "Do not believe in anything (simply) because you have heard it. Do not believe in traditions because they have been handed down for many generations. Do not believe in anything because it is spoken and rumored by many. Do not believe in anything (simply) because it is found written in your religious books. Do not believe in anything merely on the authority of your teachers and elders. But after observation and analysis, when you find that anything agrees with reason and is conducive to the good and benefit of one and all then accept it and live up to it."[26] By truly living up to these words of the Buddha, the monks would also become an overwhelming inspiration to the laity.

According to a news item in Asia Times,[27] a 32-year Sinhalese Buddhist monk, Atambagaskada Kalyanatissa, has shown a true Buddhist leadership in the Sri Lankan war zone. According to the news item, he lives in a frontier village just two kilometres from the army's defenses in the northern Wanni region of the country, and provides shelter, food and care to Tamil children orphaned by the war. This humanitarian mission began when he visited a close-by Tamil refugee camp. While he was at the camp, an orphaned infant, Kuganeshan, took to him and refused to leave him when he was ready to go. The monk felt compelled to take the child with him. Later a number of Tamil widows who were unable to provide for their children begged the monk to look after their children. As a result, the number of children under the monk's care has since grown. The monk told the Asia Times that he now gets some donations from non-governmental agencies toward the expenses involved. According to him, even the soldiers in the nearby military camps have started to "keep aside a little bit of the rice and vegetables they get to cook each day and send it across."[28] The same news item reports that a Tamil boy, given up by his widowed mother by the name Samitha Himi, told the Asia Times, "I come from a Christian Tamil family, but was so moved by the environment here, and the example of Thero (monk), that I decided to follow in the footsteps of the Buddha."[29] He has decided to become a Buddhist monk himself. This is a classic example of how the Sangha can be part of the solution to the worsening relationship between the warring communities in Sri Lanka.

Ultimate Awakening

In the aftermath of the military successes of the LTTE in the early 2000, President Kumaratunga put the country on a war footing and proposed an unprecedented devolution package modelled on the Indian federal system. She first discussed the package with the leaders of the main opposition party, the UNP, and got their support before tabling it in the legislature. The leader of the UNP, Ranil Wickremesinghe, was also the Leader of Opposition in the legislature at the time. This was the first time ever that the leaders of both main political parties agreed on a common legislative formula to end the ethnic crisis. It was also a strategic move by President Kumaratunge, as any such devolution package would need at least two-thirds majority support in the legislature to become law. When the package finally appeared in the parliamentary agenda, the government wanted the legislators to vote on it after a short debate. This, however, did not happen; the moment the contents of the bill became common knowledge there were widespread opposition and protests.

The opposition and protests against the devolution bill came from many political and non-political organizations in the country. From among the political parties in the country, the Marxist JVP and the Sinhalese extremist SU took the lead in the protests that followed. At the same time, the Buddhist monks gathered in thousands to show their opposition. One monk staged a public hunger strike for days, until the government withdrew the package from the parliament. The UNP, the main opposition party that had first consented to the package later changed its position in support of those who protested against it. Those who protested argued that the devolution package proposed to give excessive powers to the regions and reduce the rights of the Sinhalese living in the northeast province of Tamil majority. The protesters also argued that the package proposed to grant citizenship to all Indian Tamils who had come to the country before 1964, ignoring the repatriation package earlier agreed between Sri Lanka and India. In addition, they argued that the implementation of the devolution package would change the demographic composition of the upcountry against the mainstream Sinhalese, and distribute land in the island disproportionately in favour of the minority Tamils, with 30 percent of land made available to a mere six percent of the population. The protesters also showed their dismay at the way the government was rushing the bill through parliament. First, only the leaders of the two main parties knew the contents of the package. The other MPs and the public came to know the details of the package only after the government tabled it in the parliament. It was a document of 209 pages, and the government wanted to make it law after only three hours of debate. The protesters saw it as undemocratic and a complete sell-out to the minority Tamils.

Some critics expressed serious concerns on the new constitution envisaged by the devolution package. According to these critics, the basic underlying principles and concepts of the package hinged on the existing linguistic, communal, and racial differences in the country. The package states that "a citizen shall not be discriminated against on the grounds of ethnicity, religion, language, caste, gender, sex, political and other opinion, national or racial origin, mode of acquisition of citizenship, ..." But the extent of the linguistic majority in a Region (whether less than or more than seven-eighths of the total population in a Region) is the basis for the language policy of that Region. Even the election of the Vice Presidents is going to be on a communal basis. Most significantly, the constitution envisaged by the package completely ignores the fundamental need to separate the legislative, executive and the judiciary powers of the country. The legislature, the parliament, elects the president, the chief executive of the country. Then, the President appoints the officers of the judiciary, including the Chief Justice, and functions as the chief executive of the country. The parliament also elects two Vice Presidents. The parliament elects the President with not less than 50 percent support from all its members. A Vice President, however, needs only a simple majority in the house, subject to a quorum of mere 20 MPs; the total number of MPs is 225. The constitution envisaged by the package clearly states, "In the Republic, sovereignty is in the people and is inalienable." But it removes even the very right of the people to elect a President of their own choice. The election of the Indian President by that country's legislature has no relevance to the Sri

Lankan constitution envisaged by the package; the Indian President is only a constitutional President with no executive powers, while the Sri Lankan President envisaged by the package will be the chief executive of the country.

The new constitution envisaged by the package or any of its revised versions retaining the above basic features will only make the current ethnic crisis more complicated and complex, further destroy democracy in the country, and act as a recipe for anarchy. What is blatantly clear from the devolution package and the politics that followed in the country is that both its leading political parties, the SLFP and UNP, and others who coalesce with them in forming government, are in search of solutions to the ethnic crisis through mere mathematical innovations of the country's demographic composition. In the first place, it was this type of politics that created the ethnic crisis in the country. So, it is difficult to believe that the same type of politics can now bring a lasting solution.

The irony of the situation is that the proposals for a federal system of government for Sri Lanka made before independence had no opposition or protests from the Sinhalese Buddhist community in the country. In fact, as mentioned earlier, proposals for a federal system first came from the Sinhalese Buddhist leaders who represented the Kandyan kingdom. They tabled a proposal for a federal system at the Donoughmore Commission in 1927, and reiterated it at the hearings of the Soulbury Commission in 1946. Then immediately after independence S. J. V. Chelvanayagam founded the Federal Party, advocating federalism, in 1949. Kandyans and Sri Lankan Tamils in the north, who had their own identities as separate kingdoms before colonialism, proposed federalism as a means to a meaningful system of governance for independent Sri Lanka. It was a system that they thought would bring about unity in diversity, among all the peoples of the country. For the last fifty years, the leaders of the SLFP and UNP have, however, not only rejected federalism as a means to achieve unity in the country as one nation, but also have turned the ordinary people against it with fear mongering tactics (The only exception in this regard is the failed attempt of President Kumaratunga to introduce some form of federalism in 2000). As a result there is a misconception in the country today that only a unitary system of government could keep it together, making federalism an anathema, especially among the majority Sinhalese. Every time any one of the two main political parties, the UNP and the SLFP, attempted to work closely with the

Federal party, the other portrayed it as one trying to divide the country. This happened during the last five decades, election after election. Whether the leaders of these two major parties will have the courage and vision to work together in the future for a genuine federal system of government is unpredictable.

The UNP government that returned to power in December 2001 appears to have a new approach to the ethnic crisis. In this latest approach to the crisis, the government wants to first achieve normalcy in the country with the help of a cease-fire agreement with the LTTE, and thereafter to begin conciliatory talks to find a lasting solution to the crisis. There were similar cease-fire arrangements before, not once but three times. These cease-fire arrangements were in place during the times of negotiations for solutions to the ethnic crisis in the country between the government and the LTTE. When these negotiations broke down, the cease-fires also ended. According to critics, every time this happened, the LTTE resumed its separatist war with more force and vigour than ever before.

In its latest approach to the ethnic crisis, the new (UNP) government has not tried to first agree with the leaders of the main opposition party in the legislature, the PA led by the SLFP, on any particular solution to the ethnic crisis. Instead, the new government has simply called for support from the leader of the PA, the incumbent executive president of the country, for the peace process it now proposes. This is a deviation from the approach to a legislative solution to the crisis President Kumaratunge had in 2000. The new, UNP government and the LTTE formalized their latest cease-fire agreement with a Memorandum of Understanding (MOU) signed between the two parties on 22 February 2002. Appendix 7 gives the full text of the MOU. The reader may compare the contents of the MOU with that of the cease-fire agreement signed between the previous (PA) government and the LTTE in 1995 given in Appendix 8. The 2002 MOU is an open-ended agreement to bring normalcy to the country and facilitate the establishment of the LTTE as a political organization in the north and east of the country, now under government control. This agreement requires the two parties to recognize their respective ground positions as of the date of the MOU and to maintain a zone of separation of a minimum of 600 metres. Each party, however, reserves the right of movement within 100 metres of its own defense localities. By the conditions of the MOU, both parties have agreed to set up an international monitoring mission under the name "Sri Lankan Monitoring Mission," (SLMM) headed by an appointee of the Royal Norwegian

Government. The main function of the SLMM is to enquire into any instance of violation of the terms and conditions of the MOU, and to play the role of the de facto final authority on any dispute between the two parties.

The international community welcomed the signing of the MOU by the Sri Lankan government (Prime Minister Ranil Wickremesinghe) and the LTTE (Velupillai Prabhakaran). Many countries, including the United States of America, the United Kingdom, and Japan expressed the hope that both parties to the MOU would observe the agreement, creating an environment conducive to negotiations for a lasting solution to the ethnic crisis in Sri Lanka.

Within Sri Lanka, the MOU received mixed reactions. President Kumaratunge, the executive president of the country and the leader of the main opposition party in the legislature (PA) expressed her surprise and concern over the contents of the MOU. She also has expressed her opinion that Prime Minister Ranil Wickremesinghe had no authority to sign such a document on behalf of the government, as the existing constitution empowers only the President of the country to declare peace or war. Prime Minister Wickremesinghe had neither obtained the prior approval of the President nor had divulged the contents of the MOU to the President until after the LTTE leader had signed it. In addition, President Kumaratunge expressed the view that it was "improper and undemocratic"[30] for the Prime Minister to go ahead and sign such an important agreement without first informing the cabinet and the parliament of its contents. She has said that the signing of the MOU by the Prime Minister is "violative of practices by the consensual politics of cohabitation"[31] of her (PA) executive presidency and the (UNP) government. President Kumaratunge has further pointed out that the MOU has some articles that could impinge on national security, give special privileges to LTTE to conduct political activities in the northeast in preference to other Tamil groups already politically organized in the area, and change the role of the Norwegian government from being a facilitator to a mediator or arbitrator. She has been very critical of giving the final authority in resolving any dispute that may arise between the government and the LTTE to a foreign country or national. This, she has insisted, is wholly inconsistent with the sovereignty of Sri Lanka.[32] Despite her objections to the specific clauses in the MOU, President Kumaratunge has reiterated her continued dedication to peace and the approval of a cease-fire reached by mutual agreement.

The leaders of the radical Marxist JVP and the hardline nationalist SU have also opposed the contents of the MOU and the validity of the Prime Minister's signature on the document on behalf of the government. The JVP, which has 16 seats in the present parliament, has taken the position that it was wrong for the UNP government to enter into such an agreement with the LTTE without consulting the people of the country. The JVP says that the new UNP government has not got a clear mandate from the people at the December 2001 election to solve the ethnic crisis, as it claims; the UNP has received only 45.6 percent of the total votes cast and won only 109 of the 225 seats in the legislature. Under any event, the JVP says, the MOU paves the way for the LTTE to create a separate state. The JVP has taken up this matter to the Court of Appeal, seeking an order to nullify the MOU agreement. In addition, it has organized a series of public protests against the signing of the agreement.

The Sinhala Urumaya, which has no representation in the present parliament, has also sought a court order to nullify the MOU agreement, and started to organize its own protest rallies against the signing of the agreement. In addition to the JVP and the SU, two other organizations have sought a court order to nullify the MOU agreement. All those who have chosen to challenge the MOU agreement in the Court of Appeal base their arguments on two main grounds. Firstly, Prime Minister Ranil Wickremesinghe has no authority to enter into such an agreement on behalf of the government under the present constitution; this is one of the objections to the MOU by President Kumaratunge as well. Secondly, any agreement reached with the LTTE in its present proscribed status would not be valid under the country's laws.

From among the political parties or groups in the northeast, the strongest objection to the MOU has come from the Eelam People's Democratic Party (EPDP). Currently, it has two members of parliament in the legislature. Its Secretary General, Douglas Devananda, has pointed out that the MOU suggestion to disarm EDPD (along with other paramilitary groups in the North and the East: TELO, EPRLF and PLOTE) and to allow its cadres to integrate with the country's armed forces to serve outside the North and the East is anti-democratic. He has stressed the point that the EPDP, which was part of the armed struggle in the seventies and eighties, had given up arms following the Indo-Sri Lanka Agreement of 1987 in the belief that a lasting solution to the ethnic crisis could be found through democratic means. According to him EPDP members need arms to protect them from the LTTE that has a frightening record of political assassinations, fratricides and threats and harassment of those who oppose it. The EPDP does not believe that the LTTE would not resort to such activities in the future and that the leaders and the cadres of the LTTE have all of a sudden become genuine democrats. In a speech given in the country's legislature on Tuesday, 11 March 2002, Devananda has said, "If Prabhakaran is a true democrat, then I will not have to carry arms."[33]

The objection to the MOU from organizations and individuals not directly affiliated with the political parties or groups in the country is not insignificant. The most noticeable among such organizations are those of the Buddhist monks. The National Bhikku Front, that has a membership spread throughout the country, has taken the lead in expressing the monks' objection. It has pointed out the need to get the people and the civil organizations of the country fully involved in any peace process right from its very beginning. At a general meeting of the Front held on 14 march 2002 in Colombo, the secretary of the Front, Kalawelgala Chandraloka, has reiterated that the Front objects to several conditions in the cease-fire agreement reached between the government and the LTTE.[34] How this and other organizations of Buddhist monks would react to specific suggestions for a lasting solution to the ethnic crisis in the peace talks expected to follow the MOU is unpredictable. If history is anything to go by, it is difficult to believe that the Buddhist monks of the country would accept a solution agreed to between the government and the LTTE, unless the monks were not a party to peace talks.

The first monk who became a member of parliament (December 2001 election), Baddegama Samitha, has, however, commended the MOU in the legislature and wanted the talks for a political solution to the ethnic crisis between the government and the LTTE to begin as soon as possible. This, however, was neither an expression of the position of his political leader (President Kumaratunge) nor a true representation of the Buddhist monks in the country.

The specific Clauses in the MOU (Appendix 7) that have become most contentious issues among its critics include 1.2, 1.3, 1.4, 1.5, 1.6, 1.8 and 3.2. The Clause 1.2 disallows the government armed forces to conduct aerial bombardment and offensive naval operations against the LTTE under any circumstances. The Clause 1.3 states that the Sri Lankan armed forces shall continue to perform their legitimate task of safeguarding the sovereignty and territorial integrity of Sri Lanka without engaging in offensive operations against the LTTE. Critics say these two clauses together remove the ability of the government armed forces to stop the LTTE cadres from intercepting LTTE arms shipments in the territorial waters of Sri Lanka, and that this could lead to further strengthening of the LTTE military power during the cease-fire. The critics also point out that the LTTE's insistence on these clauses clearly shows that it is not accepting the principle of Sri Lankan sovereignty and the right of the government forces to defend the Sri Lankan Nation, especially at sea.

Clauses 1.4, 1.5 and 1.6 establish defense localities for the two sides, the government and the LTTE, in the war zone of the country with a demarcation line separating them. According to these clauses, where localities are not clearly established, the areas controlled by the government and the LTTE on 24 December 2001 shall continue to apply as their respective localities. Where there is contention, the SLMM headed by the Norwegian government will draw the demarcation lines. There is no specific validity period for these demarcation lines. They are open-ended, just like the cease-fire itself. Critics say such open-ended demarcation lines would legitimize the existence of a separate area of the country for the LTTE, dividing it into two sections on a permanent basis.

Clause 1.8 requires the government to disarm Tamil paramilitary groups (EPDP, TELO, EPRLF, and PLOTE) within 30 days, and to offer to integrate individuals in these groups into the government armed forces for service outside the Northern and Eastern Province. At least one of these paramilitary groups, the EPDP, which currently controls the islets of Delft and Kayts in the North, has openly objected to this condition. As quoted earlier in this chapter, Douglas Devananda, the Secretary General of the EPDP has explained to the legislature the reasons for the objection to this condition by his group. Critics say that this condition would make the LTTE the only armed Tamil group in the north and east, effectively eliminating all of its armed rivals. There is no agreement to surrender arms by the LTTE at any given time.

Clause 3.2 gives the representative of the Royal Norwegian Government appointed as the Head of the SLMM the final authority regarding the interpretation of the MOU agreement, subject to the acceptance of the two parties to it. Critics say this would surrender the sovereignty of the Sri Lankan nation to foreign forces, with attempts to replace the laws of the country by a code of international law that has no relevance to Sri Lanka and its people.

Most of the objections to the peace process have come from a belief among the Sinhalese that the government and the LTTE are trying to find a lasting solution to the ethnic crisis behind their back, keeping them in the dark. Critics say that the ongoing attempt to find a lasting solution to the ethnic crisis has been secretly masterminded by three people: Ranil Wickremesinghe (Prime Minister), Velupillai Prabhakaran (LTTE leader) and John Westbourg (Norwegian facilitator representing the international community). According to the critics, these three people have already agreed on a final solution, and are following a common strategy to implement it, whether or not the people of the country, especially the Sinhalese majority, accept it. Gunadasa Amarasekera, a well-known Sinhalese writer, has characterized the government's latest peace process with a pithy Sinhalese saying 'Diyaredden bella kapanawa,'[35] which illustrates "how one is decapitated or destroyed without his being aware of what is happening to him."[36] Some critics believe that President Kumaratunge is also a willing participant of the latest peace process. That is why, they say, she has openly admonished her PA party members to abstain from criticizing the ongoing peace process, and not to bring it up as a contentious issue at the local government elections which took place in March 2002.

It is most certain that any solution acceptable to the LTTE and Tamil people in the north and east would require significant changes to the constitution of the country. According to the existing constitution, this is possible only with the approval of the country's legislature with at least a two-thirds majority. For this the UNP government requires the full support of the PA, the main opposition party in the parliament led by President Kumaratunge. Whether the PA would finally give its support in the legislature at the right time is certainly not predictable. Going by the past and present dynamics of the two-party political system in the country, it is unlikely that a majority of the PA members of parliament would act differently. At the same time, the LTTE has a proven record of reviving and further strengthening its military resources during cease-fires and returning to war with a demand for a separate state. In this difficult situation, the government appears to be relying on world opinion as a last resort. According to Christine Jayasinghe, Prime Minister Ranil Wickremesinghe "is banking on a 'safety net of world opinion' if his tightrope act is ruined by either a belligerent President (PA) or warring rebels."[37]

Even in the unlikely scenario where the UNP and the PA leaders agree to give the required two-thirds majority approval in the parliament to a solution acceptable to the LTTE, there is no guarantee that the forces outside the legislature would not prevent it from happening as in 2000. It is not prudent to assume that the popular support given to a cease-fire arrangement, like the one in force now, is an indication of automatic acceptance of any solution agreed between the government and the LTTE by the people. For example, the Maha Nayake Theros (Prelates of Buddhist clergy) of the three Chapters (Nikayas) issued a strongly worded open letter on 20 April 2002, protesting a number of proposals between the government and the LTTE to be implemented before the upcoming peace talks. This statement said, ".. It appears to us that the so-called peace process initiated with the MOU now in place is primarily aimed at the establishment of Eelam rather than achieving real peace. Hope of peace therefore has completely collapsed." [38]

Cease-fires themselves are not the solutions to the ethnic crisis. They only help create an atmosphere conducive to talks among the warring parties on possible solutions. Any attempt by the government to implement a solution not acceptable to the general public by trying to take them unawares, as already suggested by some critics, is both undemocratic and fraudulent. Thus the path to a lasting solution to the ethnic crisis in Sri Lanka is much more complex than what it appears.

NOTES

1. V. Suryanarayan. (2001, June 9). Land of the displaced. Frontline [Online]. Volume 18, 15 paragraphs. Available: http://www.frontlineonline.com/fl1812/18120610.htm [2001, June 10].
2. Ibid.
3. Ibid.
4. The constitution of Sri Lanka at the time of its independence in 1948. A royal commission headed by Lord Soulbury and appointed by the Colonial Office in London in 1944 had recommended it. The commission's recommendations were based on a daft constitution prepared by Sri Lankan ministers and the submissions made to the commission on behalf of minority interests in Sri Lanka.

5. Sri Lanka News – Colombo Page [Homepage of ColomboPage Sri Lankan Internet Newspaper],[Online]. (2001, November 11 – Last Update). Available: http://www.colombopage.com/ [2001, November 11].
6. Sri Lanka News – Colombo Page [Homepage of ColomboPage Sri Lankan Internet Newspaper],[Online]. (2001, May 25 – Last Update). Available: http://www.colombopage.com/ [2001, May 25].
7. Sri Lanka News – Colombo Page [Homepage of ColomboPage Sri Lankan Internet Newspaper],[Online]. (2001, May 25 – Last Update). Available: http://www.colombopage.com/ [2001, May 25].
8. Dana means Offerings.
9. Seela means morality and physical discipline-
10. Parithyaga means generosity.
11. H. L. Seneviratne, The Work of Kings: The New Buddhism in Sri Lanka, (Chicago, 1999), pp. 252-253.
12. Ibid., pp. 206-207.
13. Ibid., p. 245.
14. Robert Zimmerman, Enchantment of the World: Sri Lanka, (Chicago, 1992), p.60.
15. Ibid., pp. 59-60.
16. H. L. Seneviratne, The Work of Kings: The New Buddhism in Sri Lanka, (Chicago, 1999), p. 36.
17. C. R. de Silva, Sri Lanka: A History, (1st edn., New Delhi, 1987), p.71.
18. Ibid., p. 73.
19. Ibid., p. 75.
20. G. S. Thind, Our Indian Subcontinent Heritage, (Burnaby, Canada, 2001), pp. 356-357.
21. Ibid., p. 358.
22. Ibid., P. 423.
23. Reuters, "20,000 Shake Off Indian Caste System," The Vancouver Sun, Canada, November 5, 2001, P. A7.
24. Sugita Katyal, "Converts' aim: destroy the caste system," National Post, Canada, November 5, 2001, P. A15.
25. H. L. Seneviratne, P. 20. The reference to Tambiah in this quotation is to his book "World Conqueror" (Cambridge, CUP, 1976)
26. Edwin Ariyadasa (ed.), Light of Asia, (Illustrated Version, Singapore, 1996), np.

27. Kumudini Hettiarachchi. (2001, August 3). Sinhalese Monk raises Tamil Orphans. Asia Times [Online], 8 paragraphs. Available: **http://www.atimes.com/ind-pak/CH03Df01.html** [2001, August 4].

28. Ibid.

29. Ibid.

30. The Sunday Times [Homepage of The Sunday Times, Colombo], [Online]. (2002, February 24). Available: **http://www.is.lk/times/this/frontm.html** [2002, February 24].

31. Ibid.

32. Sri Lanka News – Colombo Page [Homepage of ColomboPage Sri Lankan Internet Newspaper],[Online]. (2002, March 3 – 8:13 p.m.). Available: **http://www.colombopage.com/** [2002, March 3].

33. News10 [Homepage of Island – Sri Lankan newspaper], [Online]. (2002, March 11). Available: **http://www.island.lk/2002/03/11/news10.html/** [2002, March 11].

34. Sri Lanka News – Colombo Page [Homepage of ColomboPage Sri Lankan Internet Newspaper],[Online]. (2002, March 15 – Last Update). Available: **http://www.colombopage.com/** [2002, March 15].

35. The Island [Homepage of The Island, Colombo], [Online]. (2002, March 6). Available: **http://www.island.lk/2002/03/06/midwee05.html** [2002, March 6].

36. Ibid.

37. Christine Jayasinghe, "Calling a Truce," India Today, March 11, 202, p.50.

38. Lanka Truth [Homepage of Lanka Truth, Colombo], [Online]. (2002, April 20). Available: **http://www.lankatruth.com/** [2002, April 21].

CHAPTER 4: A NEW BEGINNING

This chapter discusses a possible political solution to the ongoing ethnic crisis in Sri Lanka and a democratic way of implementing it with the support of its people. It is a solution that would not only resolve the current problems experienced by the ethnic minorities, but would also give an opportunity to all the peoples of the country to enjoy the fruits of political independence and real democracy for the very first time. All this is possible, however, only with a new beginning for the country as a multi-ethnic independent nation, instead of the continuation of the same old politics that brought about the present crisis situation.

Such a new beginning must have a new vision for the country to see it fit for all its peoples and their future generations to live in peace and harmony as free and equal citizens. The country had a good opportunity to have such a new beginning at the time of independence in 1948. But it failed to take advantage of the opportunity at the time or thereafter, because of the divisive, chauvinist politics of post-independent leaders of the country, as discussed in previous chapters. The political independence the country received in 1948, through constitutional amendments of the departing colonial power, the British, resulted in the transfer of political power to Sri Lankans. But it didn't bring about any significant change to the divide-and-rule system of governance perpetrated by the colonial powers. The Sri Lankan elite rulers who received independence (and their dynastic-type successors) ruled the country since independence the way the colonialists ruled before them. These Sri Lankan elite leaders made some significant changes to the country's constitution during the last fifty years. All such changes, however, by and large, contributed to further segregation of the people on the basis of their linguistic and ethnic differences.

Recognize and Accept Diversity

A meaningful new beginning is possible only with a revived awareness and recognition of the linguistic, religious and ethnic diversity that now exists in the country. There was a time, when the whole country was, by and large, a homogeneous Sinhalese Buddhist society. This is now mere history, and is not the case any more. Present Sri Lankan society consists of many ethnic groups, religions, and languages. The different ethnic groups include Veddhas, Sinhalese, Sri Lankan Tamils, Indian Tamils, Moors,

Malays, and Burghers. The different religions in the country include
Buddhism, Hinduism, Christianity, and Islam, and its languages
include Sinhalese, Tamil and English. The two tables below show
the extent of the country's present ethnic and religious divide, based
on the 1981 census. The census subsequently taken by the
government is not complete.

Table 2: Population by ethnic group.

Ethnic Group	Population in 1000s	% of total population	Remarks
Sinhalese	10,979.4	74.0	Low country Sinhalese 42.8% & Kandyan Sinhalese 29.2% (based on 1971 census)
Tamils	2,705.6	18.2	Sri Lankan Tamils 12.7% & Indian Tamils 5.5%
Moors	1,046.9	7.0	
Malays	47.0	0.3	
Burghers & Eurasians	39.4	0.3	
Others	28.4	0.2	Includes Veddhas
TOTAL	14,846.7	100.0	

Source: Department of Census and Statistics, an abstract from
'Table 18 – Population by ethnic group, census years,' Statistical
Abstract of the Democratic Socialist Republic of Sri Lanka
1992, (Colombo, Sri Lanka, 1993), p.46.

The Sinhalese are predominantly Buddhists, and the Tamils are
predominantly Hindus. The Christians include Burghers, and the
descendents of Buddhists and Hindus who converted to Christianity
during the colonial period. The Kandyan Sinhalese are descendents
of those people who belonged to the former Kandyan kingdom,
which remained as a sovereign nation till 1815. The rest of the
Sinhalese are Low Country Sinhalese. The census taken in 1981 did
not classify the Sinhalese into these two groups.

Table 3: Population by religion, 1981 census.

Religion	Population in 1000s	% of total population
Buddhism	10,288.3	69.30
Hinduism	2,297.8	15.48
Christianity	1,130.6	7.61
Islam	1,121.7	7.56
Others	8.3	0.05
TOTAL	14,846.7	100.00

Source: Department of Census and Statistics, an abstract from 'Table 22 – Population by religion, census years,' Statistical Abstract of the Democratic Socialist Republic of Sri Lanka 1992, (Colombo, Sri Lanka, 1993), p.50.

A close review of the present ethnic distribution shows that the Low Country Sinhalese are predominantly concentrated in the maritime Southern and Western Provinces; the Kandyan Sinhalese in the Central, Sabaragamuwa, Uva, North-Western and North-Central Provinces; and Sri Lankan Tamils in the Northern and Eastern Provinces. Over the last few centuries, a significant number of Sri Lankan Tamils have settled in the capital city of Colombo and other areas of Sinhalese majority. The Indian Tamils are scattered throughout the central region: Central, Sabaragamuwa, and Uva Provinces. The Muslims are scattered throughout the island, with some concentration in the southern half of the Eastern Province. As said before, the Eastern Province had temporarily merged with the Northern Province, subject to a future referendum, for an interim period for the purpose of establishing one Provincial Council in the area pursuant to 1987 Indo-Sri Lanka agreement.

It is interesting to note that these different ethnic, religious and linguistic groups, except Veddhas, have descended from foreign migrants in the island of one kind or another. Some of these settlers came to the island more than two thousand years ago, some more than a thousand years ago and some only some centuries ago. These settlers came from many parts of the world, and brought into the country their languages, religions, and ways of living. They have also brought their energy, creativity and hope. There are many other countries in the world with similar historic backgrounds, and they too have ended up with similar multi-ethnic, multi-linguistic, and multi-religious societies. Some of these countries, including the Unites States of America, Canada, and Australia, receive and accept thousands of people from foreign lands as new immigrants every year. Once accepted as new immigrants they become eligible to apply for citizenship of these countries in a matter of a few years; the legal requirement in Canada in this regard is just over four years. Once a new immigrant becomes a citizen in any of these countries, he or she would be entitled to all the rights and freedoms that any other citizen of that country enjoys.

Culturally, countries of such multi-ethnic societies have developed in two distinct ways. In some of these countries, like the United States of America, the distinct cultures of the different ethnic groups have entered the melting pot through a process of assimilation and appropriation. In others, like India, the distinct ethnic groups retained their own cultural identities in an atmosphere of multi-culturalism and peaceful co-existence through accommodation and mutual respect. The historical evidence of Sri Lanka suggests that the initial settlers by and large may have chosen the former path of a melting pot with a countrywide Sinhalese Buddhist civilization. This situation, however, later changed. The different ethnic groups in today's Sri Lanka seem to prefer to retain their separate cultural identities, more than ever before. In this situation, it is imperative that all ethnic groups in the country fully accommodate and respect each other, whether their ancestors had been there for thousands of years, hundreds of years, or have just arrived. Such accommodation and mutual respect will have the power to unite all the peoples as Sri Lankans, and bring peace to this troubled land; something the ongoing bloody war has failed to do for decades.

In a society of such accommodation, mutual love and respect, no one particular ethnic group should expect any special rights or privileges over those of any other. Every group, no doubt, would desire to work for further advancement of its own language, religion and culture. What one group does to fulfil such desires, however, should not stand in the way of any other. This can happen only if there are equal opportunities, rights and freedoms for all ethnic groups for their individual advancement.

Service to Buddhism

Sri Lanka always had and will have a special place in the Buddhist world. Sri Lanka is the cradle of Theravada Buddhism, which is closest to doctrinal Buddhism. It is also the oldest Buddhist society in the world. It has an excellent record of preserving and nurturing Buddhism during times of ascendancy of Brahminical and other Hindu orthodoxy and orthopraxis throughout the Indian subcontinent, from about the fifth century AD. No doubt, all Buddhists in the country, both the clergy and the laity, wish to continue to work for the advancement of their religion. It is a just and natural cause for the Sinhalese Buddhists. Any new political system in the country should and must create an environment where they could pursue this cause without any form of intimidation or reprisal. At the same time, it is equally important to recognize similar aspirations of all other religious groups now present in the country. Enshrining Buddhism in the country's constitution, giving it a 'foremost place,' is in a way a disservice to Buddhism in the contemporary context of a multi-religious society. It would create a sense of antagonism and dislike, instead of understanding and respect, toward Buddhism and Buddhists among those who belong to other religions. This, in fact, was what actually happened in the country after the 1972 constitutional changes. Buddhism would always develop with the more understanding and respect it receives from the people of other religious faiths. Any act by any government in any country to defeat that purpose would only hurt Buddhism and Buddhists, not only in that country but also in the rest of the world.

In the Sri Lankan situation, Critics say that the enshrining of Buddhism in the country's constitution giving it a special place by the SLFP led government in 1972 was a mere act of political maneuvering to appease the Buddhist majority in the country. It looks very much similar to the act of enacting the Sinhala Only Act of 1956 to appease the Sinhalese by a previous SLFP led government. It may be interesting to note here that the British who introduced constitution writing to Sri Lanka did not have any written constitution of its own. This, however, has not lowered the status of the predominant religion in that country in any manner.

A government could achieve best results in bringing about peace and harmony among all the religious groups in a country by sticking to secular policies. This is what D. S. Senanayake, the first Prime Minister of independent Sri Lanka, appeared to have tried to do and failed, at the time of 1948 independence. The first Marxist parties, the LSSP and the CP, in Sri Lanka also advocated secular policies from the time of their inception in the thirties and forties. The main opposition to secularism in the country came from the Sinhalese-Buddhist nationalist force lead by S. W. R. D. Bandaranaike. Secularism requires governments to refuse to mix politics with religion. Bandaranaike and his followers did just the opposite. Secularism also means skepticism in regard to religion in the general sense. But this is not what a government should do. On the contrary governments should respect all religions, but should also refuse to mix their power and politics with religion. Only then government policies and programs serve the best interests of all the people of the country, belonging to all religions. Under any event, no government in any country should put the interests of any one particular group of people, selected on any basis, ahead of others. Treating one particular group differently would not only divide a country, but would also make that group a target of criticism by all others, both within and outside the country.

Therefore, it is imperative that any future revision to the constitution of Sri Lanka must address this issue, by removing the special status it now offers to Buddhism. This would not lower the importance or the significance of Buddhism in Sri Lanka or elsewhere in the world. At the same time by having it in the constitution giving it "the foremost place" and state protection, would not necessarily benefit Buddhism. Sri Lankans can learn a lot from Indian experience in this regard. The national emblem of India is a replica of the Lion of Saranath (Lion Capital) near Varanasi (Benares) in Uttra Pradesh. Emperor Ashoka (King Piyadasi) erected the Lion Capital in the third century BC to mark the place where the Buddha gave his first sermon of peace and emancipation to the world. The Lion Capital has four lions resting on a lotus in full bloom together with a symbol of 'Dharmakchakkra' that depicts the eight-fold path leading to final emancipation, Nirvana, taught by the Buddha. India has never changed this national emblem. It has, however, not helped retain Buddhism. Today, not even one percent of the total Indian population considers themselves Buddhist. At the same time more and more people are attracted to Buddhism in countries where there were no Buddhists before. For example in North America, during the last decade of the twentieth century, the number of Buddhist meditation centres has grown ten-fold, from over two hundred to over two thousand.

It is interesting to note here what specific advice Emperor Ashoka may have given to his subjects on religious tolerance. S. Dhammika, the spiritual director of the Buddha Dhamma Mandala Society in Singapore quotes a translation of one of the ancient edicts proclaiming Ashoka's reforms and policies, "Beloved-of-the Gods, King Piyadasi, honours both ascetics and the householders of the religions, and he honours them with gifts and honours of various kinds. But Beloved-of-the-Gods, King Piyadasi, does not value gifts and honours as much as he values this .... that there should be growth in essentials of all religions. Growth in essentials can be done in different ways, but all of them have as their root restraint in speech, that is, not praising one's own religion, or condemning the religion of others without good cause. And if there is cause for criticism, it should be done in a mild way. But it is better to honour other religions for this reason. By so doing, one's own religion benefits, and so do other religions, while doing otherwise harms one's own religion and the religions of others. Whoever praises his own religion, due to excessive devotion, and condemns others with the thought 'Let me glorify my own religion,' only harms his own religion. Therefore contact (between religions) is good. One should listen to and respect the doctrines professed by others. Beloved-of-the-Gods, King Piyadasi, desires that all should be well-learned in the good doctrines of other religions." (The Edicts of King Ashoka, Buddhist Publication Society, Kandy, Sri Lanka, DharmaNet Edition, 1994).

Equality of Languages

The government's approach to language should not be discriminative. Language is the basic tool people have to communicate among themselves and between them and the government. There are three main languages, Sinhalese, Tamil, and English, spoken in modern Sri Lanka. Most people speak only one language, Sinhalese or Tamil. Both the Sinhalese (74% of the total population) and Tamils (18.2%) have learnt English as a secondary language to varying degrees. Less than five percent of the Sinhalese and Tamils in the country, however, have become proficient in English. The Sinhalese living in the Tamil areas and Tamils living in the Sinhalese areas mostly speak both languages. Among the rest, neither the Sinhalese nor the Tamils appear to be willing to lean each other's language. A requirement for Tamil public servants to learn Sinhalese under the Sinhala Only Act of 1956 backfired on the government with strong protests and civil disobedience. The proportion of the population that can speak all the three languages is very small.

Before 1956, the official language of the country was English. The medium of instruction in the secondary and post-secondary institutions in the country was also mainly English. At the time, students from both communities, Sinhalese and Tamil, willingly learned English. They studied together in the same class rooms at colleges and universities, shared common dreams for the future of their country, and wanted to see the right person in the right job, irrespective of one's language or religion. The English language, thus, established a strong, common link between the two communities in a significant way. The government also appointed English teachers to elementary schools to teach English as a second language, preparing the young to do their secondary and post-secondary education in English. Initially the opportunities to learn English and to enter higher learning institutions were limited to those who lived in urban centres, less than 20 percent of the total population. Later with the introduction of free education and the increase of well-equipped secondary schools in rural areas these opportunities started to reach the rural residents as well. This trend of events, however, changed after 1956.

The S. W. R. D. Bandaranaike government that came to power on a Sinhalese-Buddhist nationalist platform in 1956 shifted the language of instruction in secondary and post-secondary institutions to Swabasha, meaning one's own language - mainly Sinhalese or Tamil. Only the pure and applied sciences at post-secondary level continued in English. This change in the medium of instruction to Swabasha had two major effects. Firstly, the students pursuing higher education lost contact with the rest of the world. Now they had to depend only on what the teachers taught in the classroom and books and other literary material written in vernacular languages. There was very little of such material in vernacular languages, and the ones available were not being updated as knowledge advanced through research and studies in the other parts of the world. All this clearly showed that the SLFP led government wrongly mixed politics, not only with religion, but also with education. One may argue how Japan continued to use its vernacular language as the medium of instruction at all levels of education and yet became one of the most industrialized nations in the world. There is a debate as to how Japan could do that. Some argue that Japan could do it because it was never colonized. others believe that the cultural factors peculiar to Japan gave it a capacity to absorb modern technology from the West. It is also notable that Japan has remained a developed nation in the world for centuries, especially since 1868. As a result, Japan was able to develop science and technology in its own language. It has developed side by side with the other developed countries as an equal partner in the technological advancement of the world. Sri Lanka's situation is very different.

Secondly, by changing the medium of instruction in schools and colleges to Swabasha, Sri Lanka lost the strong, common link that existed among its Sinhalese speaking and Tamil speaking communities. This has slowly and surely lessened the interaction between the two communities. Students of each linguistic community studied in isolation. As if all this was not enough, the government-approved books to teach history in Sinhalese elementary schools spread the germs of resentment and hatred in the innocent minds of the young Sinhalese against Tamils in the country. No doubt it is important to teach history in schools. However, the way of teaching history was not correct. It is important to teach history in a constructive manner, preparing the young not to live in the past, but to live in the present and the future.

Because of the chauvinist nature of their politics, post-independent rulers downplayed the importance of English not only in the field of education, but also as far as its use as an international language. No one can ignore the fact that Sri Lanka, like any other country in the world, needs an international language to communicate with the rest of the world. Today what is going on in the rest of the world influences practically everything in a country. Modern technology will only continue to bring the world closer and closer together. In this situation, only through an effective means of communication with the rest of the world would a country be able to gain from comparable advantages elsewhere and protect its citizens from what is inexpedient. For best results toward this, it is important that all the people in a country, not a selected few, become proficient in an international language.

For Sri Lanka English is the most logical international language. Already it had been the state language of the entire country from 1833 to 1956. Although this situation had changed with the introduction of the Sinhala Only Act of 1956, English has continued to play a dominant role in the affairs of the country, especially among its professionals, academics and the political elite. As a result, English has now become the language of authority and power in the country, although it is not its state language any more. But the country's public education system established after the Sinhala Only Act continues regardless, not recognizing this reality. Keeping a vast majority of the people not proficient in English or any other world language is an act of blind-folding them and of believing that the rich and the powerful who are proficient in the English language are wiser and smarter than the rest of its people. This situation, however, helps the rich and the powerful in the country, as they send their children abroad for education in English. Upon return, these children take the place of their parents and become the next generation of elite.

Going by the above, it is imperative that the government of Sri Lanka gives an equal opportunity to all its citizens to lean English. This does not mean that the government should ignore the importance of the country's vernacular languages. Every one of the three languages in the country, Sinhalese, Tamil and English, has, an important role to play in its affairs. The country must have a language policy that gives every citizen a clear choice to use any of the three languages in dealing with the country's legislative, judiciary or administrative institutions. At the same time, everyone in the country should be given an opportunity to learn both vernacular languages, Sinhala and Tamil, in addition to English, and pursue secondary (say after Grade five) and post-secondary (training colleges, technical colleges and universities) education in the English medium. This would help most Sri Lankans, if not all, gain proficiency in the English language in a matter of few years, and communicate and interact across their ethnic boundaries as well as with the rest of the world. Record keeping in all government institutions can be in English, with an administrative ability to translate any document into Sinhalese or Tamil upon request. All public servants at all levels who have direct dealings with the public in performing their duties must be trilingual, with at least working knowledge in the second vernacular language, Tamil or Sinhalese.

In schools, the child's first language should be the medium of instruction from the kindergarten to Grade five. Parents should be able to freely decide any language as the child's first language. English and the second vernacular language should be introduced as the second and third languages from about Grade Three, and English should eventually become the medium of instruction from about Grade Six. The opportunities to pursue language studies in all the three languages should continue throughout the secondary education, and thereafter.

Learning the student's first language until Grade ten should become compulsory, but the learning of the second vernacular language - after Grade Two - should not become compulsory, although it would be to the advantage of the student to do so. At the same time, the incumbent public servants should have a moratorium period of sufficient length of time, say 10 years or so, to acquire the language skills they now lack to qualify as trilingual. Implementation of such a language policy would establish a new system of governance in the country, guaranteeing equal opportunities for all its citizens in anything and everything, irrespective of the language one claims as his or her mother tongue. Such equal opportunities in the context of language will be more beneficial to the country and all its peoples than any form of enshrinement of one or more of the vernacular languages in the country's constitution.

By virtue of the fact that the people of the country speak the three languages, Sinhala, Tamil and English, they all become the national languages of the country. At the same time they should all be recognized as the official languages, with equality of status, rights and privileges as to their use in its legislative, judiciary, and administrative institutions. Any particular recognition given to the three languages in or outside the country's constitution must reflect this situation. It would be insane to give any form of special recognition in the country's constitution to any one particular language above the others.

The usage of the English language as a medium of instruction for higher education would reconnect Sri Lankans with the rest of the world, giving them once again the ability to gain from the comparative advantages of technologies developing elsewhere in the world. This would also lead to the gradual disappearance of elite-groups in the society with special privileges just because of their proficiency in English.

The Concept of Homeland

For some years now Sri Lankan Tamils have been asking for a separate homeland in the north and east. The main reason for this demand is that Sri Lankan Tamils traditionally occupied this region of the country for some centuries. Their Jaffna kingdom, which started in the latter part of the thirteenth century, never included what later became the eastern province. Throughout the period of the Jaffna kingdom, the Eastern Province remained a part of the

Kandyan kingdom. Sri Lankan Tamils later settled in this area, especially after it came under the Portuguese and other colonial rulers. Peasants in the Eastern Province, however, appear to have a history from the late pre-colonial period. During the time of the colonial rulers Sri Lankan Tamils had also moved to various other parts of the country, in particular to the Capital, Colombo, and its suburbs. According to critics, a significant number of Sri Lankan Tamils live outside the area now claimed as a Tamil homeland. These Sri Lankan Tamils mostly live in concentrated pockets within Sinhalese areas. There are similar, isolated pockets of other communities too, including Muslims, Indian Tamils and Veddhas, within Sinhalese areas. Even within the Eastern Province, there is a significant concentration of Muslims in its southern half. It is still not known whether these Muslims would like to be a part of a Tamil homeland that the Sri Lankan Tamils claim. The Indian Tamils who are concentrated in the upcountry Sinhalese area want nothing short of what Sri Lankans Tamils would get in the north and east. This means, the proclamation of a Tamil homeland in the north and east would eventually lead to similar demands by the Indian Tamils in the up country. Then the Muslims too may follow suit. This type of politics will only lead to further communal divisions and conflicts in the country, and will certainly not help bring about national consolidation among its peoples. The best solution to this situation is to make all of Sri Lanka a homeland for all of its peoples: Sinhalese, Sri Lankan Tamils, Muslims, Burghers, Indian Tamils, and others. Once this concept is accepted, everyone in the country should have the same rights and freedoms to settle in any province, district, or village of his or her choice. In government programs of colonist settlements, the decision where one goes and settles should be made not by the government, but by the settler himself or herself. The government should not assume the power to control the rights and freedoms of the individual in any manner.

The Adivasis

When it comes to arguments on homeland, the Veddha community needs special attention due to two main reasons. Firstly, they are the aboriginal people of the country, who represent a direct link to the first people who inhabited the island. According to archaeologists, the first people of the island date back to prehistoric times. S. U. Deraniyagala writes in his research paper entitled Pre-and Protohistoric Settlements in Sri Lanka, that "There is secure evidence of settlements in Sri Lanka by 130,000 years ago, probably by 300,000 BP and possibly by 500,000 BP or earlier."[1] As stated earlier in this book the historian K. M. de Silva also believes homo sapiens probably first appeared in Sri Lanka about 500,000 BC. Going by all this, the historic significance of Veddhas' homeland in the island is unique, and is not comparable with that of any other ethnic or linguistic group in the country. Apart from the Veddhas, the rest of the present Sri Lankans are descendents of those who came into the country comparatively recently from foreign lands, mainly India, as invaders and migrants.

Secondly, the Veddhas had never been an integral part of any kind of rule established in the country by those who had come from outside or any of their descendents. Instead, the Veddhas (who did not opt to assimilate with the foreign invaders or migrants) have continued to rule themselves, and have always lived independent of the power politics of outside rule by Sinhalese, South Indians, European colonialists, or post-independent rulers. Over the years, these outside rulers and their governments have exploited them, and harassed them for violating laws they never knew existed. More importantly they have lost many of their homelands to agricultural expansion, especially in the Eastern and North Central Provinces and in the southeast part of the country. The much-publicized Mahaweli Development Scheme, for which the present two main political parties in the country, the SLFP and UNP, claim credit, was the biggest single project of destruction of the homelands and jungle retreats of the Veddha community. At the time of writing this book, the Veddha community was specifically complaining that part of their ancestral homeland had become Maduruoya National Park. Governments seem to continue with this trend, regardless of the competing interests of the Veddha community. In response to all this, the Veddha community appealed to the government to be simply left alone and to be allowed to pursue a peaceful lifestyle of their choice in their traditional homelands. Governments in power have, however, continued to ignore such appeals in the name of 'development.' The current Veddha chieftain Uruwarige Vanniya has no faith in any of the main political parties or their leaders. When asked about the December 2001 election, he said, "Best thing is to go to the jungle and wait till the elections are over."[2] According to Faith Ratnayaka, Veddhas are now trying to take their grievances to the United Nations for an amicable solution. Ratnayaka writes, "They (the Veddhas) are preparing to appeal personally to the United Nations, in Geneva, where the Working

Group for Indigenous Populations will consider their case." [3] The rest of the Sri Lankan society does not have to wait for a decision from the United Nations to give the right place to the Veddha community in Sri Lanka. It is incumbent upon the rest of the Sri Lankan society to accept and respect the Veddha community as the aboriginal people of their country, and give its members their due place in it, by not interfering or infringing upon their rights and freedoms in their traditional homelands. The members of the Veddha community should no longer remain ignored, ignorant, and labouring under abject poverty. They must be allowed to live with dignity and to shape their future the way they want. In an interview with the BBC Sandeshaya, Chieftain Uruwarige Vanniya has requested that the next round of constitutional amendments should clearly define the rights of the Veddhas in the country. This is a just request that needs to be considered with the seriousness it deserves.

Citizenship

It is also very important to find a final resolution to the issue of the present stateless Tamils of South Indian origin in Sri Lanka. These "stateless' people, some 200,000, are descendents of South Indian Tamils brought into the country as manual workers by British planters in the nineteenth and early twentieth centuries, when both India and Sri Lanka were under British rule. It was British responsibility to find an amicable solution to the plight of these people at the time it considered granting dominion status (independence) to Sri Lanka in 1948. The British, however, ignored this issue and transferred power to Sri Lankan leaders to decide on the future of these people. The Sri Lankan leaders at the time were more interested in replacing the British in the positions of power at the earliest opportunity, rather than finding a lasting solution to the plight of these people who became stateless in 1949. Even after more than five decades of independence, the Sri Lankan leaders have not yet fully resolved this issue.

The total number of Tamils of South Indian origin now living in the plantation sector is about 1.2 million. At the time of independence, no other group of people in the country, including Sri Lankan Tamils, was prepared to accept them as Sri Lankan citizens. The post-independent governments wanted to repatriate them through negotiations with neighbouring India, their country of origin. In 1964, the two countries agreed that Sri Lanka would grant citizenship to 375,000 of them and India would take back the balance (at the time) 600,000. After a long period of bureaucratic wrangling and politics, the government of Sri Lanka started to send some of the affected people back to India by ferry in 1981. Then the civil war that broke out in 1983 brought the ferry service between the two countries to an abrupt halt, putting in jeopardy the plight of about 200,000 Indian Tamils, who were about to become Indian citizens.

These 200,000 people and their descendents cannot get government jobs in Sri Lanka, as they are not Sri Lankan citizens. Their chances of finding employment in the private sector are not any better. Their children cannot find places in the government universities. They do not qualify for financial assistance from government aided programs for anything. Above all, they do not enjoy the franchise, and this has made them a forgotten lot in a country where they have lived and worked for generations, with no serious attention from any one who can make a difference.

This is certainly not an acceptable situation. If the Indian government is still willing to honour its 1964 agreement and the 200,00 affected people and their descendents are still eager to become Indian citizens, the Sri Lankan government must consider this matter as one of top priority and do everything within its power to see it happen. If travel by sea is not feasible, the government should take them to their chosen destination by other means. At the same time, the Sri Lankan government must give its citizenship to those who do not wish to be Indian citizens or are not accepted by the Indian government for whatever reason. These 200,000 affected people and their descendents deserve much better than what they are now going through, being neither here nor there.

The British should not stay completely out of the scene, despite the arrangement they made with Sri Lankan leaders, transferring to them the responsibility to find a solution to this complex problem. It is a problem the British themselves created, affecting the lives of not only these 'stateless' people of Indian origin, but also of the Sinhalese peasants, specially in the Kandyan areas, who lost their traditional lands to British colonial plantation projects. Great Britain can clear its name on this problem only after it has been satisfactorily resolved on both these fronts: the 'stateless' people of Indian origin; and the tormented Sinhalese peasantry. Great Britain should have the courage to rise to the occasion and face this challenge in the present political context of the region and the world, and be an active party to a meaningful and lasting solution to this aged problem in Sri Lanka.

Democracy

Now let us look at democracy, what Sri Lanka needs and lacks most. Democracy is the key to any meaningful change in a country. Sri Lanka is not an exception to this basic fact. Democracy is rule by the people, all the people in a country, as against rule by a monarch or dictator (autocracy) or by a group of few (oligarchy). Although the current system of governance in Sri Lanka is oligarchic in nature, democracy is not completely foreign to traditional Sri Lankan village life. For example, let us examine how people in a traditional Sri Lankan village construct and use a community well for the purposes of domestic water supply. All the villagers meet and discuss among themselves different potential well sites and techniques of well construction. These discussions normally continue until they reach a decision by consensus on where and how to develop the well. After that, they all work together to construct the well. After its construction, the well serves anyone and everyone in the village, without discrimination. No one would be restricted from using the well on the ground that he or she had not been in favour of the well site or the method of construction finally chosen. The writer is aware that Julius Nyerere, a former President of the Republic of Tanzania in Africa quoted the same example to show how democracy works in an African village setting. It works the same way in Sri Lanka or any other South Asian country. All the people in the community participate in making decisions for the benefit of all. After arriving at a decision, they work together to implement it for the good and benefit of all. Decisions that seriously affect one or more sections of the population, however, are not democratic, even if all the people in a community have participated in arriving at them.

One of the basic underlying principles of democracy is that no one person or a group of persons is wiser than all the people together in a community; the bigger the participation, the better the decisions. Getting everyone involved in the decision making process helps resolve difficult problems and situations in an amicable manner. At national level, it is not possible for all the people in a country to get together and discuss every issue that comes up. That is why many countries have established representative models of governance, where, instead of all the people, a sizeable number of elected representatives meet and take decisions on their behalf. It is only a way to put democracy to work. At times of difficult issues, some governments still reach people at large, beyond their houses of representatives for decision making. One good example was the way Zambia changed its customary laws of succession in the eighties. It had many tribes, and each tribe had its own traditional laws of succession it had jealously guarded and passed on from one generation to the next. Any attempt to change the customary laws through the House of Representatives (parliament), without prior support from the people at large, would have led to tribal conflicts and wars. Instead of doing that, the government first led a series of discussions and debates, both formal and informal, on the need to change the customary laws among the people of the country as such. Students and teachers debated in schools, colleges and universities. Outside schools, colleges and universities, men and women debated in every nook and corner of the country, in their village meeting places, farms, factories, offices, markets, hospitals, and so on. The media, newspapers, radio and television publicized these discussions and debates as much as possible. All this helped create awareness among the people as such as to why their customary laws needed change, what the options were, and the advantages and disadvantages of each option. Only after completing such a process the government brought in a bill in the House of Representatives for debate among the elected representatives with a view to changing the customary laws of succession by law. Finally the parliament passed the bill, making new laws of succession, avoiding inter-tribal or any other form of conflicts on the matter. This clearly shows the power of democracy.

If democracy is rule by the people, it certainly implies some basic pre-requisites for its meaningful realization. These pre-requisites address four main areas: 1. Political freedom, including freedom of thought and speech, 2. Political equality, 3.Political education and maturity, and 4. Respect for human life. Democracy will not succeed in any society, if any one or more of these prerequisites are not present. The first two prerequisites of political freedom and equality are two sides of the same coin, as one depends on the other. Under political freedom, people should be able to freely criticize the government in power and its actions, individually or collectively. The media should be free from any form of control by the government. The judiciary should not be subordinate to the government, so that one could challenge any of its decisions in a court of law. The political equality should not be limited to universal franchise. Any person should be able to think freely, come to any political decision, criticize the government in power, form and lead any political party, and seek election to any political position.

The third pre-requisite is political education and maturity. This is very important not only for political leaders, but also for the general public. Sri Lankans have chosen to build a democratic system of government for their country. Even after five decades of independence, however, they appear not to have a thorough understanding of what democracy really means and the different democratic models of government developed elsewhere. One of the major reasons for this is the continued indoctrination of the people by the post-independent leaders of the country to gather support for their dynastic-type elite rule. In doing this they have continued to reject the proposal for a federal system of government for Sri Lanka, which is more appropriate for its multi-ethnic and multi-cultural society. No government elected to power since independence made any significant effort to educate the masses politically, preparing them for the future.

The fourth pre-requisite for democracy is respect for human life. In a democracy, any person should be able to think freely, come to any political decision, criticize the government in power, form and lead any political party, and seek election to any high political position without his or her life being threatened. Then only, and only then, the people are able to effectively take part in its political process. The numerous disappearances, kidnappings, and killings of media personnel and others who criticize the government in Sri Lanka show that the country is lacking this pre-requisite.

Democratic Models Developed Elsewhere

Democracy has the power to prevent bloody wars and the formation of terrorist movements. It also has the power to bring together different ethnic, linguistic and religious groups to live in peace and harmony, as members of one family. It has come about through a long political evolutionary process in the world. It is the best form of rule for any country in the modern world. In their efforts to establish democratic rule, different countries have devised different political systems or models. The British have evolved a representative system. In this system, the largest group of representatives in the parliament that agrees on a common political platform, in the form of a single political party or a coalition of two or more different political parties, forms the "Government." The remaining representatives who sit in the parliament form the

"Opposition," and they too may belong to one or more political parties. At times of elections, all the candidates who seek election appear before the masses under different political parties, and seek support for their individual party- platforms. There can also be independent candidates, who do not belong to any political party. The elected independent candidates either join the government or become part of the opposition. All the representatives, both in government and opposition, meet in the parliament, debate on the issues of the country and make decisions for its future, on behalf of its entire people. A cabinet of ministers selected by the leader of the governing party from the sitting members of the legislature becomes the executive body of the country. The leader of the governing party functions as the 'first among equals' in cabinet, and is called Prime Minister. The country runs unitarily, with all its governing powers concentrated in one centre, Westminster, London.

In this system, one becomes a representative in the house of legislature by having the highest number of votes cast at an election in his or her favour, on a first-past-the-post basis, in a territorially defined electorate. In time, this has lead to under-representation of women, minorities, aboriginal peoples, the physically handicapped, and the like in the legislatures of many countries that adopted this system. In addition, the strength of the number of representatives in the legislature representing a political party or an independent group has failed to reflect the actual strength of support it has in a country. For example, under this system, a political party or an independent group with 50 to 60 percent support in the country can end up in occupying even 90 percent of the seats in the legislature.

As a remedy to this situation, some countries have evolved a proportionate representative model. In this model of governance, the number of representatives allocated to an electoral district could be shared between all the political parties and independent groups in proportion to the votes cast in their favour at an election. Many countries, including Sri Lanka, have adopted this new way of electing their legislative representatives. This has, however, led to difficulties in electing stable governments with a clear-cut majority in the legislature. In order to avoid this situation, some countries are trying to find a middle ground between the proportionate representative model and the first-past-the post system. For example, Germany elects half of the 300 members of its legislature on the-first-past-the-post basis and the other half on the basis of proportionate representation. Germans do this with the help of an additional ballot to choose the preferred political party or independent group at the election time. The Italian legislature allocates 75 percent of its seats on the first-past-the-post basis, and the remaining 25 percent on the proportionate representative basis. Despite the fact that there are only 25 percent of the legislative seats on proportionate representation, Italy has failed to elect stable governments for some decades now. It has changed its government eight times within the last twenty years, in 1981, 1983, 1987, 1992, 1994, 1996, 1998, and 2001.

The system of government evolved by Americans is different. In their system, the people elect their "representatives" just like in the British system, but these representatives do not have the responsibility to form government or executive. People elect their government separately by electing a President and a Vice President through an 'Electoral College.' President and Vice President cannot come from the same region or State of the country; they must come from two different States. The President so elected appoints members of his cabinet from among competent men and women in the country forming the administration. These cabinet members are responsible to the people not directly but through the President. Candidates for the positions of Representatives as well as President and Vice President contest the elections on the strength of their political party manifestoes. There can be independent candidates seeking election as representatives or even as President and Vice President.

In their system of government, Americans do not run their country as a unitary state as in the case of Great Britain. Instead, what they have is a federal system of government in the form of a union of a number of different states within the same country. The Governor is the chief executive of the state, parallel to the President at the state level. The state Governors elected by the people in their respective jurisdictions keep control of local affairs, and the central government led by President handles the affairs common to all the States. In executing his duties, the President gets advice and consent from the Senate, one of the two legislative bodies at national level. The other legislative body at national level is the House of Representatives or simply the House; both these legislative bodies at national level together constitute the country's Congress. These legislative bodies at national level are comprised of elected representatives from all the States. There are similar legislative bodies at State level as well: the State Senate and the State House of Representatives. The President is the head of the executive. Representatives have legislative powers. The Supreme Court and such lower courts as the Congress may from time to time ordain and establish have the judicial powers of the country. The President appoints judges for the courts.

Federal systems of government appear to serve democracies of diverse communities better than a unitary system. India, which is the largest democracy in the world, has a federal system. It has helped bring about unity in diversity, with each one of its several states of unique linguistic and cultural distinction controlling its own affairs, while maintaining a bond with all the other states in the country as equal share holders of their common Indian heritage. All matters of regional interest come under the jurisdiction of state governments, and those that are of common interest to all the states come under the jurisdiction of the central government. Thus the central government and the state governments share the legislative powers of the country.

Canada is yet another democracy having a similar federal system of governance. The West Indians and Inuits were the first inhabitants of this vast country. From the early 1600s people from France came and settled in it. They occupied some parts of what are now the Provinces of Quebec, Nova Scotia and New Brunswick. Then came the English-speaking settlers, who first lived to the north and the west of these French settlers and later spread all over what is now Canada. These early English-speaking settlers came from a number of foreign lands, including England, Ireland, Scotland, Wales, and the United States of America. Since then more and more French and English speaking people had came and joined these early settlers, and are still continuing to do so. Meanwhile, from about the late nineteenth century there had also been immigrants from the countries in Asia, including China and India. Immigrants also came from all other parts of the world. The Chinese helped complete the great railway that runs across from the Atlantic Ocean to the Pacific. The railway opened the land locked central Prairies as well to new comers. In time, the Canadian society became a good mix of people who came from all over the world. Whoever came to the country brought with them their languages, religions, and cultures, making it a land of unique multi-cultural heritage. Over a quarter of the present population in the country treat French as their mother tongue, and the rest of the population belonging to numerous other ethnic and linguistic groups, speak mostly English. The government of Canada treats both the languages, English and French, as its official languages.

The central government of Canada is responsible for matters that affect all Canadians, including national security, sovereignty, citizenship, foreign policy, national economic policy, currency and postal services. There are 10 Provincial or Territorial governments at regional level, which are responsible for matters that affect people locally, including education, child welfare, health care, and highways. In some situations, the federal government and Provincial governments share responsibilities. These common areas include agriculture, justice, the environment, and the protection of human rights. Canada is still a constitutional monarchy. The Queen of the United Kingdom is queen of Canada. She is the official head of state of Canada. She is the constitutional head of the executive. A Governor General appointed by her on the recommendations of the Prime Minister of Canada acts on behalf of the queen as her local representative. The Canadian Parliament and the Provincial or Territorial legislatures share the country's legislative powers. The Prime Minister of Canada is the head of the Canadian government. A Premier heads each Provincial government. The Territories, only two: Yukon Territory and Northwest Territories, are each governed by a Commissioner, who represents the Government of Canada, and an elected territorial assembly. At elections people vote on party lines to elect their representatives to the Canadian Parliament, Provincial Legislatures and the Territorial Assemblies. It is not uncommon to see some independent candidates as well at these elections.

There are carefully crafted special provisions in the Canadian constitution to protect all citizens from the possible misadventure of majorities in governments, claiming authority over the rights of the individual. These special provisions include aboriginal treaty rights, minority language rights, and a comprehensive Charter of Rights and Freedoms. One of the significant underlying assumptions of these constitutional provisions is the principle that all humans should be free to pursue their ideals and vision to realize their individuality. This has helped Canada develop a pluralistic society of free men and women evolving multiculturalism under the umbrella of Canadian nationalism.

The Canada's road to such a brand of nationalism has not been without problems. At the times of constitutional changes in the country, French Quebecers asked for special recognition (as one of Canada's two founding peoples) and extra powers, including veto power over future constitutional amendments. Quebecers were never successful in these demands. Prime Minister Elliott Trudeau, a Quebecer himself, took the lead to amend the country's constitution in 1982, introducing a special charter of rights and freedoms, and spoke vehemently against such demands of Quebecers. He saw the emerging Quebec nationalism as just another form of ethnic tribalism. He was of the opinion that countries were not worth preserving, if their governments were not required to respect and advance the rights and freedoms of all their people in the same manner. Politicians in Quebec who stood for special recognition and extra powers did not, however, give up on their demands. On the contrary, they pursued those demands and even further aggravated them with a call for separation of Quebec from Canada. The Parti Quebecois, the political party of French-Canadian nationalists formed in 1970, won control of the Quebec provincial legislature in 1976, and remained in power till 1985. For the next nine years it remained in the opposition and returned to power in 1994. It also succeeded in winning the next provincial election held in 1998. Despite these electoral victories of the Parti Quebecoris, the support for the nationalist movement of Quebec appears to be shrinking. In 1980, Quebecers rejected a call for an independent Quebec, called sovereignty-association, in a provincial referendum by 60 percent of the votes. The Meech Lake Accord signed in 1987 made some progress on the Quebec demand for separatism, but collapsed in 1990. In 1992, Canadians defeated a national referendum on a constitutional reform package recognizing some of the Quebec's demands. In 1999 polls suggested that support for Quebec secession had shrunk to about 40 percent of Quebec voters. Then in the 2000 national election the Bloc Quebecoirs, the counterpart of Parti Quebecoirs at national level, received fewer votes in Quebec than the country's main national party, Liberal Party, for the first time since 1980. In January 2001, Lucien Bouchard, who founded the Bloc Quebecoirs in 1990 and played the roles of the Leader of the Official Opposition in the Canadian (national) parliament from 1993 to 1996 and leader of Parti Quebecoirs and Premier of Quebec from 1996 to 2000, finally resigned from politics, complaining about the lack of adequate support for the separatist cause in Quebec.

The political system in Switzerland is the most democratic system in the modern world. It is a federal state consisting of 26 regional governments (considered as 20 "full" cantons and six "half" cantons for the purpose of representation in the federal legislature). These regional governments have fiscal autonomy and the right to manage their own affairs. They enjoy all powers not specifically delegated to the federal, national or central government. Municipal governments come under the jurisdiction of the regional governments. The central government has a bicameral legislature (Council of States – 46 members and National Council – 200 members), similar to the one in the United States. The legislature elects seven of its members to the highest federal executive body in the country called the Federal Council for four-year terms. These seven members of the Federal Council serve in place of a single chief executive of the country. Each year the legislature elects from among the seven Council members a President and a Vice President purely on the basis of seniority. The constitution does not allow the renewal of this mandate for the following year. In addition the Councilor who becomes President for one year is not able to seek the position of Vice President the following year. Traditionally, the Councilor who performs as Vice President one year becomes President the next year. The President of the Council becomes the President of the country, but not the Head of the State. The Head of the State is the entire Federal Council. The Councilors act collectively in all matters. In the federal legislature, each chamber elects from its members a President and two Vice Presidents for a period of one year. These mandates too are not renewable for the following year, just like in the case of President and Vice President of the Federal Council. There are similar executive councils and legislatures in the regional governments.

According to available statistics on the language divide in the country, 64% speak German, 19% French, 8% Italian, 1% Romansh, and 8% other languages. German, French, Italian, and Romansh, all are national languages. Three of them: German, French and Italian are official languages. Romansh is also an official language for communicating with persons whose language preference is Romansh. According to the religious divide, 46% are Catholics, 40% Protestants, 5% others, and 9% no religion. The country's constitution does not enshrine any one religion with any kind of special status. The Swiss citizens can demand a popular vote through a referendum on laws passed by the country's legislature. If 50,000 or more people (about 1% of the total population) request a vote on a law passed by the legislature, the government has no choice but to hold a referendum. The people have the power to accept or reject (veto) the law. The Swiss citizens also have a right to ask for a popular vote on a new issue altogether. This requires a written petition by at least 100,000 people (about 2%

of the total population). By this process the people in the country can ask for a change in government policy or even a change to the country's constitution.

In all the above democracies, England, the U. S. A., India, Canada, and Switzerland there is more than one political party. But it is not the number of political parties in a country that decides whether it is democratic or not. The ancient Greeks who came up with the idea of democracy for the first time never imagined it that way. The word democracy comes from the Greek words "DEMOS' meaning people and 'KRATOS' meaning rule. Thus, the degree of democracy in a country depends not on the number of political parties it has, but on the extent of effective participation of the people in its decision making process. Some countries have one-party systems of government, which, they say, are also democratic. Initially, even the United States of America had a one-party system of governance, until the time of Thomas Jefferson, who organized what is now known as Democratic Party of that country. George Washington, a great symbol of democracy, did not have an opposition party for some time. All the communist countries, including China, Cuba, and some African countries continue with one-party systems of governance. Communist leaders defend the system vehemently. Nikitha Krushchev of former communist USSR once said, "..The Soviet society is a society of working men, peasants and intellectuals with their roots in the people, united by a community of interests and a singleness of purpose. The interests of the Soviet people are expressed and upheld by one party – The Communist Party. .... This is what accounts for the absence of any other parties in our country..." [4] It is common knowledge, however, that the Communist rule has been established in these countries only through a process of suppression and oppression of their other political movements and parties. But in some African countries, single-party systems have been established through dissolution, mergers, and by absorption of the opposition parties to the government. It is, however, important to understand that no leader or party in any country ever got a mandate from its people for such political unification among different political parties. Once the leaders of political parties coalesced to form a single-party system in a country, its people had to live with it, whether they liked it or not. Those who did not like it had been left out of the decision making process in the country. Professor Arthur Lewis, a political philosopher who studied one-party systems in West Africa, once wrote, " ..Single party system fails in its entire claim. It cannot represent all the people, or maintain free discussions or give stable government or above all reconcile the differences between the different regional groups. .. It is partly the product of the hysteria of the moment of independence, when some men found it possible to seize the state and suppress their opponents. It is a disease from which West Africa deserves to recover. .." [5] In defending his one-party rule in Nigeria, its former Prime Minister, Sir Abubakar Tafewa Balewa, had once said, ".. I have told people all along that we are not ripe for a system of government in which there is a fully pledged opposition. In Nigeria no party can agree to be in opposition for long. A political opposition in the Western accepted sense is a luxury that we cannot afford. You see today in parliament – there the MPs are performing, some of them, some of the duties of the opposition. So they can. Let them criticize let them condemn this government – let them say anything they like. The trouble is that the Nigerian Member of Parliament wants to criticize the government and to be in it at the same time. Democracy, democracy – what is it? There is American democracy, British democracy – Why not Nigerian democracy? I wish we could find that..." [6] According to critics, one-party system appears to have taken the shape of self-perpetrating organs of the ruling leaders.

Sri Lanka has developed a multi-party democracy with a unitary system of government. It started with a governing system similar to that of Great Britain at the time of its independence in 1948 based on a constitution enacted in 1946. It has since introduced changes to the way of governing the country through two major constitutional revisions in 1972 and 1978. The 1972 revision changed the country's status from being a Dominion of the British Empire to a free and independent Republic, removed the protection afforded to minorities by the 1946 Soulbury (independence) constitution, and proclaimed that the "Republic of Sri Lanka shall give to Buddhism the foremost place" and that "it shall be the duty of the State to foster and protect Buddhism." These revisions also proclaimed that "The Official Language of Sri Lanka shall be Sinhala, as provided by the Official Language Act No.23 of 1956." According to the 1972 revised constitution, there would be a President nominated by Prime Minister. The President so nominated by Prime Minister would act as the constitutional Head of the State, the Executive and the Government, and as the Commander-in-Chief of the Armed Forces. He or she would also appoint the officers of the judiciary. There were no changes to the unitary form of government or to the way of electing representatives to the parliament on the basis of territorial representation.

The 1978 constitutional revisions paved way for a Gaulist model of government with an elected President, a Prime Minister from the parliament and proportional representation in the house by a complex polling system of voting for political parties as well as candidates. According to these revisions, the President elected by the people of the country is the Head of the State, the chief executive of the country and the head of the country's government. The President is also the Commander-in-Chief of the Armed Forces. He or she appoints Prime Minister and Ministers of the cabinet from among the members of parliament, and the judges of the judiciary. No person twice elected to the office of President shall qualify to seek election to that office thereafter. These revisions did not bring about any change to the way of running the country as a unitary state. The 1978 constitutional revisions retained the special place given to Buddhism and Sinhala by the 1972 constitution.

The form of democracy that evolved in the country through these constitutional measures has not helped bring about a lasting solution to its ever-worsening ethnic crisis. Since independence in 1948, the grievances of the Tamil minority have gradually grown in both number and magnitude. This in turn has significantly changed the character of the demands of the Tamil minority in the country over the last fifty years. Its demand prior to independence was to have a fifty-fifty representation in the house of representatives: fifty percent of the seats in the house of representatives to be reserved for minorities and the other fifty percent for the mainstream Sinhalese, purely on communal grounds. Then, after a short spell of "responsive cooperation" till about 1953, the Tamil minority as a whole gave up the fifty-fifty demand and concentrated on a new demand of federalism. This has later changed to complete secession by civil war by 1976. Ever since, the war has continued with no apparent solution in the foreseeable future. Although the war is confined to the north and east, it has become a threat to democracy in the whole country. Post-independent governments that failed to bring about a peaceful solution to the ethnic crisis in the country by democratic means are primarily responsible for this unfortunate situation. Today, the country is devoid of all four basic prerequisites of democracy discussed before: 1. Political freedom, including freedom of thought and speech, free media, and an independent judiciary, 2. Political equality, 3. Political education and maturity, and 4. Respect for human life.

A fresh approach to resolve the ethnic conflict and to establish an effective democratic system in the country is possible only on a solid foundation of equal rights and freedoms for all its peoples. Unequal rights and freedoms in the country must be a thing of the past. There is no question, the country's constitution needs revision, correcting its present imbalances on the rights and freedoms of the individual and building an effective democratic system of governance. The constitution of the country should not give special status to any one particular language or religion, based on the mathematical innovation of its demographic composition. It is important to give official language status to all the three major languages in the country: Sinhalese, Tamil and English. Any person in the country should be able to attend to his or her day to day affairs in a language of his or her choice. According to available statistics, 99.8 percent of the total population of the country treat Sinhalese, Tamil, Malay or English as the mother tongue. Even a person belonging to the rest of the population, including the Veddha community should be able to communicate with the government in his or her own language.

Any new change to the country's constitution must also address all the other contentious issues that have led the country to its present abyss: aboriginal rights, homeland, citizenship and franchise, ethnicity, religion, and democracy. Sri Lanka is unique as far as the nature of the complexity and diversity of its society. Therefore, no one particular form of government good for another country can be equally good for Sri Lanka. No doubt, Sri Lanka must be prepared to learn from experiences elsewhere in the world. At the same time, it is equally important, if not more important, that it learns from its own experiences, both failures and successes. From its own experiences over the last five decades, it has become very clear that any more tinkering with the existing unitary form of government one way or the other will not result in lasting peace and development. Sri Lanka needs a new beginning altogether. It is a beginning delayed for more than fifty years. This new beginning must start with a newly formulated form of government that can effectively meet all the above challenges.

In choosing a new form of government, Sri Lankans surely do not look for anarchism or totalitarianism of any kind. What Sri Lankans need is a democratic system of government that guarantees the rights and freedoms of the individual. It must be a government that voluntarily places firm limits on its own powers that affect the rights and freedoms of individuals. In addition, the government must have proper judicial and legislative systems that can effectively work out conflicts among individuals or groups of individuals. The country's constitution and laws must clearly lay down the rules for resolving all such conflicts. The need to preserve the constitution and the laws of the country must be a primary objective of its political system.

Sri Lankans must weigh the pros and cons of both the unitary and federal systems of governance, before they finally make a choice. The unitary system keeps the principle governing powers at a centre. In this system, the government so centralized creates the regional and local governments. The regional and local governments have only those powers the government at the centre gives them. The United Kingdom and some of its former colonies in Asia and Africa have such unitary systems. The other countries of unitary systems include France, Italy, North Korea, and Cuba. In federal systems, a central government and regional governments share the governing powers. Such systems of government evolve when a number of regions (States or Provinces or Districts) federate in order to establish a nation. Both the central and regional governments get their governing powers from the people they govern. The countries that have federal systems of government include the United States of America, Canada, India, Australia, Austria, Brazil, Mexico, and Switzerland. The federal systems of government require effective decentralization, and this in turn helps rule out the possibility of totalitarianism under such systems.

There can be a parliament, Prime Minister, executive president, and a number of political parties competing at elections under any of these government systems, unitary or federal. For example, there are executive presidents in both unitary France and the federal United States. The unitary United Kingdom has a two-party system similar to that of the United States. At the same time, governments of any particular political ideology, such as communism, socialism, capitalism or any other, could exist under both unitary and federal systems. For example, among the communist countries, the former USSR had a federal system, while China still continues with a unitary system.

Historically Sri Lanka had been mostly a non-unitary state. The periods of single rule during the times of early monarchs had been extremely rare. Even on those rare occasions, the rulers had not brought the entire country under one administration. There were three distinct kingdoms at the time the first European colonial rulers, the Portuguese, came into the country. They captured two of the kingdoms, the Jaffna kingdom and Kotte kingdom, and ruled them with separate administrations. The Dutch who ousted the Portuguese continued with the same separate administrations. The English who replaced the Dutch managed to bring the entire country under their rule in 1815, and started to administer the country the same way, now with three separate administrations, one for the former Jaffna kingdom, one for the former Kotte kingdom, and the other for the newly conquered Kandyan kingdom. The British, however, changed this situation in 1833 by introducing a unified system of administration for the entire country. Ever since the country retained a unitary form of government with an all-island administrative and political structure. Time has proved that it is a structure that lacks the ability to bring about harmonious living of all the ethnic groups in the country as one nation, despite many attempts of decentralization of administration and devolution of some governing powers to regions. The devolution package proposed by President Kumaratunge, as already discussed, would not change this history. What the country now needs is not decentralization of administration or devolution packages striving to maintain the present unitary status quo, but a federal system of governance per se, giving real political power to regions on all matters, other than those of all-island interest.

A New Democratic Model for Sri Lanka

The people of Sri Lanka themselves must finally decide what kind of a democratic governing system is best for them, depending on the needs and aspirations of all its peoples. In their search for a better governing system, Sri Lankans have so far not made any significant progress. The constitutional changes implemented since independence have given too much of governing powers, first to the parliament and then to the executive president. In the process there also has been too much blending of the legislative, executive and judiciary powers of the country. The changes proposed by the 2000 'devolution package' would make the judiciary and the executive powers subjugated to the legislature. Any new governing system for Sri Lanka must uphold the basic principle of separation of powers: legislative, executive and judiciary. A presidential federal system would be better for Sri Lanka, as someone elected by the entire country would lead it. There should be, however, adequate checks and balances in the system to make sure that no one becomes President without considerable support from all the regions in the country. A group of about four persons representing all the major ethnic groups and regions in the country serving together in an executive council as in Switzerland in place of a single chief executive, would have an added advantage. Along with a chief executive (or an executive council) elected by its entire population, Sri Lanka could have a federal system of governance, with three levels of government: federal, regional, and municipal. The regions should have autonomy to run their own affairs, except for those of common interest to the entire country. Lastly, it goes without saying that the country should also remain as a sovereign republic.

Let us now examine in some detail the basic features that could constitute such a presidential, federal, republic model for Sri Lanka, with three levels of government: federal, regional and municipal. The federal government could have other names, like central government or national government. The discussion below would use only one of these names: central government. The central government and regional governments would share the legislative powers of the country, and the municipal governments (now 308 in all: 14 Municipal Councils, 37 Urban Councils, and 257 Pradesheeya Sabhas) would come solely under the jurisdiction of the regional governments. The regional governments could be at provincial or district level. If they are to be at provincial level, each of the former northern and eastern provinces could have a separate regional government, like all other provinces. It would be better still to organize the unit of regional governments at district level, so that every district could have a separate regional government. This would establish self-governance and autonomy, within a federal system of governance, to each of the present 25 Districts. Such a move would enable the minority groups locally concentrated in different districts, like the Indian Tamils in Nuwara Eliya District and the Muslims in Amparai District, to have a greater say on matters affecting their lives and to play a greater role in the country's polity, like any other ethnic or linguistic group.

The regional unit discussed here is different to that of the federal proposal made at the 1927 and 1944 Royal Commissions. The regional units proposed then were made on the basis of the boundaries of the three separate kingdoms that existed at the time the first colonial power came to the island. This was in recognition of the character of the demographic composition of the country at that time, which is no longer the same. Any present proposal made in this regard need to take into account the character of the current demographic composition of the country as discussed above.

Elections to national and regional legislative bodies would be on the basis of proportional representation. The election unit for proportional representation at both national and regional elections would be the district. If the regional governments were at provincial level, the proportional representative election unit for the national senate (explained later) would become the province, not the district. The election of the members of municipal bodies too would be on the basis of proportional representation. The proportionate representative election unit of a municipality would be the entire area under its jurisdiction or a sub-area within it. Such an approach would further minimize under-representation and alienation of minorities in governments at all levels: central, regional, and municipal. It would be important to investigate the need to elect one-half (or any other proportion) of the number of representatives on the basis of proportionate representation and the other half on the first-past-the-post basis - as done in Germany – for all or at least some of the legislative bodies.

The central government at national level would have a central executive body called the National Council and a national legislature elected by the people, and a judiciary appointed by the National Council and ratified by the legislature. The National Council would have four members elected by the entire country to six-year terms. They would serve in place of a single chief executive. Each of the four members would assume the role of the president of the National Council for one-fourth of their common six-year term, eighteen months. The president of the National Council would also become the President of the country, but not its Head of the State. All four members of the National Council together would constitute the Head of the State.

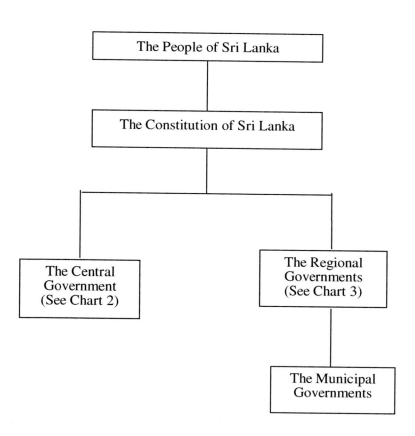

Chart 1: The Three Levels of Government

The People of Sri Lanka

The Constitution of Sri Lanka

The Central Government (See Chart 2)

The Regional Governments (See Chart 3)

The Municipal Governments

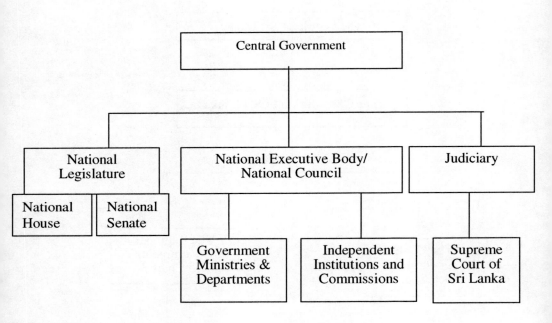

Chart 2: The Central Government

Central Government

National Legislature

National House

National Senate

National Executive Body/ National Council

Judiciary

Government Ministries & Departments

Independent Institutions and Commissions

Supreme Court of Sri Lanka

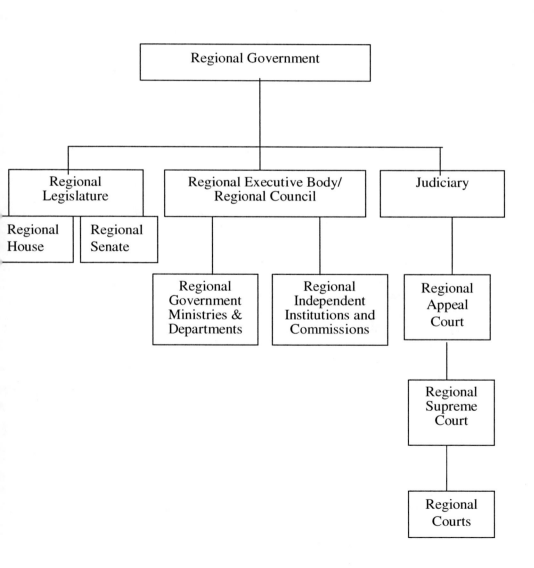

Chart 3: The Regional Government

The four National Council members would come from four different Districts, and would include at least one from the present Western or Southern province, Northern or Eastern Province, and the rest of the country. Such an arrangement would encourage every political party seeking election to the National Council to include members from the different regions and the country's minority communities onto its presidential slate. The 1981 census figures show that the western and southern provinces together have a population almost equal to that of the rest of the country, less the Northern and Eastern Provinces. The Northern province and Eastern province are predominantly occupied by Sri Lankan Tamils. For a political party or an independent group to win a National Council election, it would be required to get at least 20 percent of the votes cast in every province.

A National Council elected by the people of the country would cease to exist, even if one of its members resigns. If a member of the Council becomes incapacitated for performing Council duties by death or any other reason, the rest of the Council would appoint a replacement. Such replacement would be from the same District as that of the member incapacitated or from another District other than those of the remaining members. If all the members of the Council become incapacitated for performing their duties at the same time, the people of the country would elect a new National Council.

The national legislature would be bicameral with two separate bodies, say a House of Representatives (herein after referred to as the House) and a Senate, both elected by the people. One of the two bodies, say the senate, would consist of a certain number of members from each region, while the other, the house, have members elected on a population basis. Two National Council members other than its incumbent president would chair the two legislative bodies, one each. These National Council members, however, would not have legislative powers. But they could be useful in passing a bill in the legislature when it gets into a deadlock with a fifty-fifty division. The national Council member who would not act as president or a chairperson of a legislative body would focus his or her energies on inter-regional matters and national consolidation. These roles of the National Council members also would be limited for a period of eighteen months. Under no circumstances would a National Council member be allowed to assume the same role, as its president or otherwise, for two consecutive eighteen-month periods.

Regional governments would function in a way similar to the central government, with a regional executive body and a bicameral legislature (the House and the Senate) elected by the people and a judiciary appointed by the executive body and ratified by the legislature. The regional executive body would consist of three members coming from three different sub-regions of the region. For example, if the regional governments were at provincial level, the three regional executive members would come from three different districts. The president of the executive body would assume the role of the Governor of the regional government. Each of the three members of the regional executive body assumes the role of its president and the Governor of the region for one-third of its six-year term, two years. Two members of the executive body would chair the two regional legislative bodies. Under no circumstances would a regional executive council member assume the same role, as its president or otherwise, for two consecutive two-year periods.

The central government and regional governments of the country would share the legislative powers of the country. Both levels of governments would derive their power directly from the people themselves. The country's constitution would clearly define the powers both delegated and forbidden to the central government as well as regional governments. The powers neither delegated to the central government by the constitution nor forbidden to the regional governments would be reserved to the regions or to the people of the country at large.

The powers delegated to the central government would cover all common areas of interest to Sri Lankans. These areas would include the nation's defense and security, national Army, Navy and Air Force, calling forth the regional militia, if any, to execute the laws of the country, suppress insurrections and repel invasions, foreign affairs, treaties with other countries, administration of the federal justice system, foreign loans, national financial institutions, elections, commerce, foreign trade, taxation, customs duties, money supply, interregional transport, national railways, civil aviation, shipping and navigation, ocean-waters, ports and harbours, fishing in the ocean waters, posts and telecommunication, inter-regional irrigation and other development projects, national standards for professions and occupations, national archives and museums, archeology, national heritage, the environment, national parks, acquisition of private property, national public service commission, and services to provinces.

The powers forbidden to the central government would include passing laws to punish a person without trial, collection of captivation-taxes, such as a poll tax or a head tax, laying a tax or duty on articles exported from any region, and passing laws preferential or discriminatory to any particular person, group of persons, region or sub-region in the country.

The powers delegated to the regional governments would cover areas such as public safety; maintenance of law and order (police and militia); enforcement of criminal law; direct regional taxation to raise revenue for a regional purpose; borrowing money on the sole credit of the region; administration of justice in the region; regional public service commission; management and sale of the public lands within the region and of the timber and wood thereon; settlement and colonization; agriculture and agrarian services; animal husbandry; irrigation within the region; fish and wildlife; the environment; forests; taxes on mineral rights; public and reformatory prisons; health; welfare; education; municipal institutions within the region; licenses and permits for commercial places and motor vehicles; incorporation of companies within the region; solemnization of marriages in the region; property and civil rights in the region; trade and commerce, excluding foreign trade; co-operatives; business; labour, ports and harbours, other than those managed by the federal government; rural and urban development; cultural activities; regional libraries and museums; regional tourism; and acquisition of private property for the purposes of any matter falling under regional powers.

The powers forbidden to the regional governments would include treaties, money supply, navy or airforce, engaging in war, taxing imports and exports, and passing any kind of discriminatory laws. Regional governments would have no powers to deprive any person of life, liberty or property without due process of law or deny to any person within their jurisdictions the equal protection of the laws.

There would be conjunctive areas, such as the environment, where both the central government and the regional government have a role to play. In addition, the central government would get involved in matters assigned to regional governments, which may require national action or more financial resources than what regional and municipal governments could provide. Going by experience elsewhere, the country as a whole would benefit by vesting in the central government the responsibility for health care, higher education, and social welfare, as a means to maintain common, national standards in these vital areas. In education, the national government's role would, however, be limited to setting broad, national policies and standards and funding. The regional governments would be responsible for curriculum development and regulations. There would be School Boards at regional level to administer the running of primary and secondary schools.

The executive power at central level would be vested in the four-member National Council directly elected by the people for a limited term of six years. The National Council would be the Head of the State and the commander in chief of the Army, Navy and Air Force of Sri Lanka, and of the militia of the regions, if any, when called into national service of the country. The National Council would make treaties, appoint ambassadors, central government ministers, judges of the Supreme Court and all other officers of the central government, with the consent of the national legislature. The National council would require more than a two-thirds majority support from the legislature for treaties, and at least a simple majority support for high level appointments. The members of the National Council would have collective responsibility for the decisions they take. The Council would require the support of at least three of its sitting members to implement any major decision.

The legislative powers of the central government would be vested in the national, bicameral legislature. It would pass laws in matters that fall under the areas of jurisdiction delegated to the national government. The legislature would approve a bill only after both its bodies, the House and the Senate, have passed it in an identical form, with the same wording. Finally the National Council would have to approve the bill. The president of the National Council would either sign or veto the bill on behalf of the Council.

The House and the Senate would share the functions other than strict law making assigned to the national legislature. Such functions would include approving treaties; national government appointments, including members of the judiciary; proposing constitutional improvements and amendments; and impeaching and trying government officials. Impeaching the National Council or any of its members would be a joint task of both the bodies of the national legislature.

The executive power of the region would be vested in the regional executive body elected by the people of the region for a limited term of six years. The Governor and the two other members of the executive body would come from three different sub-regions of the region. These sub-regions could be separate districts, if regional governments were set up at provincial level. The sub-regions could be separate electoral constituencies, if the regional governments were set up at district level. Such a system would result in the representation of the different ethnic and cultural groups in regions at their highest level of decision making.

The regional executive body would command the regional militia, if any, and have the power to appoint regional government ministers, judges, and other officers of the regional government. The executive council would, however, require the consent of the regional legislature for high level appointments, including those of the judges of the Supreme Court of the region. It would be the Governor's responsibility to ensure proper implementation of the laws passed by the region. The Governor would also be able to grant pardons, call the regional legislature into special sessions, and direct the preparation of the regional budget.

The legislative powers of the regional government would be vested in the regional, bicameral legislature. Two regional executive council members would chair the two legislative bodies, one each. These executive council members, however, would have no legislative powers. But they would cast the deciding vote at times of a fifty-fifty division in the legislative bodies they chair. The regional legislature would pass laws in matters that fall under the areas of jurisdiction delegated to the regional governments. The process of law making would be similar to that of the central government. Finally the Governor would either sign or veto a bill passed by the regional legislature on behalf of the regional executive council.

The regional House and the Senate would share the functions of the regional legislature other than law making. Such functions would include approving government appointments, including members of the judiciary; proposing constitutional improvements and amendments; and impeaching and trying government officials. Alternatively one of the two legislative bodies could be responsible for all such functions other than law making. Impeaching the Governor or any other regional executive council member would be a joint task of both the bodies of the regional legislature.

The regional governments would pass their governing powers as much as possible to municipal governments within their jurisdictions. This would clearly establish a bottom-up approach to governance directed by the people at the community level.

Experience clearly shows that it would be easier to solve difficult problems, especially among different ethnic groups, at community level, rather than at higher levels. At community level, people are generally much more accommodating and tolerant with regard to differences on language, religion, ethnicity or culture. In every traditional community, people make a considerate effort to live together as members of one family, disregarding such differences that may exist among them. It is always politicians, especially at national level, who have been instrumental in creating disunity among people, based on such differences. Politicians do this in response to the demands of special interest groups and political campaign contributors, without whom their politics could come to an end. For example, the "Sinhala only in 24 hours" call that ripped Sri Lanka apart was not made by any Sinhalese community in the country, but by a politician at national level. He had made this call not in response to any such demand by any particular linguistic community as such but in response to a special interest group that was backing him. At the same time, the degree of arrogance and elitism among politicians at community level is much lesser than at national level. Thus, transferring political power to local communities as much as possible would be a definite advantage. It would give a real taste of democracy to the people at grass root level and help establish lasting peace and unity in the country.

Then, there would be provision for citizens to demand a popular vote through a referendum on laws passed by the country's legislature. If at least one percent of the total number of registered voters in the country request a popular vote on a law passed by the legislature, the government would have no choice but to hold a referendum. The people would have the power to accept or veto the law. The citizens would also have a right to ask for a popular vote on a new issue altogether. This would require a written petition by at least two- percent of the total number of registered voters. A proposal to change the constitution to amend an existing law or to deal with a completely new issue would require the same degree of support among the registered voters as would be otherwise required for the same change in the legislature.

The timing of elections to the elective bodies at municipal, regional, and central levels could be arranged in a manner to hold the resulting governments responsible for their promised platforms. For this it would be necessary to first divide all the ridings in the five government institutions (municipalities, regional House and Senate, and central House and Senate) to five different groups (say

A, B, C, D, and E) each of similar size and regional representation. Then each of the groups could elect members from its ridings to a different institution each year. This would keep four-fifths of the seats in each elective institution unaffected at any given election. The following table may help understand the electioneering process involved in such a system.

Table 4: Five-Year Unified Election Strategy

Group	Year One	Year Two	Year Three	Year Four	Year Five
A	National Senate	Regional Senate	National House	Munici-pality	Regional House
B	Regional House	National Senate	Regional Senate	National House	Municip-ality
C	Munici-pality	Regional House	National Senate	Regional Senate	National House
D	National House	Munici-pality	Regional House	National Senate	Regional Senate
E	Regional Senate	National House	Munici-pality	Regional House	National Senate

Trevor P. B. M. Moat first made a similar proposal in his paper entitled A Vision of National Unity and Improved Living standards in Canada. [6] As Moat writes, such a system "allows the electorate to support or snub parties in power on a regular basis by electing or rejecting their allies in other governing bodies or in subsequent years." [7] There is always a potential danger that the political party in power could loose up to 20 percent of the total number of seats in the elective bodies in the country in any given year. This would be a significant challenge to any government elected on proportional representative basis, as majorities over 20 percent of the total number of seats is generally rare in such situations.

Every region would have a civil court system consisting of Regional Courts, a Supreme Court, and a Court of Appeal. The Regional Courts would hear cases involving disputes that arise or defendants residing within their respective judicial districts, and those involving claims up to a specified amount. The Supreme Court would hear appeals from Regional Courts and cases of any judicial district and of claims of higher amounts. The Court of Appeal would hear appeals from the Supreme Court. The Supreme Court of Sri Lanka would be the highest level appellate court in the country. It would hear appeals from the Regional Courts of Appeal.

All law enforcement functions would be the responsibility of police authorities. These authorities would function as three groups. Firstly, there would be a national police force responsible to the central government enforcing throughout Sri Lanka laws made by or under the authority of the central legislature. Secondly, there would be a regional police force responsible to the regional government administering justice within regions. Thirdly, municipalities, especially the larger ones, would have a municipal police force responsible to a police commission appointed by the regional government. The national police force would also provide police services to regions and municipalities upon their request under specific policing agreements between the national police force and them. Any such policing agreement between the national police force and municipalities would need the approval of the respective regional governments. The regional police force would have the responsibility to police those municipalities within its region not required, by statute, to have their own police services - especially in the rural areas. In addition, the regional police force would provide its services to other municipalities on request and with specific contracts drawn up with the regional force. The police forces at all levels would be committed to and be involved with community based policing. Such community based policing would include school liaison programs, community relation units, victim services operations, bicycle patrol, and community watchdog groups.

There would also be a security intelligent service agency to protect the national security interests of the country and safeguard all its citizens. This would be a civilian intelligent service with no law enforcing powers. This agency would have national secrets to protect, but would not be a secret organization. The main task of this agency would be to investigate and report on threats to the security of Sri Lanka. While performing its functions, the agency would respect the laws of the country and protect human rights. All its operations would come under close control of the central government.

The National Council of the country would have the power to summon, prorogue and dissolve any one or both of the national legislative bodies, the House and the Senate, at any time. The

National Council would also have the power to remove a regional executive council from office and appoint an interim regional executive council to hold office until a new executive council was duly elected within a specified period of time, say six months. Every regional executive council would have the power to summon, prorogue and dissolve any of the legislative bodies within its regional jurisdiction, the regional House and the regional Senate. An interim executive council appointed by the National Council would have all the executive powers vested in the regional executive council.

The National Council would have the power to declare war and peace. The National Council would also have the power to declare a state of emergency for the entire country or a portion thereof in accordance with the provisions of the country's constitution. With the declaration of emergency for a part or the whole of a region or country, the National Council would have the power to call the militia of any region into the national service.

Checks and Balances

There would also be adequate checks and balances in the proposed federal governing system to enrich and foster bonds of oneness among the different regions of the country. These checks and balances in the governing system would include the following:

Prohibition of discriminatory laws: The country's constitution, the supreme law of the country, would have adequate provisions to prevent the enactment of any form of discriminatory laws, against a person or group of persons belonging to a particular language, religion, ethnicity or culture, by governments at central, regional or municipal level.

Guarantee of fundamental rights and freedoms for all: The country's constitution would guarantee the fundamental rights and freedoms for all people, without exceptions. The fundamental rights would include 1. Democratic rights, 2. Mobility rights, 3. Legal rights, and 4. Equality rights (women's rights included). The fundamental freedoms would include 1. Freedom of conscience and religion, 2. Freedom of thought, belief, opinion and expression, including the freedom of the press and other media of communication; 3. Freedom of peaceful assembly; and 4. Freedom of association.

Unanimous consent for and veto powers over some constitutional amendments: The country's constitution would clearly outline the procedure required to follow in amending it. Amendments that do not alter the intent and purpose of the new, federal constitution as far as its fundamental democratic, federal structure, people's fundamental rights and freedoms and equal treatment to all languages, religions, ethnic backgrounds, and cultures, would require only two-thirds majority consent from the national legislature. All other amendments to change any of the features of the democratic, federal structure of the new constitution or to modify the clauses that deal with the fundamental rights and freedoms or equality status of all languages, religions, and the like would require the unanimous consent of the national legislature. In both situations, the consent of the national legislature would mean the consent of the required degree of support, two-thirds or unanimous as the case may be, from both the legislative bodies at national level, the national House and the Senate. As in any other case, the National Council would have to finally endorse the amendments, so passed by the legislature.

Emphasis and promotion of common values: There would be programs specially designed to emphasize and promote common values among Sri Lankans living in all its regions, such as family, local community, mutual respect, caring and sharing, equal opportunities, justice, liberty, human rights, freedom, self-governance and democracy. By these programs, similarities among all the peoples of the country would become more evident than their differences. This would help bring all the peoples of the country together as a proud nation of an adorable national spirit brightly ornamented with those shared values. Family would be the main building block of society, and there would be deliberate action to enhance its strength and security.

Student Exchange Programs: There would be student exchange programs across the country, especially at secondary and post-secondary educational levels. The central government would sponsor these programs, and give opportunities to students in every region to study in an outside region. This would help develop friendships among Sri Lankans across the country.

Promotion of mutually beneficial trade among regions: The central government would run programs especially designed to promote trade among regions to their mutual benefit. This would facilitate each and every region in the country to plan and implement its economic production goals taking into account the comparative advantages of its resources, and market its products to the entire country. Such a strategy would help every region achieve accelerated growth patterns, and jointly boost the national economy in an unprecedented manner.

Equalization Program: This program would offset the economic disparities among the different regions in the country that may result due to the differences in the strengths of their respective economies. This program would be nationally sponsored and financed, and would help establish in the regions of weaker economies the same benefits as in the ones of stronger economies. It would involve regional development, equalization payments, and a national network of social security, based on the relative needs of different regions and their resources. Equalization payments in the critical areas of health, education, the environment, and the like would always receive highest budgetary priorities at central government level. Regions would have equal accessibility to benefits and transfer payments.

The above checks and balances to enrich and foster bonds of oneness among the different regions of the country complete the basic features that could constitute a federal, presidential republican model for Sri Lanka. All the features discussed in the model are important. By living in Canada, the author has been able to think objectively, free from any influence of the existing divisive politics in Sri Lanka in developing the model. The author does not assume that it is in a final form for implementation; instead, he only believes that it would widen the horizon of the scope of debates on constitutional changes now needed.

It is left to the Sri Lankans living in Sri Lanka to finally decide how best to use this model in improving their country's constitution. It is they who should decide on the final form of the constitutional changes the country now needs. For example having a national executive council in place of a single president is good in principle. However, whether the council should comprise of two, three or four members is debatable. On the one hand, an odd number (say three or five) of members may be more workable, as this would not lead to a 50-50 split within the council on any issue. On the other hand, having four members would have a better representation of the people as discussed earlier. Having four members, in fact, can even result in national executive councils with 50 percent of its members representing the country's minorities, at least occasionally. If, however, the decision is to have three members, they should come from the three different regions suggested in the model. Such regional representation at the highest executive level in the country would be consistent with the traditional divisions of the three different kingdoms existed before the arrival of the European colonialists.

At the same time, the regional governments could be at the provincial or district level. The country has nine provinces (if North and East taken separately) and 25 districts. In this situation, one might think that having regional governments at provincial level is better, as governments at district level may appear to be too many. Having regional governments at district level would, however, have added advantages, especially in favour of the scattered minorities in the country, as discussed in the model. Going by similar experience elsewhere 25 regional governments in a federal state of Sri Lanka would not be too many. For example, Switzerland, which is smaller in size, has 26 regional governments (cantons) that retain attributes of sovereignty. Its land area is less than two-thirds of that of Sri Lanka, and its total population is not even one half of Sri Lanka's.

The model, with or without further improvements, would have the power to bring about a lasting solution to the current ethnic crisis. It would offer a non-communal approach to any kind of communal conflicts in the country. It would not decide the fate of any linguistic, religious or ethnic minority based on mathematical innovations of the country's demographic composition. Instead, it would help evolve a new Sri Lankan society with equal rights and freedoms for all its peoples.

The new form of government envisaged by this model would not only bring about a lasting solution to the current ethnic crisis, but would also make Sri Lanka a superb democracy in the world. The reader might notice that some other democracies in the world, including India, Canada, Australia, Switzerland and the United States of America already have many features of the model under consideration. This has come about as the author has taken into account experiences outside Sri Lanka in developing the model, with no special preference to follow the governing system of any particular country. The author believes that the model proposed for Sri Lanka is best suitable for the specific needs of Sri Lankans.

With the implementation of such a new governing model, Sri Lankans should be able to free themselves from the current institutional structure in the polity and administration of their country that has kept them away from real solutions to their problems. It is a structure Sri Lankans should have abolished at the time of independence in 1948. But this has not happened. So, Sri Lankans should do it now. Once implemented, the proposed new governing model would put an end to the present centralized, dynastic and elite rule of Sri Lanka, and give a taste of real democracy to its entire people for the very first time. In such a democratic governing model, people would be closer to their governments at all levels, more than ever before, and would be able to influence decision-making affecting their present and future well-being in their villages, towns, municipalities, districts, provinces, and country. Then, the development-needs of rural areas in the country would get the same attention as those of its towns and cities. The policies of trilingualism and secularism inherent in the model would enable every person in the country to live free of any kind of intimidation from a language or religion not akin to him or her, irrespective of where one lives.

In such a new governing system, there would be much greater involvement of the public at large in the formulation of the country's national policies, than now. The minorities in the country, based on language, religion or ethnicity, would begin to enjoy the same rights and freedoms as those of the majorities. There would be a visible presence of all different ethnic groups in the key positions of the governing institutions of the country, both political and administrative, at all levels. Any one in the country, a Sinhalese, Tamil, Muslim, Burgher, or a Veddha, would be able to enter politics at the grass roots level and climb his or her way up to the highest executive level of the country merely on merit. All ethnic groups in the country, the Sinhalese, Sri Lankan Tamils, Muslims, Indian Tamils, Burghers, Veddhas, and others, would come to the front and centre of the country's polity. They all would have equal opportunities in anything and everything in the country. This would end the present marginalization of the country's minorities in its affairs, and give birth to a new nation of proud Sri Lankans of many languages, religions and ethnic and cultural backgrounds, all enjoying the same rights, freedoms and opportunities. Only a road to such a meaningful, new Sri Lankan nation can bring about hope for a lasting solution to the current ethnic crisis.

This governing model also has checks and balances to ensure that the right people are there in the right positions to run the country. For example, the need for the President or National Council to get advice and consent of the national legislature in making appointments to the national cabinet and other high positions in the executive, judiciary and administrative sectors of government would prevent the wrong people in strategic positions. This would help Sri Lanka take advantage of the skills and abilities at the highest levels in the country in running its affairs, free from nepotism, political maneuvering and misadventures. This, in turn, will help rebuild much needed trust between the country's government and the people it serves.

With the new opportunity for all Sri Lankans to learn and work in English, the 'sky would not be the limit' for their future generations. Sri Lankans would not be left behind the technologically advancing world. Instead, they would begin to keep abreast with the rest of the world, and become active partners in making the world a better place for all its inhabitants.

Process for Change

It is important to note that the change of the governing system of Sri Lanka from its present centralized form to such a federal model could come about only through a major amendment to its constitution. According to the existing constitution, any amendment to it is possible only with a two-thirds or larger majority support in the legislature. This, however, cannot come about in the current political climate, as long as public opinion is against such a change. What happened to the devolution package bill in the legislature in 2000 clearly indicates that there is a dominant section of the public who would go to any extent to derail efforts to implement such a change. Legislators, both individually and as political parties, would simply succumb to public pressure, as their political future hinge on public opinion. If a political party in power or opposition goes against public opinion, it will have to face the wrath of the people at the next election. Thus, in the final analysis, the real power to implement or not to implement such a change to the constitution of the country lies with its people. This is a fact of life most people simply do not notice.

Therefore, it is critical for the people of the country to understand all options available for further improvement of the constitution of their country. After all, the country and its constitution belong to its people and not to its politicians and the public is far more intelligent than politicians are inclined to believe. However, the people of the country never had an opportunity to fully understand the related issues and discuss among themselves how to improve the governing system of the country for the benefit of all its citizens. What they have so far heard and seen is mostly the propaganda material of the chauvinist and dynastic-style power struggles of the political elite. So, it is critically important to have a process of political education and involvement of the people to give them the ability to make well-informed decisions about the future of their country.

The people of Sri Lanka should not wait for any particular leader, either in government or opposition, to ceremoniously initiate such a process of political education and involvement. People must initiate the process on their own with discussions and debates among themselves on the future of their country, wherever they meet and talk: farmers and fishermen in their villages; students and teachers in their schools, colleges and universities; others in their workshops, factories, offices, prisons; and so on.

Such discussions and debates should constitute a deliberate, rational and democratic process, involving all the people of the country, in an atmosphere of reason, cooperation, goodwill and mutual respect. It should unleash objective and dispassionate discussions and debates among the people on possible solutions to their current problems and what constitutional changes could be beneficial for the future of their country. In these discussions and debates, Sri Lankans should ask themselves the following three basic questions:

- What kind of country do they think they now have in terms of its geography, demographic formation, constitution, system of government, and the like?
- What kind of country do they think they should have?
- What kind of constitutional changes do they think should happen to build the kind of country they think they should have?

The research community and the academics in history, political science, sociology, cultural anthropology and other related subjects have a very important role to play in all this. Their primary role should be to educate the public by analyzing the different political and governing systems in the world and by drawing parallels and comparisons with the present governing system in Sri Lanka. The media has an equally important role to play in these discussions and debates. It can introduce regular constitutional debates and discussions in local and national newspapers, radio and television programs, and the like. At the same time, it can publicize the debates and discussions going on elsewhere, and try to reach the unreachable.

The government of Sri Lanka too has a role to play in facilitating this political education process of the people. It can prepare and distribute upon request a discussion and debate kit containing the basic questions people should be asking at the discussions and debates, reporting sheets, and the like to interested groups. It can also run toll-free telephone hotlines with specially trained operators to express their opinions on the subject matters in question. Further, the government can run special programs to encourage poets, artists, drama groups, and the like to boldly put forward their ideas about the future of the country in their own creative, artistic way. While all this is going on, the government can distribute through post offices, schools and other learning institutions the details of different proposals for constitutional changes made by individuals and organizations in all three languages. Such details can appear in the form of questions and answers, especially those of sensitive nature, not leaving room for misinterpretation by any extremist groups.

One might question how long such a process would take. The Author's own experience elsewhere in similar situations suggests that the time needed for such a process would not be as long as one would first think. Once the process starts, it would develop fast, reaching all parts of a country. As a result, the time such a process would take could be as short as one year, depending on the extent of voluntary contribution to the process. Under any event, in the absence of such a process, the post-independent leaders of the country have failed to develop a meaningful governing system acceptable to all its peoples for more than five decades now. Sri Lanka should have had such a public process in the late forties as part of an exercise to plan a proper governing system for the newly independent Sri Lanka. If this did happen at that time, the country would not have faced an ethnic crisis like the one of today.

Such a process of discussions and debates would fulfill an important pre-requisite to democracy: political education. It will liberate the people from the bond of the present chauvinist, dynastic and elite politics, and create a peaceful environment for the necessary democratic and constitutional changes the country now needs. As the people have already discussed and learnt the pros and cons of all possible scenarios by the time of the actual changes, there would be no more surprises to incite unmanageable protests against them. In such a scenario, the public opinion would surely build in favour of a new constitution to establish a system of government acceptable to all the peoples of the country. With such a process of political education, Sri Lankans would be able to invent the best ever democratic form of government for a multi-ethnic and multi-linguistic country such as theirs.

The process for change pursued by the political leaders is very different. It appears to have no important role for the general public of Sri Lanka. It starts with secret talks among the leaders of the political parties and the separatist group(s) and ends in the legislative assembly. These political leaders have engaged foreign governments, first the government of India and later the Royal Norwegian Government, as a facilitator of these secret talks. The Sri Lankan leaders have also sought assistance from the rest of the international community to strike a deal between the two warring parties, and appear to depend on a safety net of world opinion as a last resort to succeed in their secret talks. Thus the political leaders of Sri Lanka expect the whole world to participate in their secret talks with the LTTE, in one way or another. The only group of people on Earth deliberately left out of the participation of these secret talks is the general public of Sri Lanka.

The plan of the country's leaders has always been to first strike a secret deal with the warring parties and then try to enact it in the legislature by securing the needed two-thirds support among the legislators. Getting two-thirds support in the legislature for anything is, however, difficult, due to the extent of division within the legislature on party lines, especially between the two dominant parties, the UNP and the PA. In government, the leaders of both these major parties have appeared to depend on acts of political backstabbing, underhand deals, and even bribery, to overcome that difficulty.

Perhaps these leaders may not see through their dynastic and elite lenses anything wrong in such a process for change. If it succeeds, Sri Lanka would have a "solution" to its ethnic crisis acceptable to Norway, Sweden, Denmark, the United Kingdom, the United States of America, and perhaps the entire international community. Then, the political leaders of Sri Lanka may even qualify for the Noble Prize for peace in the eyes of the international community. The only hitch here is that a solution so reached may still not be acceptable to a majority of the Sinhalese, Tamils, Muslims, Burghers, and Veddhas of Sri Lanka. Thus the process of change pursued by the political leaders of Sri Lanka robs Sri Lankans of their democratic rights and might put them in a worse situation than ever before.

Every time the UNP or the PA forms a government after an election, it claims to have a clear mandate from the people of the country to solve its ethnic crisis. At no election, however, have any of these political parties told the public how it intends to do that in specific terms. Thus the general public never knows the specific proposals these parties make at the secret meetings with the LTTE. Nevertheless, the government formed by either party expects full cooperation from the public for what it agrees with the LTTE at their secret meetings. If the general public rise up against the position taken by the government, critics say, it would resort to its old tactics of rule by emergencies and curfews, repression and terror, detaining people without trial, intimidating innocent people, harassing political opponents, silencing the media, passing retroactive penal laws, setting up special courts, and by making the ordinary people of the country look up to its leaders in reverence and supplicate before them.

During every cease-fire arranged between the government and the LTTE, the people have enjoyed a spell of peace. The rulers at the times of these cease-fires have always tried to convince the people that the country is now ready for permanent peace, knowing very well that the slightest disagreement with the LTTE would end the cease-fire. Cease-fires are, no doubt, important, but they are not the solution to the ethnic crisis of Sri Lanka.

NOTES

1.   S. U. Deraniyagala. (1996, September 8).Pre-and protohistoric Settlement in Sri Lanka. Proceedings of the X111 Congress,

Forli'-Italia [Online]. Volume 5, 22 paragraphs. Available: http://members.tripod.com/~hettiarachchi/dera1.html   [2001, March 24].

2. Sri Lanka News – Colombo Page [Homepage of ColomboPage Sri Lankan Internet Newspaper],[Online]. (2001, November 7–Last Update). Available: http://www.colombopage.com/ [2001, November 7].

3. Veddhas-Virtual Library Sri Lanka [Homepage of Virtual Library of Sri Lanka], [Online]. (2001, March 24). Available: http://members.tripod.com/~hettiarachchi/dera1.html   [2001, March 24].

4. Herath Ranbanda, Democratic Socialism, (Matale, 1979), pp. 34-35.

5. Ibid., p. 35.

6. Ibid., p. 36.

7. Frank Stronach (ed.), As Prime Minister, I Would....., (Toronto, 195), p.29.

8. Ibid.

CHAPTER 5: CONCLUSION

This book has examined in detail the different aspects of the Sri Lankan ethnic crisis, including its historic context, the factors that influence it, and a peaceful, democratic means to end it. Initially, Sri Lanka was under the rule of chieftains and monarchs for thousands of years. During this period, dynastic wars and family feuds characterized the country's political landscape. Later, three European colonial powers ruled the country, the first two only partially. The rule of these colonial powers lasted for four and a half centuries, until Sri Lanka became independent in 1948. The 1948 independence did not reinstate native chieftains and monarchs. Instead, it gave the people of the country the power to rule themselves. For effective and meaningful realization of self-rule, however, the country first needed a new, democratic system of government with equal rights, freedoms and opportunities for its people. What is blatantly evident from this book is that this has not materialized. In place of such a new, democratic governing system, the politics of the post-independence leaders have evolved into an oligarchic ruling system dominated by a few dynastic-type elite leaders, disguised as democracy. In their post-independence power struggles, these leaders have resorted to archaic, divisive politics based on ethnicity and language. Fifty years of such divisive politics has now resulted in a deadly ethnic crisis with civil wars and suicide bombings.

It is the people of the country that are paying the price for the failures and misadventures of the post-independence leaders. Today the people are divided on the basis of ethnicity and language more than ever before. There has been no meaningful program for national consolidation and integration. Minorities are attempting to resort to separatism as the only way to live with dignity in their own country. Hatred by hatred and an eye for an eye have become the adorable tools of conflict resolution. The 20-year LTTE separatist war claims at least 10 human lives a day, except during times of cease-fire. The civilians living on both sides of the warfront suffer from the cessation of civil society and the indiscriminate killing of innocent people, extortion, kidnappings, and rape. People everywhere in the country have a growing sense of fear, uncertainty and despair about the future of themselves and their children. The government is on the verge of insolvency. The country's economy has melted down to the rock bottom. The cost of living has skyrocketed. The rate of inflation is exceptionally high. The Sri Lankan Rupee has dived down to its lowest value ever.

What the people in every part of Sri Lanka want is a quality of life in an environment of peace and harmony. The experience so far, however, clearly shows that it is simply not possible under the present governing system. Further attempts to continue with the same governing system would only worsen the current crisis and all the above impairments that go with it. The specific long-term solution to the ethnic crisis through a new governing system suggested in this book would correct this unfortunate situation. It is a solution not to take the country back to chieftains and monarchs or to any new form of colonialism. It is a solution for Sri Lanka and its people to go forward into the 21st century as a united, multi-ethnic, independent, secular, democratic nation. This is a new approach to the present ethnic crisis, which needs to be implemented not through secret talks among leaders, but through open and direct participation of the people of the country. This solution was developed on the strengths of the proven successes of democracies in plural societies throughout the world. It can give a new life to Sri Lanka and its entire people. It is certainly not a solution forced upon the people of Sri Lanka. It must be left to the Sri Lankans living in Sri Lanka to decide on its final form.

In working for a peaceful, democratic solution to the current ethnic crisis, the people of Sri Lanka must have faith in themselves and in the power of truth and love, instead of guns and ammunition. They need to first understand and accept the historic and present context of the crisis, however unpleasant it might be. This would enable them to establish a solid foundation for the future of their country on the strength of truth and love. Sri Lankans should and must start thinking that they all together constitute one big family, and start loving each other across the borders of ethnicity, language and religion in a true spirit of "One Lanka –One Nation, One Nation – One Family." With such a change of heart, Sri Lankans should be able to contemplate what has happened in the past and exchange ideas among themselves on their country's future in a dispassionate and objective manner. Then only they will be able to make well-informed decisions as to what needs to be done to make their country a place fit to live in for all. This book gives the basics necessary for such an exchange of ideas among the people of Sri Lanka.

In short, this book shows a path to a peaceful and democratic solution to the bloody ethnic crisis in Sri Lanka. It is a path all Sri Lankans should explore at this darkest hour of their country's history. The author wishes that Sri Lankans would have the courage and vision to take up this challenge and become a shining example to the world of a country that solved a bloody ethnic crisis in a peaceful manner.

APPENDIX

Appendix 1: The Kandyan Convention

At a Convention, held on 2nd day of March, in the year of Christ 1815, and the Singalese year 1736, at the Palace in the City of Kandy, between His Excellency Lieutenant-General Robert Brownrigg, Governor and Commander-in-Chief in and over the British Settlements and Territories in the Island of Ceylon, acting in the Danle and on behalf of His Majesty George the Third, King, and His Royal Highness George Prince of Wales, Regent of the United Kingdom of Great Britain and Ireland, on the one part, and the Adikars, Dissaves, and other principal chiefs of the Kandyan provinces, on behalf of the inhabitants, and in presence of the Mohottales, Coraals, Vidaans, and other subordinate head men from the several provinces, and of the people then and there assembled, on the other part, it is agreed and established as follows:

Ist. That the cruelties and oppressions of the Malabar ruler, in the arbitrary and unjust infliction of bodily tortures, and the pains of death, without trial and sometimes without an accusation or the possibility of a crime, and in the general contempt and contravention of all civil rights, have become flagrant, enormous, and intolerable; the acts and maxims of His Government being equally and entirely devoid of that justice which should secure the safety of his subjects, and of that good faith which might obtain a beneficial intercourse with the neighbouring settlements.

2nd. That the Rajah Sri Wickreme Rajah Sinha, by the habitual violation of the chief and most sacred duties of a sovereign, has forfeited all claims to the title, or the powers annexed to the same, and is declared fallen and deposed from the office of king; his family and relatives, whether in the ascending, descending, or collateral line, and whether by affinity or blood, are also for ever excluded from the throne; and all claim and title of the Malabar race to the dominion of the Kandyan provinces is abolished and extinguished.

3rd. That all male persons being, or pretending to be, relations of the late Rajah Sri Wickreme Rajah Sinha, either by affinity or blood, and whether in the ascending, descending or collateral line, are hereby declared enemies to the government of the Kandyan provinces, and excluded and prohibited from entering those provinces, on any pretence whatever, without a written permission for the purpose, by the authority of the British government, under the pains and penalties of martial law , which is hereby declared to be in force for that purpose; and all male persons of the Malabar caste, now expelled from the said provinces, are, under the same penalties, prohibited from returning, except with the permission before mentioned.

4th. The dominion of the Kandyan provinces is vested in the sovereign of the British empire, and to be exercised through the Governors or Lieutenant-Governors of Ceylon for the time being, and their accredited agents, saving to the Adikars, Dissaves, Mohottales, Coralls, Vidaans, and all other chief and subordinate native head men, lawfully appointed by authority of the British government; the rights, privileges, and powers of their respective offices, and to all classes of the people the safety of their persons and property, with their civil rights and immunities, according to the laws, institutions, and customs established and in force amongst them.

5th. The religion of Boodhoo, professed by the chiefs and inhabitants of these provinces, is declared inviolable; and its rights, ministers, and places of worship, are to be maintained and protected.

6th. Every species of bodily torture, and all mutilation of limb, member, or organ, are prohibited and abolished.

7th. No sentence of death can be carried into execution against any inhabitant, except by the written warrant of the British Governor or Lieutenant-Governor for the time being, founded on a report of the case made to him through the accredited agent or agents of the government resident in the interior, in whose presence all trials for capital offences are to take place.

8th. Subject to these conditions, the administration of civil and criminal justice and police, over the Kandyan inhabitants of the said provinces, is to be exercised according to established forms, and by the ordinary authorities, saving always the inherent right of government to redress grievances and reform abuses, in all instances whatever, particular or general, where such interposition shall become necessary .

9th. Over all other persons, civil or military, residing in or resorting to these provinces, not being Kandyans, civil and criminal justice, together with police, shall, until the pleasure or His Majesty's government in England may be otherwise declared, be administered in the manner following:

First, All persons, not being commissioned or non-commissioned military officers, soldiers, or followers of the army, usually held liable to military discipline, shall be subject to the magistracy of the accredited agent or the agents of the British government, in all cases except of murder, which shall be tried by special commissions, to be issued from time to time by the governor for that purpose. Provided always, as to such charges of murder wherein any British subject may be defendant, who might be tried for the sanle by the laws of United Kingdom of Great Britain and Ireland, in force for the trial of offences committed by British subjects in foreign parts no such British subject shall be tried on any charge of murder, alleged to have been perpetrated in the Kandyan provinces, otherwise than by virtue of such laws of the United Kingdom.

Second, Commissioned or non-commissioned military officers, soldiers, or followers of the army, usually held amenable to military discipline, shall, in all civil and criminal cases, wherein they may be defendants, be liable to the laws, regulations, and customs of war, reserving to the governor and commander-in-chief, in all cases falling under this ninth article, an unlimited right of review over every proceeding, civil or military, had by virtue thereof, and reserving also full power to make such particular provisions, conformable to the general spirit of the said article, as may be found necessary to carry its principle into full effect.

lOth. Provided always, that the operation of the several preceding clauses shall not be contravened by the provisions of temporary or partial proclamation published during the advance of the army; which provisions, in so far as incompatible with the said preceding articles, are hereby repealed.

11 th. The royal dues and revenues of the Kandyan provinces are to be managed and collected for His Majesty's use, and the support of the provincial establishment, according to lawful custom, and under the direction and superintendence of the accredited agent or agents of the British government.

12th. His Excellency the Governor will adopt provisionally and recommend to the confirmation of his Royal Highness the Prince Regent, in the name and on behalf of His Majesty, such dispositions in favour of the trade of these provinces, as may facilitate the export of their products, and improve the returns, whether in money, or in salt, cloths, or other commodities, useful and desirable to the inhabitants of the Kandyan country
.

God save the King!
By His Excellency's command,
JAMES SUTHERLAND,

Dep. Secretary.

Source: Henry Marshall: *Ceylon.*

Appendix 2: Bandaranaike–Chelvanayagam Pact

The following are the two joint statements issued by the Prime Minister and representatives of the Federal Party on 26 July 1957.
Statement of the general principles of the agreement between the Prime Minister and the Federal Party.

"Representatives of the Federal Party have had a series of discussions with the Prime Minister in an effort to resolve the differences of opinion that had been growing and creating tension.

" At an early stage of these conversations it became evident that it was not possible for the Prime Minister to accede to some of the demands of the Federal Party.

"The Prime Minister stated that from the point of view of the Government he was not in a position to discuss the setting up of a federal constitution of regional autonomy or any step which would abrogate the Official Language Act. The question then arose whether it was possible to explore the possibility of an adjustment without the Federal Party abandoning or surrendering any of its fundamental principles and objectives.

" At this stage the Prime Minister suggested an examination of the Government's draft Regional Councils Bill to see whether provision could to made under it to meet reasonably some of the matters in this regard which the Federal Party had in view.

"The agreements so reached are embodied in a separate document.

"Regarding the language issue the Federal Party reiterated its stand for parity, but in view of the position of the Prime Minister in this matter they came to an agreement by way of an adjustment. They pointed out that it was important for them that there should be a recognition or Tamil as a national language and that the administrative work in the Northern and Eastern Provinces should be done in Tamil.

"The Prime Minister stated that as mentioned by him earlier, it was not possible for him to take any step which would abrogate the Official Language Act.

USE OF TAMIL

" After discussions it was agreed that recognition of Tamil as the language of a national minority of Ceylon, and that four points mentioned by the Prime Minister should include provision that, without infringing on the position of the Official Language Act, the language of administration in the Northern and eastern provinces should be Tamil and that any necessary provision be made for the non- Tamil speaking minorities in the Northern and Eastern provinces.

"Regarding the question of Ceylon citizenship for people of Indian descent and revision of the Citizenship Act, the representatives of the Federal Party put forward their views to the Prime Minister and pressed for an early settlement.

"The Prime Minister indicated that the problem would receive early consideration.

"In view of these conclusions the Federal Party stated that they were withdrawing their proposed satyagraha.

REGIONAL COUNCILS
"(A) Regional areas to be defined in the Bill itself by embodying them in a schedule thereto

"(B) That the Northern Province is to form one Regional area whilst the Eastern Province is to be divided into two or more regional areas.

"(C) Provision is to be made in the Bill to enable two or more regions to amalgamate even beyond provincial limits; and for one region to divide itself subject to ratification by Parliament Further provision is to be made in the Bill for two or more regions to collaborate for specific purposes of common interest.

DIRECT ELECTIONS
"(D) Provision is to be made for direct election of regional councilors. Provision is to be made for a delimitation commission or commissions for carving out electorates. The question of MP's representing districts falling within regional areas to be eligible to function as chairmen is to be considered. The question of Government Agents being Regional Commissioners is to be considered. The question of supervisory functions over larger towns, strategic towns and municipalities is to be looked into.

SPECIAL POWERS
"(E) Parliament is to delegate powers and to specify them in the Act. It was agreed that Regional Councils should have powers over

specified subjects including agriculture, cooperatives, lands and land development, colonization, education, health, industries and fisheries, housing and social services, electricity, weather schemes and roads. Requisite definition of powers will be made in the Bill.

COLONIZATION SCHEMES

"(F) It was agreed that in the matter of colonization schemes the powers of the Regional Councils should include the power of select allottees to whom lands within their area of authority shall be alienated and also power to select personnel to be employed for work on such schemes. The position regarding the area at present administered b~ the Gal Oya Board in this matter requires consideration.

TAXATION BORROWING

"(G) The powers in regard to the Regional Councils vested in the Minister of Local Government in the draft Bill to be revised with a view to vesting control in Parliament wherever necessary.

"(H) The Central Government will provide block grants to the Regional Councils. The Principles on which the grants will be computed will be gone into. The Regional Councils shall have powers of taxation and borrowing.

Appendix 3: Dudley Senanayake–Chelvanayagam Pact

Mr. Dudley Senanayake and Mr. S.J. V. Chelvanayagam met on the March 24th 1965 and discussed matters relating to some problems over which the Tamil- speaking people were concerned, and Mr. Senanayake agreed that action on the following lines would be taken by him to ensure a stable Government.

1. Action will be taken early under the Tamil Language Special Provisions Act to make Tamil as the Language of administration and of record in the Northern and Eastern provinces. Mr. Senanayake also explained that it was the policy of his party that a Tamil-speaking person should be entitled to transact business in Tamil throughout the Island.

2. Mr. Senanayake stated that it was the policy of his party to amend the Language of the Courts Act to provide for legal proceedings in the Northern and Eastern Provinces to be conducted and recorded in Tamil.

3. Action will be taken to establish District Councils in Ceylon; vested with powers over subjects to be mutually agreed upon between the two leaders. It was agreed, however that the Government should have power under the law to give directions to such Councils in the national interest.

4. The Land Development Ordinance will be amended to provide that all citizens of Ceylon be entitled to the allotment of land under the Ordinance. Mr. Senanayake further agreed that in the granting of land under colonization schemes the following priorities be observed in the Northern and Eastern provinces.

(A) Land in the Northern and Eastern Provinces should in the first instance be granted to landless persons in the District;

(B) Secondly to Tamil speaking persons resident in the Northern and Eastern Provinces, and;

(C) Thirdly to other citizens in Ceylon, preference being given to Tamil citizens in the rest of the Island.

Dudley Senanayake   S.J.V. Chelvanayagam
March 24th 1965

Appendix 4: Indo-Sri Lanka Agreement, 1987

The President of the Democratic Socialist Republic of Sri Lanka, His Excellency Mr. J.R. Jayawardene and the Prime Minister of the Republic of India, His Excellency Mr. Rajiv Gandhi having met at Colombo on 29 July 1987.

Attaching utmost importance to nurturing, intensifying and strengthening of traditional friendship of Sri Lanka and India and acknowledging the imperative need of resolving the ethnic problem of Sri Lanka and the consequent violence and for the safety, well being and prosperity of people belonging to all communities in Sri Lanka.

Have this day entered into the following Agreement to fulfil this objective.

In this context.

desiring to preserve the unity sovereignty and territorial integrity of Sri Lanka:

acknowledging that Sri Lanka is a multi-ethnic and a multi-lingual plural society consisting, *inter alia,* of Sinhalese, Tamils, Muslims (Moors) and Burghers:

1.3 *recognizing* that each ethnic group has a distinct cultural and linguistic identity which has to be carefully nurtured.

1.4 *also recognizing* that the Northern and the Eastern Provinces have been areas of historical habitation of Sri Lankan Tamil speaking peoples, who have at all times hitherto lived together in this territory with other ethnic groups:

1.5 *conscious* of the necessity of strengthening the forces contributing to the unity, sovereignty and territorial integrity of Sri Lanka and preserving its character as a multi-ethnic multi-lingual and multi-religious plural society in which all citizens can live in equality, safety and harmony and prosper and fulfil their aspirations:

2. Resolve that:

2.1 Since the Government of Sri Lanka proposes to permit adjoining Provinces to join to form one administrative unit and also by a Referendum to separate as may be permitted to the Northern and Eastern Provinces as outlined below.

2.2 During the period, which shall be considered an interim period, (i.e. from the date of the elections to the Provincial Council, as specified in para 2.8 to the date of the referendum as specified in para 2.3) the Northern and Eastern Provinces as now constituted, will form one administrative unit, having one elected Provincial council. Such a unit will have one Governor, one Chief Minister and one Board of Ministers.

2.3 There will be a referendum on or before 31st December, 1988 to enable the people of the Eastern Province to decide whether:

(a) The Eastern Province should remain linked with the Northern Province as one administrative unit, and continue to be governed together with the Northern Province as specified in para 2.2 or

(b) The Eastern Province should constitute a separate administrative unit having its own distinct Provincial Council with a separate Governor, Chief Minister and Board of Ministers.

The President may, at his discretion decide to postpone such a referendum.

2.4 All persons who have been displaced due ~o ethnic violence, or other reasons will have the right to vote in such a referendum. Necessary conditions to enable them to return to areas from where they were displaced will be created.

2.5 The referendum when held will be monitored by a committee headed by the Chief Justice: a member appointed by the President nominated by the Government of Sri Lanka: and a member appointed by the President, nominated by the representatives of the Tamil speaking people of the Eastern Province.

2.6 A simple majority will be sufficient to determine the result of the referendum.

2.7 Meetings and other forms of propaganda, permissible within the laws of the country will be allowed before the referendum.

2.8 Elections to Provincial Councils will be held within the next three months, in any event before 31st December 1987. Indian observers will be invited for elections to the Provincial Council of the North and East

2.9 The Emergency will be lifted in the Eastern and Northern Provinces by August 15, 1987. A cessation of hostilities will come into effect all over the Island within 48 hours of the signing of this Agreement All arms presently held by militant groups will be surrendered in accordance with an agreed procedure to authorities to be designated by the Government of Sri Lanka.

Consequent to the cessation of hostilities and the surrender of arms by militant groups, the Army and other security personnel will be confined to barracks in camps as on 25th May 1987. The process of surrendering of arms and the confining of security personnel moving back to barracks shall be completed within 72 hours of the cessation of hostilities coming into effect.

2.10 The Government of Sri Lanka will utilize for the purpose of law enforcement and maintenance of security in the Northern and Eastern Provinces the same organizations and mechanisms of Government as are used in the rest of the country.

2.11 The President of Sri Lanka will grant a general amnesty to political and other prisoners now held in custody under the Prevention of Terrorism Act and other Emergency laws, and to combatants, as well as to those persons accused, charged and/or convicted under these laws. The Government of Sri Lanka will make special efforts to rehabilitate militant youth with a view to bringing them back into the mainstream of national life. India will co-operate in the process.

2.12 The Government of Sri Lanka will accept and abide by the above provisions and expect all others to do likewise.

2.13 If the framework for the resolutions is accepted, the Government of Sri Lanka will implement the relevant proposals forthwith.

2.14 The Government of India will underwrite and guarantee the resolutions, and co-operate in the implementation of these proposals.

2.15 These proposals are conditional to an acceptance of the proposals negotiated from 4.5.1986 to 19.12.1986. Residual matters not finalized during the above negotiations shall be resolved between India and Sri Lanka within a period of six weeks of signing this Agreement These proposals are also conditional to the Government of India co-operating directly with the Government of Sri Lanka in their implementation.

2.16 These proposals are also conditional to the Government of India taking the following actions if any militant groups operating in Sri Lanka do not accept this framework of proposals for a settlement, namely,

(a) India will take all necessary steps to ensure that Indian territory is not used for activities prejudicial to the unity, integrity and security of Sri Lanka.

(b) The Indian Navy/Coast Guard will co-operate with the Sri Lanka Navy

in preventing Tamil militant activities from affecting Sri Lanka.

(c) In the event that the Government of Sri Lanka requests the Government of India to afford military assistance to implement these proposals the Government of India will co-operate by giving to the Government of Sri Lanka such military assistance as and whell requested.

(d) The Government of India will expedite repatriation from Sri Lanka of Indian citizens to India who are resident here, concurrently with the repatriation of Sri Lankan refugees from Tamil Nadu.

(e) The Governments of Sri Lanka and India will co-operate in ensuring the physical security and safety of all communities inhabiting the Northern and Eastern Provinces.

2.17 The Government of Sri Lanka shall ensure free, full and fair participation of voters from all communities in the Northern and Eastern Provinces in electoral processes envisaged in this Agreement. The Government of India will extend full co-operation to the Government of Sri Lanka in this regard.

2.18 The official language of Sri Lanka shall be Sinhala. Tamil and English will also be official languages.

3. This Agreement and the annexure thereto shall come into force upon signature.

IN WITNESS WHEREOF we have set our hands and seals hereunto.

DONE in COLOMBO, SRI 1ANKA, on this the Twenty Ninth day of July of the year One Thousand Nine Hundred and Eighty Seven, in duplicate, both texts being equally authentic.

Junius Richard Jayawardene
President of the Democratic
Socialist Republic of
Sri Lanka

Rajiv Gandhi
Prime Minister of
the Republic of
India

ANNEXURE TO THE AGREEMENT

1. His Excellency the President of Sri Lanka and the Prime Minister of India agree th1't the referendum mentioned in paragraph 2 and its sub-paragraphs of the Agreement will be observed by a representative of the Election Commission of India to be invited by His Excellency the President of Sri Lanka.

2. Similarly, both Heads of Government agree that the elections to the Provincial Council mentioned in paragraph 2.8 of the Agreement will be observed by a representative of the Government of India to be invited by the President of Sri Lanka.

3. His Excellency the President of Sri Lanka agrees that the Home Guards would be disbanded and all paramilitary personnel will be withdrawn from the Eastern and Northern Provinces with a view to creating conditions conducive to fair elections to the Council. The President, in his discretion, shall absorb such paramilitary forces which came into being due to ethnic violence into the regular security forces of Sri Lanka.

4. The President of Sri Lanka and the Prime Minister of India agree that the Tamil militants shall surrender their arms to authorities agreed upon to be designated by the President of Sri Lanka. The surrender shall take place in the presence of one senior representative each of the Sri Lanka Red Cross and the Indian Red Cross.

5. The President of Sri Lanka and the Prime Minister of India agree that a joint Indo-Sri Lankan observer group consisting of qualified representatives of the Government of Sri Lanka and the Government of India would monitor the cessation of hostilities from 31 July 1987.

6. The President of Sri Lanka and the Prime Minister of India also agree that in terms of paragraph 2.14 and paragraph 2.16 (c) of the Agreement, an Indian Peace Keeping Contingent may be invited by the President of Sri Lanka to guarantee and enforce the cessation of hostilities; if so required.

PRIME MINISTER

July 29, 1987

Excellency,

Conscious of the friendship between our two countries stretching over two millennia and more, and recognizing the importance of nurturing this traditional friendship, it is imperative that both Sri Lanka and India reaffirm the decision not to allow our respective territories to be used for activities

prejudicial to each other's unity, territorial integrity and security. ,

2. In this spirit, you had, during the course of our discussions, agreed to meet some of India's concerns as follows:

(i) your Excellency and myself will reach an early understanding about the relevance and employment of foreign military and intelligence personnel with a view to ensuring that such presences will not prejudice Indo-Sri Lankan relations;

(ii) Trincomalee or any other ports in Sri Lanka will not be made available for military use by any country in a manner prejudicial to India's interests;

(iii) The work of restoring and operating the Trincomalee Oil Tank Farm will be undertaken as a joint venture between India and Sri Lanka;

(iv) Sri Lanka's agreement with foreign broadcasting organizations will be reviewed to ensure that any facilities set up by them in Sri Lanka are used solely as public broadcasting facilities and not for any military or intelligence purposes.

3. In the same spirit, India will:

(i) Deport all Sri Lankan citizens who are found to be engaging in terrorist activities or advocating separatism or secessionism;

(ii) Provide training facilities and military supplies for Sri Lankan security forces.

4. India and Sri Lanka have agreed to set up a joint consultative mechanism to continuously review matters of common concern in the light of the objectives stated in para 1 and specifically to monitor the implementation of other matters contained in this letter.

5. Kindly confirm, Excellency, that the above correctly sets out the agreement reached between us.

Please accept, Excellency, the assurances of my highest consideration.

Yours sincerely,

Rajiv Gandhi

His Excellency Mr. J.R. Jayawardene
President of the Democratic Socialist
Republic of Sri Lanka
Colombo.

This is to confirm that the above correctly sets out the understanding
reached between us.
Please accept, Excellency, the assurances of my highest
consideration.

J.R. Jayawardene
President

His Excellency Mr. Rajiv Gandhi,
Prime Minister of the Republic of India
New Delhi.

Appendix 5: Chronology Since 1983

1983: Tamil nationalist movements in India started to arm and train
LTTE cadres. Sometime during the same period, V. Prabhakaran,
the leader of the LTTE, is believed to have moved to the Indian
State of Tamil Nadu.

14 May 1985: LTTE gunned down 46 Sinhalese civilians at
Anuradhapura, a holy Buddhist site.

8 July 1985: The government and the LTTE held their first peace
talks in Bhutan. These talks failed. As a follow up, President
Jayewardane, later proposed at the 1986 Summit of the South Asian
Area for Regional Co-operation (SAARC) in Banglore, India, a
three-fold proposal to end the ethnic problem. The main points in
this proposal, which was much publicized as 'the Trifurcation
Proposal,' were 1. Ampara District where the majority were not
Tamils to be separated from the Eastern province and annexed to
adjoining Uva Province, 2. The rest of the Eastern Province to have
its own Provincial Council, and 3. The Northern province to stand
on its own as a separate Province, as before. The LTTE flatly
refused to accept this proposal as well.

21 April 1987: A bomb blasted in Colombo killing more than 100
people.

26 May 1987: The government launched the 'Operation Liberation,' a major army combat against the LTTE. The Indian government intervened in this event and first sent by boat some food and other essential supplies to the people affected by the raging war between the government forces and the LTTE, on June 3, 1987. The Sri Lankan government refused to allow the supplies into the country. Then on the next day the Indian government sent five aircraft to the island and dropped tonnes of relief supplies to the affected areas from the air, in complete violation of Sri Lankan air space.

5 July 1987: The LTTE carried out its first suicide bombing, killing 39 troops at the Nelliyady army camp in the north of the country.

July 1987: The government gave one more concession on the contentious issues discussed at the 1985/6 peace talks. It agreed to provide a temporary merger of the northern and eastern provinces in the country, on condition that a referendum in the eastern province would finally decide whether such a merger should be made permanent. In response to this concession, the LTTE insisted on two pre-conditions for the renewal of peace talks: 1. The withdrawal of Sri Lankan government troops to the positions they occupied before 'Operation Liberation,' and 2. All Tamil refugees to be allowed to resettle in their own areas. When the government accepted the two conditions, the LTTE added two more pre-conditions to any future peace talks: 1. LTTE was not prepared to return its weapons, and 2. Its opposition to the proposed Eastern Province referendum to make the temporary merger of the northern and eastern provinces permanent.

29 July 1987: The governments of India and Sri Lanka signed a pact to end Tamil separatism in Sri Lanka. The pact required the LTTE to surrender its arms and an Indian peacekeeping Force (IPKF) to replace the Sri Lankan Security forces in the Northern and Eastern Provinces of the island. Following the pact, the Sri Lankan government set up Provincial Councils to partially decentralize political administration of the island.

10 October 1987: Despite what was expected of the pact, the LTTE refused to surrender its arms and, instead, resumed the separatist war, taking on Indian troops, the Indian Peace Keeping Force (IPKF).

23 February 1990: The government (now President Premadasa, UNP) began the second round of peace talks, and asked the IPKF to leave the country.

24 March 1990: The IPKF started to leave the country, leaving large areas of northern Sri Lanka under LTTE control.

10 June 1990: The LTTE abandoned peace talks and once again resumed its separatist war.

2 March 1991: A car-bomb blast killed Defense Minister Ranjan Wijerathne and 18 others in Colombo.

21 May 1991: A suicide bomber, alleged to be a LTTE cadre, blew up Rajiv Gandhi, the Prime Minister of India.

22 June 1991: A suicide bomber, alleged to be a LTTE cadre, drove a truck packed with explosives into the military Operations Headquarters in Colombo, killing 21 and wounding 114 others.

1992: India banned the LTTE after the 1991 killing of Prime Minister Rajiv Gandhi.

16 November 1992: A suicide bomber, alleged to be a LTTE cadre, blew up Clancy Fernando, the Sri Lankan Navy Commander.

1 May 1993: A suicide bomber blew up President Premadasa and 23 others at a May Day rally in Colombo.

13 October 1994: The government (Prime Minister Chandrika Kumaratunge) began the third round of peace talks with the LTTE.

24 October 1994: A suicide bomber, alleged to be a LTTE cadre, blew up Gamini Disanayake, the main opposition (UNP) presidential candidate, and 56 others in a political rally in Colombo.

9 November 1994: Chandrika Kumaratunge (PA) won the presidential election and became President.

7 January 1995: The cease-fire agreement signed between President Kumaratunge and the LTTE leader, Velupillai Prabhakaran, came into effect from 7 January 1995.

19 April 1995: After about six months of peace talks, the LTTE resumed its separatist war by bombing two navy boats. In response, the government renewed its military attacks on the LTTE under a banner of 'war for peace.' While fighting the war, the government asked for support to eradicate terrorism, safeguard democracy in the country, and to liberate Tamils from the dictatorship of the LTTE.

2 December 1995: Jaffna, the main stronghold of the LTTE in the North, fell to Sri Lankan army. At the height of the war in Jaffna hundreds of thousands of people fled the town without any specific destination, and ended up in refugee camps both within and outside the country.

31 January 1996: A LTTE suicide bomber drove a truck packed with explosives and destroyed a part of the Central Bank building in Colombo, killing 91 people and wounding 1,400.

18 July 1996: LTTE overran a major army camp in Mullaitivu, killing 1,200 troopers.

24 July 1996: A commuter train had a bomb blast near Colombo killing 70 people and wounding 600.

15 October 1997: Suicide bombers drove a truckload of explosives and devastated the Twin-Tower World Trade Centre building, killing 18.

25 January 1998: Suicide bombers devastated the holiest Buddhist shrine in the country, The Temple of the Tooth in Kandy in the central Province, killing 16 people.

1998: Sri Lankan government banned the LTTE after the attack on the Temple of the Tooth on 25 January 1998.

29 January 1998: The government held local elections in Jaffna for the first time since 1983. But the elections failed to provide a viable political process.

5 March 1998: A bus bomb exploded in Colombo's commercial area of Maradana, killing 37 people and wounding 250 others.

17 May 1998: An assassin, alleged to be a LTTE cadre, murdered the mayor of Jaffna, who belonged to TULF.

6 August 1998: The government declared a nation-wide state of emergency "in the interests of the public security."

6 September 1998: The LTTE offered to recommence peace talks on condition of third party mediation. The government rejected the offer and continued with the war.

11 September 1998: A bomb blast rocked the municipal council building in Jaffna, killing the mayor and 11 others.

29 July 1999: A suicide bomber, alleged to be a LTTE cadre, gunned down Neelan Thiruchelvam, a TULF MP and a key figure in the government sponsored peace efforts, in front of his own house.

18 September 1999: Few suspected LTTE cadres attacked three villages killing more than 50 people.

18 October 1999: President Kumaratunge ruled out peace talks with the LTTE for the time being.

18 December 1999: Two separate bomb blasts in election rallies in Colombo killed 38 people, and injured President Kumaratunge.

21 December 1999: Chandrika Kumaratunge got re-elected as President at the presidential election with 51.1 percent popular vote.

5 January 2000: A suicide bomber, alleged to be a LTTE cadre, detonated explosives strapped to her body outside the office of the Prime Minister, killing 13 people and injuring another 28.

27 January 2000: A powerful bomb blasted in the main post office in Vavunia in the North, leaving many casualties.

1 February 2000: The Norwegian government came to play an intermediary role in putting a new peace package before the LTTE.

2 March 2000: A woman suicide bomber, alleged to be a LTTE cadre, detonated explosives near a vehicle carrying Piyal Abesekara, the top military commander in Trincomalee District in the Northeast. Abesekara escaped the attack, but his driver was killed.

10 March 2000: A bomb blasted on the Ceremonial Drive to parliament, killing 23 people, including some policemen.

23 April 2000: According to government sources, the LTTE took control of the Elephant Pass military base in the Jaffna peninsula. This prevented further movement of the government troops by road to the Jaffna peninsula from the south.

4 May 2000: The government puts the country on a war footing, assuming new powers under the country's Constitution.

8 May 2000: The government turned down a truce offer by the LTTE to enable government troops to evacuate from the Jaffna peninsula.

11 May 2000: The government banned live broadcasts of all television and radio programmes on the separatist war.

17 May 2000: A powerful bomb blasted in the eastern town of Batticoloa, killing over 20 people and injuring another 75.

5 June 2000: Suicide bombers sunk a navy gunboat in the north, killing five people.

7 June 2000: A suicide bomber, alleged to be a LTTE cadre, assassinated C. V. Goonarathne, a senior cabinet minister in the government, and 20 others in Colombo.

14 June 2000: A suicide bomber, alleged to be a LTTE cadre, killed himself and two civilians when knocked down by a cyclist while trying to attack an air force bus carrying 50 troopers.

26 June 2000: Six suicide bombers sunk a merchant vessel, the M. V. Mercs Uhana, off the northern coast.

30 June 2000: The Supreme Court of the country ruled that the imposition of media censorship by the government was illegal.

8 August 2000: The government postponed a parliamentary vote on a crucial devolution bill modelled on the Indian federal system. The main opposition party, UNP, had first agreed to support the bill, but later changed its mind due to significant opposition to the bill from the majority Sinhalese.

16 August 2000: A suicide bomber, alleged to be a LTTE cadre, killed himself and a nine-year old girl while attempting to ram into an army vehicle. Two soldiers escaped with injuries.

15 September 2000: A suicide bomber detonated explosives trapped to his body while he was being searched outside the main eye hospital in Colombo, killing seven people.

2 October 2000: A suicide bomber detonated explosives trapped to his body, killing himself and 23 others, including M. Baithullah, a Muslim candidate at the October 10 parliamentary election.

5 October 2000: A suicide bomber attacked a meeting of the ruling party in Medawachchiya in the north central, killing over 10 people.

19 October 2000: A suicide bomber detonated explosives trapped to his body while being questioned outside the main Town Hall in Colombo, killing himself and injuring over 19 people. A new cabinet was being sworn in at the time of this incident.

25 October 2000: Thirty one Tamil youth aged between 14 and 23 who were detained in a rehabilitation camp in Bandarawela in the central part of the island were killed, allegedly by a mob of people from neighbouring villages. Police and army personnel deployed at the rehabilitation camp failed to protect them. This sparked a series of protests and counter mob-attacks involving Indian Tamils and Sinhalese in the upcountry. (A similar incident had occurred in the maximum security prison in the capital Colombo in 1983)

2 November 2000: Eric Solheim, the Norwegian Special Envoy to Sri Lanka, announced that the LTTE was prepared to open peace talks without preconditions. He had personally met the LTTE leader, V. Prabhakaran, a few days before. The (PA) government rejected the offer.

30 November 2000: Two powerful land mine explosions killed 14 security personnel and injured more than 16 others in Trincomalee and Vavunia.

12 December 2000: Major Paul Marks, a military expert on Sri Lanka of the United States army warned that Sri lanka's Tamil rebels could destabilise India and spread terrorism to the United States and Western Europe. The warning came in the Joint Force Quarterly, a professional military journal published for the Chairman of the Joint Chiefs of Staff of the armed forces of the United States.

25 December 2000: The LTTE declared a unilateral cease-fire, and called on the Sri Lankan government to match it. The government refused to respond to the cease-fire, and launched a series of operations and recaptured areas close to Jaffna town.

17 January 2001: Nearly 4000 Jaffna University students and staff held an event to urge the government to accept the self-determination right of the Tamils. The army had refused permission

to the event saying it was being organised by the LTTE, but event took place without incidents.

28 February 2001: The United Kingdom banned the LTTE as a "terrorist organisation," along with twenty other foreign organisations recommended for proscription. The LTTE warned that this would impose severe restraints on the Norwegian peace initiative.

25 April 2001: The LTTE ended its cease-fire after four months, and demanded that the proscription on the LTTE by the Sri Lankan government be lifted before peace talk could recommence. The government refused to give in to this demand.

1 June 2001: Ethnic riots broke out between Sinhalese and Muslims in Mawanella, a town in central Sri Lanka, leaving two dead and much of the town in ruins. This led to a week of communal unrest in many parts of the island, including the capital city of Colombo.

11 June 2001: President Chandrika Kumaratunga agreed to sign a Memorandum of Understanding (MOU) with the Sri Lankan Muslim Congress agreeing to the creation of a separate administrative district for Kalmunai. The government, however, failed to implement this agreement due to widespread protests from both Sinhalese and Tamils.

July 2001: The Sri Lanka Muslim Congress (SLMC) left the governing coalition, reducing it to a minority in the parliament.

10 July 2001: President Chandrika Kumaratunga prorogued the country's legislature (the Parliament) with effect from midnight 10 July 2001 until 7 September 2001 in an apparent bid to save her minority government from defeat in a no-confidence vote in the Parliament.

10 July 2001: President Chandrika Kumaratunga called for a national referendum on a new constitution on 21 August 2001. The details of the proposed new constitution were not released.

24 July 2001: Thirteen guerrillas, believed to be LTTE cadres, armed with machine guns and rocket-propelled grenade launchers, carried out a pre-dawn attack on the country's only international airport and the adjoining, biggest military air-base in Colombo. This attack, according to official military sources, had destroyed thirteen air crafts, including two Kfir jet fighters, one MI-24 Helicopter gun ship and one MIG-27 jet fighter, and led to 18 deaths. After the attack, the Eelam Nation website controlled by the LTTE warned that if the daring attack was possible, then there was nothing that could prevent the LTTE from carrying out an attack on the military

headquarters and cause serious damage to the city of Colombo without difficulty.

07 August 2001: President Kumaratunga postponed the referendum set for 21 August 2001 to 18 October 2001.

05 September 2001: JVP signed a Memorandum of Understanding (MOU) with the Peoples' Alliance (PA), the governing coalition under President Kumaratunga's leadership, giving its conditional support for a probationary government for one year. This support was crucial for the survival of President Kumaratunga's government after a key Muslim ally withdrew from it in June 2001.

12 September 2001: President Kumaratunga reduced her cabinet to 20 from 44 as promised in the probationary MOU with the JVP.

24 September 2001: Parliament passed the 17th Amendment to the Constitution with a two-thirds majority to appoint a Constitutional Council and four independent commissions on elections, the judiciary, police and the public service. The appointment of these special commissions was also part of the government-JVP MOU.

08 October 2001: Parliament decided to take up the debate of a no-confidence motion against the government proposed by the UNP on 11 October 2001. Within a day or two more than ten government members, including some key cabinet ministers, crossed over to the opposition, showing a clear defeat for the government.

10 October 2001: President Kumaratunga dissolved the one year old parliament, elected on 10 October 2001 for a six-year term, thus preventing the opposition from being a majority on the floor of the House. The next parliamentary general election was scheduled for 5 December 2001.

24 October 2001: LTTE triggered a huge claymore mine explosion in Nelliady killing one senior army officer and six soldiers.

01 November 2001: LTTE fighters attacked a Police Guard Point at Muttur in the Trincomalee district, killing eleven police constables and ten other security personnel around 2:10 PM.

UNP formed the next government with the support of SLMC after the 5 December 2001 election, and showed its intention to enter into fresh peace talks with the LTTE. First the two parties signed a Memorandum of Understanding for an open ended cease-fire arrangement on 22 February 2002, preparing grounds for finding a lasting solution to the country's ethnic crisis through peace-talks.

Appendix 6: Questions and Answers on the Sangha Order

(Answers given by Venerable Sona and Venerable Thitapunno)

1. Why should one become a Buddhist monk? Although there are many reasons why people become monastics in the Theravada Buddhist order- this was so even in the Buddha's time --, the *sasana* or dispensation was established with the purpose of facilitating the attainment of *nibbana* to individuals who complied with the requisites given at the *upasampada* ordination. In an ideal case it should be understood that the attainment of *nibbana* is the sole reason for becoming a member of the *sangha*.

2. What are the main goals and objectives of a Buddhist monk? As the foremost objective it is the attainment of *nibbana*. There are secondary objectives like preserving, teaching, and spreading the teachings *(Dhamma)*.

3.Is it wrong for Buddhist monks to take part in political activities? There is no specific general injunction on the part of the Buddha prohibiting monks from taking part in "political activities". One would first have to define clearly what is meant by "political activities". However, if these activities are somehow linked with wrong action, wrong livelihood or wrong speech they should not be done by monks. An example is found in Brahmajala Sutta, Digha Nikaya (D.1), where the Buddha specifies the types of livelihood and speech in which monks should not be involved, there he mentions: "Talk of kings [political talk}, ...talk of ministers [political talk}, armies, ...villages, towns and cities, countries..." This is wrong speech; "Running errands or messages for kings, ministers, nobles..." This is wrong livelihood (I would assume then that doing activities on behalf of a political party would fall under this section of the sutta).

There would be no objection if a monk, upon being asked for advice on political matters, gave advice on these matters. The Buddha himself gave advice of this nature in his time (see for example his statements as to what should be the duties of a monarch (10 *rajadhamma,* J.V.378), the duties of a Universal Emperor *(Cakkavatti-vatta, 0.111.61),* the four bases of social harmony for a king *(raja-sangahavattu,* 5.1.76; A.II.42; It.21) .In the particular case of a monk who advocates a military action (specifically suggesting that soldiers are to kill the enemy), and if a soldier acts on that advice and kills somebody , that monk who gave the advice is *parajlka* and is no longer in communion with the order.

A good indication that monks should not be involved with government (even if this is a righteous one) may be inferred from Samyutta Nikaya 4:20. In this case Mara prompted the Buddha:

"Let the Blessed One govern, let the sublime one govern, without killing and ordering execution, without confiscating and sequestrating, without sorrowing and inflicting sorrow, in other words, righteously" Needless to say the Buddha rejected this thought pointing that such thought is not fit for one who has abandoned sense desires. In general it is not proper for a monk to teach worldly knowledge such as: math, how to read & write, geography, political structures, astrology, medicine, palmistry, etc. Even acting as a school teacher, unless it is directly connected to the practice or transmission of Dhamma, would be a case of wrong livelihood for a monk.

4. If it is wrong for Buddhist monks to take part in political activities, Explain why? It depends on the specific activity (as mentioned above). To give, for example, a Dhamma talk to politicians or the military is fine.

5.Are there no checks and balances in the Buddhist Order to prevent monks from taking part in political activities or doing anything else wrong? If according to *vinaya* they misbehave and they are unrepentant they can be banished from the sangha. This happens when monks are badly behaved and won't change. If the monastery is one in which monks who are well-behaved live, the badly-behaved monk(s) will be asked to leave. In Thailand the government has power to disrobe monks who misbehave. In Canada there is no such interest in the governments to administer Buddhist affairs. In Sri Lanka it sounds that there is less control than in Thailand.

6.Is it true that the Buddha himself intervened in a war between his father's kingdom and a neighbouring one, and helped stop it? I don't recall the incident off the top of my head. If you know the canonical reference please let me know.

7. What part of the Buddha's teachings deals with the ways of governing a country? See answer to question 3 (among other teachings).

8. What are the main principles of governance the Buddha has preached? For monks it is the vinaya or rules of discipline. He did not advocate any specific system for lay societies. In his time there were different types of government in India and he did not make specific statements as to which should be favoured.

9. What basic qualities must a ruler have to govern a country well, according to the teachings of the Buddha? In connection to answer to question 3:

Four bases of *social harmony for a king:* Shrewdness in agriculture, in promotion of government officials, skilful bestowal of favours, and kindly and pleasing speech.

Ten duties of a *king:* Charity or generosity, morality, altruism, honesty, kindness, self-control, non-anger, non-violence, forbearance, and uprightness.

Twel*ve duties* of *a Universal Emperor:*
1-Rule by righteousness
Provision of ward and protection to:
2- Those in the Emperor's immediate circle,
3- The armed forces,
4-Govemors and administrative officers,
5~Royal dependants, civil servants,
6-Brahmins, householders, craftsmen, traders,
7- Town and country dwellers,
8. Religious devotees, and
9-Beasts and birds.
10-Prevention of wrongdoing in the Kingdom.
11- Distribution of wealth to the poor.
12-Seeking advice from sages, aspiring to greater virtue.

10. What advice would the Buddha give to the present Buddhist monks and rulers of Sri Lanka, if he were living and approached for advice? I think he already did that, he said:
"I address you, monks. 1 inform you monks:
All compounded things are subject to passing away,

Become consummate through non-complacency"

11. What advice would the Buddha have given to those engaged in ethnic and religious wars? He also did that, he said: "Abandon evil, cultivate the good, and purify the mind.",

Also,

"All tremble at violence; life is dear to all.
Putting oneself in the place of another,
One should not kill nor cause another to kill. *(Dhp. X,* 130)"

And also,

"Hatred is never appeased by hatred in this world.
By non-hatred is hatred appeased.
This is a law eternal. (Dhp. 1, 5)"

Apendix 7: Government-LTTE MOU, 2002

Preamble
The overall objective of the Government of the Democratic Socialist Republic of Sri Lanka (hereinafter referred to as the GOSL) and the Liberation Tigers of Tamil Eelam (hereinafter referred to as the L 1TE) is to find a negotiated solution to the ongoing ethnic conflict in Sri Lanka..

The GOSL and the L TTE (hereinafter referred to as the Parties) recognize the importance of bringing an end to the hostilities and improving the living conditions for all inhabitants affected by the conflict. Bringing an end to the hostilities is also seen by the Parties as a means of establishing a positive atmosphere in which further steps towards ne!Zoti8tinns on a lasting solution can be taken.

The Parties further recognize that groups that are not directly party to the conflict are also suffering the consequences of it. This is particularly the case as regards the Muslim population. Therefore, the provisions of this Agreement regarding the security of civilians and their property apply to all inhabitants.

With reference to the above, the Parties have agreed to enter into a ceasefire, refrain from conduct that could undermine the good intentions or violate the spirit of this Agreement and implement confidence-building measures as indicated in the articles below.

Article I: Modalities of a ceasefire

The Parties have agreed to implement a ceasefire between their armed forces as follows:

1.1 A jointly agreed ceasefire between the GOSL and the L 1TE shall enter into force on such date as is notified by the Norwegian Minister of Foreign Affairs in accordance with Article 4.2, hereinafter referred to as D-day.

Military operations

1.2 Neither Party shall engage in any offensive military operation. This requires the total cessation of all military action and includes, but is not limited to, such acts as:

The firing of direct and indirect weapons, armed raids, ambushes, assassinations, abductions, destruction of civilian or military property , sabotage, suicide missions and activities by deep penetration units; b) Aerial bombardment; c) Offensive naval operations.

1.3 The Sri Lankan armed forces shall continue to perform their legitimate task of safeguarding the sovereignty and territorial integrity of Sri Lanka without engaging in offensive operations against the LTTE.

Separation of forces

1.4 Where forward defence localities have been established, the GOSL's armed forces and the LTTE's fighting formations shall hold their ground positions, maintaining a zone of separation of a minimum of six hundred (600) metres. However, each Party reserves the right of movement within one hundred (100) metres of its own defence localities, keeping an absolute minimum distance of four hundred (400) metres between them. Where existing positions are closer than four hundred (400) metres, no such right of movement applies and the Parties agree to ensure the maximum possible distance between their personnel.

1.5 In areas where localities have not been clearly established, the status quo as regards the areas controlled by the GOSL and the LTTE, respectively, on 24 December 2001 shall continue to apply pending such demarcation as is provided in article 1.6.

1.6 The Parties shall provide information to the Sri Lanka Monitoring Mission (SLMM) regarding defence localities in all areas of contention, cf. Article 3. The monitoring mission shall assist the Parties in drawing up demarcation lines at the latest by D-day + 30.

1.7 The Parties shall not move munitions, explosives or military equipment into the area controlled by the other Party .

1.8 Tamil paramilitary groups shall be disarmed by the GOSL by D-day + 30 at the latest. The GOSL shall offer to integrate individuals in these units under the command and disciplinary structure of the GOSL armed forces for service away from the Northern and Eastern Province.

Freedom of movement

1.9 The Parties' forces shall initially stay in the areas under their respective control, as provided in Article 1.4 and Article 1.5.

1.10 Unarmed GOSL troops shall, as of D- day + 60. be permitted unlimited passage between Jaffna and Vavuniya using the Jaffna-Kandy road (A9). The modalities are to be worked out by the Parties with the assistance of the SLMM.

1.11 The Parties agree that as of D-day individual combatants shall, on the recommendation of their area commander, be permitted, unarmed and in plain clothes, to visit family and friends residing in areas under the control of the other Party .Such visits shall be limited to six days every second month, not including the time of travel by the shortest applicable route. The L TTE shall facilitate the use of the Jaffna-Kandy road for this purpose. The Parties reserve the right to deny entry to specified military areas.

1.12 The Parties agree that as of D-day individual combatants shall, notwithstanding the two- month restriction, be permitted, unarmed and in plain clothes, to visit immediate family (i.e. spouses. children. grandparents. parents and siblings) in connection with weddings or funerals. The right to deny entry to specified military areas applies.

1.13 Fifty (50) unarmed LTTE members shall as of D-day + 30, for the purpose of political work, be permitted freedom of movement in the areas of the North and the East dominated by the GOSL. Additional 100 unarmed L TTE members shall be permitted freedom of movement as of D-day + 60. As of D-day + 90, all unarmed L TTE members shall be permitted freedom of movement in the North and the East. The L1TE members shall carry identity papers. The right of the GOSL to deny entry to specified military areas applies.

Article 2: Measures to restore normalcy

The Parties shall undertake the following confidence-building measures with the aim of restoring normalcy for all inhabitants of Sri Lanka:

2.1 The Parties shall in accordance with international law abstain from hostile acts against the civilian population, including such acts as torture, intimidation, abduction, extortion and harassment

2.2 The Parties shall refrain from engaging in activities or propagating ideas that would offend cultural or religious sensitivities. Places of worship {temples, churches, mosques and other holy sites, etc.) currently held by the forces of either of the Parties shall be vacated by D-day + 30 and made accessible to the public. Places of worship which are situated in "high security zones" shall be vacated by all amled personnel and maintained in good order by civilian workers, even when they are not made accessible to the public.

2.3 Beginning on the date on which this Agreement enters into force, school buildings occupied by either party shall be vacated and returned to their intended use. This activity shall be completed by D-day + 160 at the latest.

2.4 A schedule indicating the return of all other public buildings to their intended use shall be drawn up by the Pallies and published at the latest by D-day + 30.

2.5 The Parties shall review the security measures and the set-up of checkpoints, particularly in densely populated cities and towns, in order to introduce systems that will prevent harassment of the civilian population. Such systems shall be in place from D-day + 60.

2.6 The Parties agree to ensure the uninterrupted flow of non-military goods to and from the LTTE- dominated areas with the exception of certain items as shown in Annex A. Quantities shall be determined by market demand. The GOSL shall regularly review the matter with the aim of gradually removing any remaining restrictions on non-military goods.

2.7 In order to facilitate the flow of goods and the movement of civilians, the Parties agree to establish checkpoints on their line of control at such locations as are specified in Annex B.

2.8 The Parties shall take steps to ensure that the Trincomalee-Habarana road remains open on a 24-hour basis for passenger traffic with effect from D-day + 10.

2.9 The Parties shall facilitate the extension of the rail service on the Batticaloa-line to Welikanda. Repairs and maintenance shall be carried out by the GOSL in order to extend the service up to Batticaloa.

2.10 The Parties shall open the Kandy-Jaffna road (A9) to non military traffic of goods and passengers. Specific modalities shall be worked out by the Parties with the assistance of the Royal Norwegian Government by D-day + 30 at the latest.

2.11 A gradual easing of the fishing restrictions shall take place starting from D-day. As of D-day + 90, all restrictions on day and night fishing shall be removed, subject to the following exceptions.
(i) fishing win not be permitted within an area of 1 nautical mile on either side along the coast and two nautical miles seawards from an security forces camps on the coast; (ii) fishing win not be permitted in harbours or approaches to harbours, bays estuaries along the coast.

2.12 The Parties agree that search operations and arrests under the Prevention of Terrorism Act shall not take place. Arrests shall be conducted under due process of law in accordance with the Criminal Procedure Code

2.13 The Parties agree to provide family members of detainees access to the detainees within D- day + 30.

Article 3 : The *Sri* Lanka Monitoring Mission.
The Parties have agreed to set up an international monitoring mission to enquire into any instance of violation of the terms and conditions of this Agreement. Both Parties shall fully cooperate to rectify any matter of conflict caused by their respective sides. The mission shall conduct international verification through on-side monitoring of the fulfilment of the commitments entered into this agreement *as* follows:

3- 1 The name of the monitoring mission shall be the Sri Lankan Monitoring Mission (hereinafter referred to as the SLMM)

3.2 Subject to acceptance by the Parties, the Royal Norwegian Government (hereinafter referred to as the RNG) shall appoint the Head of the SLMM (hereinafter referred to as the HOM), who shall be the final authority regarding interpretation of this Agreement,

3.3 The SLMM shall liaise with the Parties and report to the RNG.

3.4 The HOM shall decide the date for the commencement of the SLMM's operations.

3.5 The SLMM shall be composed of representatives from Nordic countries.

3.6- The SLMM shall establish a headquarters in such place as the MOM finds appropriate. An office shall be established in Colombo and in Wanni in order to liaise with the GOSL and the LTTE, respectively. The SLMM will maintain a presence in the districts of Jaffna, Mannar, Vavuniya, Trincomalee. Batticaloa and Ampara.

3.7 A local monitoring committee shall be established in Jaffna, Mannar, Vavuniya, Trincomalee, Batticaloa and Ampara. Each committee shall consist of five members. two appointed by the GOSL, two by the L TTE and one international monitor appointed by the HOM. The international monitor shall chair the committee. The GOSL and the L TTE appointees may be selected from among retire d judges, public servants, religious leaders or similar leading citizens.

3.8 The committees shall serve the SLMM in an advisory capacity and discuss issues relating to the implementation of this Agreement in their respective districts, with a view to establishing a common understanding of such issues. fu particular, they will seek to resolve any dispute concerning the implementation of this Agreement at the lowest possible level.

3.9 The Parties shall be responsible for the appropriate protection of and security arrangements for all SLMM members.

3.10 The Parties agree to ensure the freedom of movement of the SLM::M members in performing their tasks. The members of the SLMM shall be given immediate access to areas where violations of the Agreement are alleged to have taken place. The Parties also agree to facilitate the widest possible access to such areas for the local members of the six above-mentioned committees, cf. Article 3.7.

1.11 It shall be the responsibility of the SLMM to take immediate action on any complaints made by either Party to the Agreement and to enquire into and assist the Parties in the settlement of any dispute that might arise in connection with such complaints.

3.12 With lhe aim of resolving disputes at me lowest possible level, communication shall be established between commanders of the GOSL armed forces and the L TTE area leaders to enable them to resolve problems in the conflict zones.

3.13 Guidelines for the operations of the SLMM shall be established in a separate document.

Article 4: Entry into force, amendments and termination of the Agreement

4.1 Each Party shall notify its consent to be bound by this Agreement through a letter to the Norwegian Minister of Foreign Affairs signed by Prime Minister Ranil Wickremesinghe on behalf of the GOSL and by leader Velupillai Prabhakaran on behalf of the LTTE, respectively, The Agreement shall be initialled by each Party and enclosed in the above-mentioned letter.

4.2 The Agreement shall enter into force on such date as is notified by the Norwegian Minister of Foreign Affairs.

4.3 This Agreement may be amended and modified by mutual agreement of both Parties. Such amendments shall be notified in writing to the RNG.

4.4 This Agreement shall remain in force until notice of termination is given by either Party to the RNG. Such notice shall be given fourteen (14) days in advance of the effective date of termination.

Annex. A : List of goods
Annex B : Checkpoints

ANNEX A
The parties agree to ensure the flow of non-military goods to and from LTTE dominated areas of the Northern and Eastern Province, as well as unimpeded flow of such goods to the civilian population in these areas. Non military goods not covered by article 2.6 in the Agreement are listed below:
-Non military arms/ammunition
-Explosives
-Remote control devices
-Barbed wire
-Binoculars/ Telescopes
-Compasses
 -Penlight batteries
Diesel, petrol, cement and iron rods will be restricted in accordance with the following procedure and quantities:

-Diesel and Petrol
The Government Agents (GA)will register available vehicles; tractors and motorcycles in the LTTE controlled areas. The GA will calculate the required weekly amount of diesel and petrol based on the following estimate'
Trucks/Buses 250 litre/week
4 Wheels tractor 310 litre/week

2 wheel tractor 40 litre/week
Petrol vehicle 30 litre/week
Motorcycles 7 litre/week
Fishing vessels 400 litre/week

-Cement
Cement required for rehabilitation and reconstruction of Government property; registered co-operatives; or approved housing projects implemented by the GOSL and international NGOs and more affluent members of the society; will be brought in directly by relevant institutions under licences issued by Government Agents. The GA shall stipulate the monthly quantities permitted for such project based upon planned and reported progress.

Cement required for individual shops/constructions/house owners/rehabilitations-initiatives will be made available through the co-operations on a commercial basis. The monthly import for this purpose will be limited to 5000 bags during the first month and thereafter 10,000 bags/month. Individual sales by the co-operatives will be registered and limited to 25 bags per household.

-Iron Rods
Iron rods for building constructions will be brought in to the L TTE controlled areas under licences issued by the GA.
A monthly reassessment will be made to assess the possibilities of removal of the above restrictions.

ANNEX B
Checkpoints agreed in 2.7 are as follows.
-Mandur
-Paddirupur
-Kaludaveli Ferry Point
-Ambalantivu Ferry Point
-Mamunal Ferry Point
-Vanvunateevu
-Santhiveli Boat Point
-Black Bridge
-Sitandy Boat Point
-Kiran Bridge
-Kinniyadi Boat Point
-Valachenai
-Makerni

-Mahindapura
-Muttur
-Ugilankulam
-Omanthai

Appendix 8: Govternment-LTTE Cease-fire Agreement, 1995

The agreement signed between President Chandrika Kumaratunga and Velupillai Prabhakaran in 1995. The ceasefire came into effect from January 7, 1995. Declaration of Cessation of Hostilities.

The modalities for the. implementation of the agreed Cessation of Hostilities by the Government and LTTE for a specified period will be as follows.

1 There win be no offensive operations by either party during this period. An offensive operation will be considered a violation of the agreement.

2. The Security Forces and the L TTE will maintain their present positions on the ground, keeping a minimum of 600 metres between each other. However, each party would reserve the right of movement within 100 metres from their own bunker lines, keeping a minimum of 400 metres in between. Any party moving in the restricted areas would be considered an offensive operation.

3. The Navy and the Air Force will continue to perform their legitimate tasks for safeguarding the sovereignty and territorial integrity of the country, from external aggression, without in anyway engaging in offensive operations against the L TTE. or causing any obstructions to legitimate and bonafide fishing activity in specified areas.

4. Acts such as sabotage, bomb explosions, abductions, assassinations, and intimidations, directed at any political group, party or any individual win amount to an offensive operation,

5.(a)It is suggested that Committees to deal with violations of this agreement be set up to inquire into any instances of violation of the above terms of agreement. These Committees could be set up in the areas of Jaffna, Mannar, Vavuniya, Mullaitivu, Trincomalee and Batticoloa .Ampara and any other areas as deemed necessary .

{b) It will be the responsibility of these Committees to take immediate action on complaints made by eitller party to this agreement to inquire into and resolve such disputes,

(c) These Committees could comprise represent8tives drawn from Canada, Netherlands, Norway. ICRC and from a111Ong retired

Judges or Public Officers, Religious Heads and other leading citizens; all appointed by mutual agreement.

Each Committee could consist of five members viz:

Two from the Government;

Two from the L TTE ; and

One from a foreign country who win be the chairman

(e) Freedom of movement for the Committees to perform their tasks will have to be ensured by both parties to this agreement.

(f) Facilities required for the Committees to act swiftly and impartially, will have to be provided by mutual agreement.

6. Recommend establishment of communication *link* between SF and LTTE military area leaders which will enable them to sort out problems expeditiously, focally.

7. Cessation of hostilities will c~ntinlle till notice of termination is given by either party. Such notice should be given at least 72 hours before termination.

———————————

SELECT BIBLIOGRAPHY

1. Anderson, John G. (ed.) (Hong Kong, 1987), Insight Guides: Sri Lanka
2. Arasaratnam, S. (Prentice Hall, 1964), Ceylon.
3. Ariyadasa, Edwin (ed.) (Singapore, 1996), Light of Asia.
4. Austin, Dennis (London, 1994), Democracy and Violence in India and Sri Lanka.
5. _____ and Anirudha Gupta (The Centre for Security and Conflict Studies, 1988), Lions and Tigers: The Crisis of Sri Lanka.
6. Bastiampillai, Bertram and Shelton Wanasingha (Colombo, 1995), Devolution in a Multi-ethnic Society.
7. Bastian, Sunil (ed.) (New Delhi, 1994), Devolution and Development in Sri Lanka.
8. Bhaduri, Major Shankar, Major General Afsir Karim and Lieutenant General Mathew Thomas (ed) (New Delhi, 1990), The Sri Lankan Crisis.
9. Committee for Rational Development (New Delhi, 1984), Sri Lanka The Ethnic Conflict: Myths, Realities and Perspectives.
10. De Silva, C. R. (New Delhi, 1987), Sri Lanka: A History.
11. De Silva, G. P. S. H. (Colombo, 1979), A Statistical Survey of Elections to the Legislatures of Sri Lanka 1911-1977.
12. De Silva, K. M. (ed.) (University of Ceylon, 1973), History of Ceylon, Volume 3, from the beginning of the 19th Century to 1948.
13. _____ (ed.) (New Delhi, 1991), Sri Lanka, Problems of Governance.
14. _____ (London, 1981), A History of Sri Lanka.
15. _____ and S. W. R. de A Samarasinghe (New York, 1993), Peace Accords and Ethnic Conflict.
16. _____ (ICES, Colombo, 1996), Devolution in Sri Lanka- S. W. R. D. Bandaranaike and the Debate on Power Sharing.
17. _____ (HC, 1998), Reaping the Whirlwind: Ethnic Conflict, Ethnic Politics in Sri Lanka.
18. Department of Census and Statistics, Sri Lanka (Department of Census and Statistics, 1992), Statistical Abstract of the Democratic Socialist Republic of Sri Lanka 1992.

19. _____(Department of Census and Statistics, 1993), Statistical Pocket Book of the Democratic Socialist Republic of Sri Lanka 1993.
20. Dissanayake, T. D. S. A. (Colombo, 1983), The Agony of Sri Lanka: An In-depth Account of Racial Riots of July 1983.
21. Geiger, Wilhelm (trans.) (New Delhi, 2000), The Mahavamsa or the the Great Chronicle of Ceylon
22. Goldmann, Robert B. and Wilson, A. J. (London, 1984), From Independence to Statehood.
23. Gombrich, Richard and Gananath Obeyesekere (Princeton, 1988), Buddhism Transformed: Religious Changes in Sri Lanka.
24. Gunaratne, Rohan (Kandy, 1990), Sri Lanka: A Lost Revolution? The Inside History of the JVP.
25. Gunawardana, R. A. L. H. (SSA, Sri Lanka, 1995), Histotoriography in a Time of Ethnic Conflict: Construction of the past in contemporary Sri Lanka
26. Jayatileke, D. (ICES, Colombo, 1995), Sri Lanka: The Travails of a Democracy, unfinished war, protracted crisis.
27. Jayaweera, Neville (Oslo, 1991), Sri Lanka: Towards a Multi-Ethnic Democracy.
28. Jayewardene, J. R. (New Delhi, 1992), Men and Memories: Autobiographical Recollections and Reflections.
29. Jeganathan, P., and Q. Ismail (SSA, Colombo, 1995), Unmaking the Nation: The Politics of Identity and History in Modern Sri Lanka.
30. Jupp, (London, 1978), James   Sri Lanka: Third World Democracy.
31. Keuneman, Herbert (based on a manuscript by) (HK, 1987), Sri Lanka.
32. Kulandasamy, M. S. (New Delhi, 2000), Sri Lankan Crisis: Anatomy of Ethnicity, Peace and Security.
33. Manikkalingam, Ram (Social Scientists' Association, Colombo, 1994), Prudently Negotiating a Moral Peace.
34. Manogaram, C. (Hawaii, 1987), Ethnic Conflict and Reconciliation in Sri Lanka.
35. Manor, James (Cambridge, CUP, 1989), The Expedient Utopian: Bandaranaike and Ceylon.
36. Nissan, Elizabeth (Minority Rights Group International, London, 1996), Sri Lanka: A Bitter Harvest.
37. Nyrop, Richard F., Beryl Lieff Benderly, Ann S. Cort,. Newton B. Parker, James L. Perlmutter, Rinn-Sup Shinn, and Mary

Shivanandan (United States Government as represented by th Secretary of the Army, Washington, D.C., 1970), Sri Lanka: A Country Study.

38. Piyadasa, L. (London, 1984), Sri Lanka: The Holocaust and After.

39. Ponnambalam, S. (London, 1983), Sri Lanka: The National Conflict and the Tamil Liberation Struggle.

40. Powell, Geoffrey (London, 1973), The Kandyan Wars: The British Army in Ceylon, 1803-1818.

41. Sabaratnam, Laksmanan (London, 2002), Ethnic Attachments in Sri Lanka.

42. Seneviratne, H. L. (Chicago, 1999), The Work of Kings: The New Buddhism in Sri Lanka.

43. Sivarajah, Ambalavanar (New Delhi, 1996), Politics of Tamil Nationalism in Sri Lanka.

44. Stronach, Frank (Foreward by) (Toronto, 1995), "As Prime Minister, I would…"

45. Tambiah, Stanley Jeyaraja (Chicago, 1986), Sri Lanka: Ethnic Fratricide and Dismantling of Democracy.

46. Thind, G. S. (Burnaby, Canada, 2001), Our Indian Sub-Continent Heritage.

47. Thiruchandran, Selvy (HC, 1999), Other Victim of War: Emergence of Female Headed Households in Eastern Sri Lanka.

48. Wijesingha, Rajiva (New Delhi, 1986), Current Crisis in Sri Lanka.

49. Wilson, A. J. (London, 1979), Politics in Sri Lanka, 1947 – 1979.

50. _____ (Vancouver, 2000), Sri Lankan Tamil Nationalism: Its Origins and Development in the 19th and 20th Centuries.

51. _____ (Hawaii, 1988), The Break-Up of Sri Lanka: The Sinhalese – Tamil Conflict.

52. _____ (London, 1988), The Break-up of Sri Lanka: The Sinhalese-Tamil Conflict.

53. Zimmerman, Robert (Chicago, 1992), Enchantment of the World: Sri Lanka.

INDEX

ISBN 1553697793-6

9 781553 697930